SAFE
NOWHERE

Tom Bleakley

ISBN-10: 152392084X
ISBN-13: 9781523920846

TOM BLEAKLEY

Entertaining thriller that will more than satisfy.

Kirkus Reviews

Tom has done it again. This is an exciting legal thriller about a real life public health concern."

Dr. John Telford, Author

"An entertaining work of fiction about the dangers of imported generic drugs."

Dr. Wayne Dyer, Best-Selling Author

TOM BLEAKLEY

Acknowledgements

Special thanks to Anne Lynch, Paul Lynch, Dr. John Telford, Dr. Wayne Dyer, Kari Vredenburg, Rebecca Vredenburg, Dr. Carl Rasimas, Sarah Giacona, Francesca Giacona, Mandy Bush, Madison Bush, and Caitlin Bush. I am grateful to my editor, Matthew Carnicelli, for his kind advice and suggestions, as well as his moral support. Sherry Frazier has been a cheerleader for my writing efforts and her continuing encouragement and support is greatly appreciated.

I would be remiss if I failed to acknowledge the heroic efforts of Dinesh Thakur whose whistle blowing efforts in exposing the fraud and illegal activity of a major Indian drug maker served as the impetus for Safe Nowhere. Likewise, Dr. Kathy Spreen and Katherine Eban are specially acknowledged for their contributions in bringing this information to public attention. Ms. Eban's writings in Fortune are 'must reads' for anyone interested in further information about the problems with foreign generic drugs. Special acknowledgements are made to Michigan attorneys James B. Ford and Geoffrey Fieger for their heroic efforts against judicial tyranny.

Finally, special thanks to my loving wife, Mary Ellen Bleakley, whose patience and valuable advice always provides a solid foundation for my writing efforts.

TOM BLEAKLEY

Prologue

What kind of drug company would do something like this? Deepak Patel pushed himself away from the laboratory table and rubbed his eyes. This was the third drug sample he'd examined and each contained a drastically different amount of active ingredient. They were supposed to be all the same. Hell, one of the samples had three times the amount of drug stated on the package label. Another contained no drug at all. Only the third sample's dose was close to what the label claimed. Sales of the drug were booming in the United States. There would be dire consequences if users were exposed to the higher doses.

# # #

Sharon Albright looked at her husband. He was a mess. His usually impeccable business suit was dirty and torn in several places, like he'd been crawling around in the mud. He had a dazed look.

"Where have you been? Why didn't you call?"

Her husband walked closer and struck her across the face.

"Don't talk to me in that tone of voice. It's none of your damn business where I've been."

Sharon fell to the floor and started to crawl away from him. He kicked her in the ribs and she felt a sharp crack in her chest. He kicked her again.

"I'll teach you not to talk to me again like that, you bitch."

Sharon closed her eyes, rolled into a tight ball, and waited for the next kick. It never came. Instead, her husband collapsed on the kitchen floor beside her. She was too frightened to move. She lay still and waited. Nothing. She opened her eyes. Her husband lay flat on his back and stared up at the ceiling. She moved closer.

"Are you all right? Can you move?"

His eyes darted back and forth and he tried to say something.

She struggled to her feet, reached for the phone, dialed 911, and then collapsed on the floor

# # #

"My God, I've been so worried. Are you all right? Do you need me to come up there?"

Mark Stenson spoke slowly. "No need. They're going to discharge me in the morning and I'll be on the next flight out."

"What do they say?"

"I've had a heart attack. It's pretty bad, they say. I'm on some medications that'll keep me from having any further damage. I've got to watch what I eat and lose some weight but I should be all right. The doctor here said I should take at least two months before I go back to work." He paused. "And I've got to stop taking Lorital."

"I knew you shouldn't have been taking that drug. Where are your friends? Why couldn't they call and let me know what was going on?"

"I was unconscious for a whole day. They decided to keep on going. Apparently, the trip planner said that no one was going to get any money back if they cancelled on such short notice. I don't blame them. There's nothing they could have done anyway. It was a lot of money. Hell, we were fifty miles above the Arctic Circle. No cell phones up here. They probably wanted to call, but there was no service."

"Some friends."

"Don't be too judgmental. I'd have done the same thing."

"Call me back when you know what flight you're on. I'll pick you up at the airport. I'm taking you to your doctor as soon as you get here."

"No need. They told me up here that everything will be fine, so long as I follow instructions."

"Honey, I love you. I was terrified that I might never see you again."

"I love you, too." Stenson hung up the phone. He'd had a life-changing experience, and he'd come out of it better than he was before, a lot better. He smiled. It was going to be nice to get home. His life was going to be a lot different.

TOM BLEAKLEY

Chapter 1
May 2011

Katie Hornsby waited for an elevator in the lobby of the Penobscot Building in downtown Detroit. She'd graduated from the Detroit College of Law four months earlier, took the Michigan bar examination, and last week received the good news that she'd passed. Two days ago, she was admitted to the bar at a swearing-in ceremony at Wayne County Circuit Court.

Now, she needed to find a job. New lawyers were a dime a dozen, she'd heard, and the word on the street was that the chances of finding work were between slim and none for the non-connected. Several of her classmates had been hired by big law firms even before the results of the bar exam were known. They were the lucky ones. The key, she knew, was to know someone, have some personal contact that opened the door. Katie had no such friends. She didn't even know any lawyers. Instead, she'd planned a different approach. As a kid, she had tried selling magazines door-to-door, and was rarely successful, but she decided to use the cold-call techniques gleaned from that experience for her job seeking. She began her quest here in the Penobscot Building because it housed the highest concentration of law firms in the city.

She spent a few minutes looking at the building directory in the lobby and thinking about how she'd proceed. "Begin at the beginning," her dad had always said. According to the directory, there were 122 law firms in the building spanning from the eighth floor to the forty-fifth. When the elevator door opened, she pushed the button for the eighth. She'd start at the bottom and work her way up, hoping she'd get lucky before she reached the top.

The first two hours were frustrating. No one wanted to see her or talk to her, much less offer her a job. A pattern of sorts had evolved. She'd give her pitch to the receptionist at the front desk of each office. Most would give her the courtesy of listening. She'd tell them what she thought was the most impressive of her qualifications: she'd passed the Michigan bar exam with the highest score ever achieved. All she got were blank stares. She'd leave a copy of her resume and move on to the next.

She trekked up the stairs from the eleventh to twelfth floors and stood in the hallway while she caught her breath. Just down the hall, a young black woman fussed with a sign at the entrance to an office just across from the elevators.

There were four names on the sign. Katie watched as the woman removed the bottom nameplate, turned it over, and reinserted the blank side into the vacant slot. She stepped back to look over her handiwork.

Katie moved closer.

The young woman noticed her and smiled. "Can I help you?" This girl could do toothpaste commercials, she thought.

"Yes. I'm looking for a job." Katie returned the smile and nodded at the sign. "My name would look nice there."

"Is Dr. Newton expecting you? I don't remember seeing an appointment on his calendar."

"I don't have an appointment, but if there's an opening, I'd like to apply." She extended her hand. "I'm Katie Hornsby."

The two shook hands. "I'm Leslie. Let's go see if Dr. Newton will see you." She gestured toward the door. "Your timing is good.

We do need someone."

Katie followed her into the reception area and sat down.

Leslie smiled again at her. "I'll go back and check if he can see you." The variety of magazines on the table reminded Katie of her magazine-selling days. She'd have made a fortune if she'd known back then that downtown law firms subscribed to so many magazines. Leslie returned and sat down at the reception desk. "He'll be a few minutes."

Katie studied Leslie as she resumed working at the desk. The young woman fascinated her; dark-skinned, well built, petite, and sexy, Leslie radiated sensuality. She looked out of place here. She carried herself more like a celebrity than a person answering phones at a small law firm. Leslie's flawless face featured light brown eyes framed by short spiked hair.

Soon a man dressed in jeans and a black tee shirt approached. "I'm Gary Newton." He offered his hand. "Leslie tells me you're looking for a job."

Katie got up from her seat. Newton was older than he looked, about fifty, about twice her age, with neatly trimmed grey hair framed and the bluest eyes she'd ever seen. He was tall and slender and certainly wasn't dressed like a lawyer.

"I'm Katie Hornsby. I just passed the bar exam and am looking for work."

"Let's talk. Come on back."

As she passed the reception desk, Leslie winked and whispered, "Good luck."

Katie sat quietly in Newton's office while he reviewed her resume, looking around the room. The furnishings were simple and non-pretentious. A floor-to-ceiling bookcase covered the entire wall behind Newton. More than half the books in the case, Katie noted, were medical texts.

Newton looked up and whistled through his teeth. "These are impressive credentials. The highest Michigan bar exam score ever and you graduated summa cum laude from high school, college, and law school. Ever have a grade other than A?"

"No." Katie shrugged her shoulders.

"It's ironic that you're here today. Our newest associate gave notice yesterday. He's moving to Arizona. He has a job there and he's leaving in two weeks. We have an opening that needs to be filled right away."

"Leslie referred to you as Dr. Newton. Are you a medical doctor or a lawyer?"

"Both. I'm board certified in internal medicine, but I gave up the practice of medicine a few years ago. I still maintain my license. I'm also a lawyer and I specialize in handling cases against the drug industry. Eighty percent of the litigation in our firm is against the drug industry. The rest are medical malpractice cases."

"That must be very helpful…to be a doctor as well as a lawyer."

"It has its advantages. But let's talk about you. Now that you're a lawyer, what kind of law do you want to practice?"

She grinned. "I'd like to specialize in handling cases against the drug industry."

He laughed. "You catch on quick."

Katie nodded. She felt good about what was happening. She'd liked Newton instantly. His manner was gentle and she felt comfortable in his presence.

He looked at her and paused. He loved her air of casual

confidence. She was natural and authentic, not cocky or over-confident. She intrigued him. She would definitely appeal to a jury. She wasn't physically imposing but petite and slim. He couldn't tell if she wore makeup, but if she did she didn't need it. Men would definitely find her attractive and women would not be threatened by her appearance. Guys her own age, he'd guess, would say she was hot. Guys his age would suck in their bellies and stand straighter when she was around. He chuckled at the thought.

"Tel me a little about you."

"I'm a hometown girl. I was born and raised in Detroit. I am an only child. My mom died when I was four. My father raised me by himself. He died the year before I started law school. I went to the Detroit public schools, Wayne State University for my undergraduate degree, and Detroit College of Law. I love baseball. I'm a big fan of the Detroit Tigers. I love everything about the game. I remember pretty much everything about baseball I've ever heard, read or seen." She paused. "Also, I played softball in high school and college."

"We need to replace the departing lawyer quickly. I was planning on starting the search for a replacement this morning, and here you walk in unannounced. I've got a good feeling about you, and I must admit I'm terribly impressed by your bar exam score. With the thousands of lawyers who've written the Michigan bar exam over the years, you having the highest score ever made is truly remarkable. You're probably going to tell me that you paid your own way through school by working."

Katie smiled and nodded. "I did. I worked as a waitress at a small Italian restaurant on the east side of Detroit. I think it helped me learn to manage my time."

"If I let you walk out of this office without offering you a job, some other firm will snap you up in a heartbeat. When can you start?"

Katie grinned. "I'm ready right now. I know I'll do a good job."

"How about tomorrow?"

"That's perfect. I feel like I'm dreaming."

Newton reached for a legal pad, wrote on it, and passed it to her. "This is the starting salary I'm offering. It reflects the going rate for new lawyers who specialize in handling cases against the drug industry."

Katie looked at the figure. Her eyes widened.

"Are you serious?"

"It's not enough?"

"It's more than enough. I accept. Thank you very much."

She really connects with people, Newton thought, very likable. This was a special person.

"So, let's get started. Let me tell you what you'll be doing. We've just started on a big case. Do you know anything about the drug Lorital?"

Katie shook her head. "No."

"Testosterone is the hormone in men that causes men to be men. It is produced naturally in the body. Lorital is testosterone in pill form, all dressed up by the promotion of the drug as a 'fountain of youth' gimmick for men. A drug company got the bright idea to market Lorital to older men with this 'fountain of youth' approach. As men get older, their testosterone levels get lower, a natural and normal aging process. The company making Lorital has tried to make it into a disease process that needs to be treated. You know about major league baseball players using steroids, right?"

Katie nodded. "Sammy Sosa of the Chicago Cubs was one of my favorite players. I cried when I heard he'd used steroids."

"Lorital is the common man's equivalent of a major-league ballplayer using steroids. It's on the list of drugs banned by professional sports. The company has done a fantastic job of marketing it in the U.S. and it sells more than a couple of billion dollars a year. They've promoted the concept that everything that happens to a man as he gets older can be traced to insufficient testosterone. Tired in the morning? Take the drug. Can't sleep? Take the drug. Trouble with the sex life? Take the drug."

"Sounds like another Viagra."

"It's being used as another Viagra. Younger men are taking the drug to enhance their sexual performance. But big problems have surfaced with the generic version of the drug not seen with the brand-name drug. Men taking the generic drug have suffered heart attacks or strokes. We have nine cases right now against the generic manufacturer, an Indian company. Five of our clients are under fifty years old. My colleagues around the country tell me that our cases are just the tip of the iceberg. It's a big case and it's going to get bigger. In a case like this with multiple clients, there are a lot of details that need to be handled. That will be your job— to handle the details and help prepare the cases for trial under my direction."

"How will I know what to do?"

"I'll mentor you. The reason I can't do this by myself is that I've got a busy practice, other cases taking my time. You'll find that the office stays busy. We get a lot of drug cases from around the country, more than half outside Michigan. Lawyers from every state call on us to take their clients' cases. The other two lawyers in the firm are also both registered nurses and handle the medical malpractice cases. They are both so busy I couldn't think of asking them to work on Lorital. If you have question when I'm not around, you'll find either one of them helpful."

"The name of the law firm on the front door is Riley and Newton. Who is Mr. Riley? Or is it Dr. Riley?"

"Bob Riley was my partner. He died a couple of years ago. I was married to his daughter, and he was like a father to me. When we first got married, I was practicing medicine until I realized I was in the wrong profession. I started law school at night and Bob hired me after I finished and passed the bar exam." Newton laughed. "But I sure didn't have the highest bar exam result ever. Even though my marriage with his daughter fell apart after he hired me, he kept me on and taught me a great deal about being a trial lawyer. He was a great trial lawyer and a great friend. He wasn't a doctor but he sure as hell knew a lot about medicine and drugs. We tried a lot of cases together and I've kept his name on the letterhead out of respect. He died shortly after we tried a lawsuit involving the drug Serenity"

"I remember that case. It was my first year of law school and some of us went to court and watched some of it. That was you and Mr. Riley?"

Gary nodded. "Bob's name is still well-known around the country so it's sound business practice to keep his name as part of the firm name."

"It's obvious you still miss him."

"I do. He was a great guy." Newton paused. "I'm really pleased you came in today. You impress me. I think this is going to work out well. You've met Leslie already. She'll orient you to all the office details."

Katie nodded. "She was so nice to me."

"This firm couldn't run without her. She does it all." He stood and extended his hand. "Welcome aboard. By the way, are you related to Roger Hornsby?"

Katie grinned. "There's a standing joke in my family. My grandfather was named Roger Hornsby. He would always say to us grandkids, 'Ask me if I'm related to Roger Hornsby.' When we'd ask the question, he'd say, 'I am Roger Hornsby,' then he'd laugh harder than anyone else. So, my answer is, yes, I am related to Roger Hornsby."

"The baseball player?"

She shook her head. "You're asking if my grandfather was the great Roger Hornsby who batted .358 over his entire baseball career from 1915 to 1937 with the Chicago Cubs? No, but my grandfather was named after him."

"You do remember baseball trivia, don't you?" He laughed.

"Yes, I do. I usually spout off when I get nervous. But right now I'm not nervous. I'm just excited."

TOM BLEAKLEY

Chapter 2
Five years earlier

Everett Plimpf, IV was the twenty-nine-year-old great-grandson of the founder of Orex Laboratories, Inc. He stood up from his seat at the far end of the conference room table and looked around at the other members of the board. Everyone was present. He pulled his shoulders back and took a deep breath. He was tall, powerfully built and draped in an expensive custom-made suit embellished with a colored shirt and bold tie; his dark razor-cut hair was slicked back and held in place with gel. He was proud of his physique, his broad shoulders, his six-packs abs, his massive neck and forearms, his six-feet, two-inch "gym-rat" body. His friends called him "Ev." He was the youngest member of the board by more than twenty-five years. Despite the age differential, he was active in the areas it counted most: setting policy and goals for the long-term success of the company.

Plimpf cleared his throat and flexed his shoulders.

"We have a big decision to make, and it needs to be made today. Our product, Lorital, is now the most widely used form of testosterone in the United States. The product exceeds $4 billion yearly in sales and is still growing. Gentlemen, we are at a critical point in time when not making a decision about Lorital will be disastrous. In less than two years we lose our patent protection and the generic jackals will be all over us. We can't just sit around and wait for this to happen. We have to think about the long-term consequences of not being pro-active."

He scanned the others. Orex was not well served by this board. A bunch of pussies. The rest of the drug industry was expanding product lines and adapting innovative changes in a market that was rapidly growing. Orex, in contrast, was standing still. As the sales of Lorital grew exponentially over the past few years, the present board reduced the company's line of products to a handful of other drugs. Lorital was now the primary source of corporate income, and its profits were enhanced by massive cost-cutting elsewhere. Necessary decisions became no decisions. "Do nothing" had become the board's mantra. If the board didn't take action on Lorital, the company was going to be in big trouble in the near future when it started to lose business to generics of the drug. It was up to him to preserve and enhance the family legacy.

He continued. "Our marketing people tell me that current sales of Lorital will drop by eighty percent once the generics move in. The number crunchers also tell me that the testosterone market will triple in the next fifteen years. If we don't act now to protect our interests, we'll not only lose our trade sales, we'll be standing by watching the generics walk away with huge profits from the market we created. *The Wall Street Journal* reported last week that financial analysts are concerned about the long-term health of the company once the patent on Lorital expires in two years."

He paused and looked around the room, waiting. There was no reaction from the group other than scattered furtive glances cast among one another. No balls, Plimpf thought, just a bunch of followers.

"I have a plan. First, I want you all to hear about a new promotional campaign that I suggest we begin immediately. A world-renowned specialist in hormone disorders, who has done extensive research on the effects of testosterone, recommends we promote the potential use of Lorital well beyond the current indications. My research shows that if we push ahead hard in this direction, in five years potential sales will be nine times what we have today."

The group murmured among themselves.

He continued. "Next, if we can't beat the generic manufacturers, I recommend we join them. I know the most likely generic company to move into the Lorital market, and I know I can structure a deal with that company to best protect our interests. I recommend we purchase this company and use it to make and sell generic Lorital. At the same time, we'll continue to sell and promote our own Lorital under the brand name. We'll have the best of both worlds."

Plimpf stopped and looked around to assess how the others were handling the pitch. In the past, the board had rebuffed him on his suggestions of business expansion without a stated reason. He wasn't going to let it happen this time. His family held enough shares of Orex stock to make things uncomfortable for the rest of the board if they didn't go along. His father's long-term illness had created a void of leadership that young Plimpf was now moving to fill. He'd talked this plan over with his father and knew he had his support.

"It's not a question of if we should do this, but who we do it with, and when to do it," he explained. "We will have to be careful about anti-trust problems, but that's why we have Mr. Holt, our general counsel." He looked over at Timothy Holt, a big man from Texas, who nodded in return. Holt had been general counsel at Orex for the past ten years and was an old drinking buddy of his father. "He'll take care of that. We'll take control of this company by putting our own people in place, but we'll maintain the appearance of separate companies. If we do this right, no one will know that we're running the company."

He stopped again, looked around. "The money at stake is big," he said. "I have a company in mind. There's an outfit in India, Enpact Pharmaceuticals, which has a huge worldwide generic business. It's an ideal situation. Enpact has grown so fast it's spiraling out of control. It's already selling more than forty generic drugs in the U.S. Two brothers own it—the Singh brothers—and they'll sell to us in a heartbeat. As you all know, we have plenty of cash in various off-shore accounts to make this deal feasible."

His father raised his hand and waited for his son to acknowledge him. "Do they have plans for a generic Lorital?"

"If we take over the company, they sure as hell will."

The group laughed nervously.

Young Plimpf continued. "The real beauty of this plan is that Enpact is in India, and it will be damn near impossible to sort through India's laws and regulatory procedures and jump on us for anti-trust violations here in the U.S. We buy Enpact, take real control, but maintain separate corporations. Simple as that. The feds will leave us alone."

The moment was right. He looked at his father and raised his eyebrows.

"We should vote now before it's too late."

The elder Plimpf nodded. "Gentlemen, let's take a vote."

The board's vote was unanimous. Everyone voted in favor of the plan.

At the end of the week, young Plimpf and Holt headed to India and approached the owners of the privately held Enpact, the Singh brothers, with a proposal to buy the company. The brothers jumped at the opportunity. Two months later, the deal was sealed and all papers were signed. Orex's involvement in the deal was hidden by the creation of a chain of dummy corporations with charters in the Caribbean. Plimpf and Holt sat the brothers down and explained the need for secrecy and separate business entities. All banking accounts would be kept offshore. This was important. The rationale was to protect the sales of its brand name Lorital. Why would anyone ever use the brand name Lorital if it became known that the same corporation was selling generic Lorital at a much lower cost? Orex paid $1.2 billion for the company from its largest offshore account. The transaction was recorded on Orex's books as a stock dividend and transferred to another unspecified offshore account, followed by several more transfers. Each Singh brother pocketed $500 million up front from the sale of the company they'd started less than five years earlier.

To maintain the appearance of Indian management, one of the brothers, Videda Singh, would stay on as CEO. The other brother, Anugrah Singh, would move to the U.S. and put an Indian presence in lobbying efforts on behalf of the company. The stage was set. Orex became the hidden owner of one of the world's largest drug companies, a company that already sold forty percent of the generic drugs used in the U.S., and Plimpf was in the driver's seat. He'd made this venture happen and it would be an astounding success. There'd be some bumps in the road but he was prepared to do whatever it took.

# # #

By early 2011, Plimpf's plan was succeeding well beyond all expectations. Orex's trade-name sales of Lorital and Enpact's generic sales of the drug had exceeded the goals he'd set five years earlier. A year after the purchase of Enpact, Plimpf's father retired and Ev became the CEO of Orex. On several visits to Enpact's various manufacturing facilities in India over the next four years, he'd been struck by the shoddy practices he'd observed. Even as a layman without any pharmaceutical or scientific training, he could see that there was a definite need to upgrade both the physical facilities of the company and the scientific level of key personnel. He and Timothy Holt worked closely together throughout this time period and he had acquired a deep sense of trust in his general counsel. Both men recognized the need for stronger control over Enpact's activities and the two of them settled on a plan. Holt would establish a private law firm in New York in which he was the senior partner. Orex would hire him to perform all the duties ordinarily associated with being general counsel of a major corporation. In the same manner, Enpact would hire him as outside counsel to perform general counsel responsibilities for the Indian company. Holt's activities on behalf of both corporate entities were thus protected by lawyer-client privilege and the separation between the two companies could be maintained. Wearing the Enpact hat, Holt had begun a recruiting process that brought highly qualified scientists and medical personnel to India to work for Enpact after some concerns about the safety of generic Lorital had begun in the U.S.

Chapter 3
May 2011

The senior law clerk to the Chief Justice of the Michigan Supreme Court knocked gently on the door and waited until it opened.

"What is it, Stanley?"

"I've just gone over court filings for the past two weeks and there's a case I thought you'd like to hear about, Mr. Chief Justice."

"Come in and talk to me." Gerald Haley was handsome, drifting toward sixty, and reeked with the appearance of good health. Most people reacted to him negatively because he was a little too smooth, too polished, and gave off an air of superiority that suggested he was better than everyone else. His ample head of dyed black hair, held carefully in place by an abundance of hair spray, amplified the effect.

The two sat at the Chief Justice's conference table.

"Judge Steven Green, the new judge that the governor appointed to Wayne County circuit court, has been assigned a case called 'Albright versus Enpact.' It's a case involving the drug Lorital and Enpact is a company based in India."

"And why would I be interested in this?"

"Enpact's chief counsel, Timothy Holt, a classmate of yours at Yale, called to speak with you two days ago and you weren't here. Miriam passed the call to me. Mr. Holt is coming to Detroit next week and wants to take you to lunch."

The Chief Justice smiled. He knew Holt well. They partnered on Yale's national champion debate team, served as co-editors of *Yale Law Review,* and were inducted together in Skull and Bones. The two had stayed in contact over the years and went on frequent golfing, fishing, and hunting trips together. Holt was a good old boy who played his Southern heritage for all it was worth. Despite those affections, Haley couldn't help but like the man.

"By all means, have Miriam set it up. Now tell me more about the case."

Aldridge handed the Chief Justice a typed memo. "I've prepared a short synopsis of the details."

"My eyes only…right?"

"Of course, Mr. Chief Justice."

"Thank you for bringing this to my attention." The judge smiled as Aldridge left the room. After the door closed, he sat down and read the memo. He picked up the phone and dialed his secretary. "Miriam, put Judge Steven Green on the list of invitees to the ALEC golf outing. Ask Darlene at ALEC to send him an invitation. Then get him on the line for me."

# # #

Elizabeth Barrett felt like a fish out of water ever since she'd come to Enpact as the director of its clinical medicine department. The eight months had been a nightmare. An attractive but plain woman, she found it uncomfortable to be surrounded by men who treated her like a child or leered at her as though she were a piece of meat. This occurred not only in public but also at work. She found that when she spoke up she was ignored. She faced resistance from her colleagues and was made to feel unwelcome at work. It was tiring and disheartening to fight it, but she got up every day and worked hard at her job. She minimized her exposure to such indignities. She worked alone at her desk from early morning to late evening, seven days a week. Although some contact was inevitable, she limited professional and work contacts to phone conversations. The two-year commitment to Enpact, notwithstanding the lucrative employment contract that brought her to India, was going by slowly. Too slowly.

She didn't know how much more she could take. She couldn't decide which was worse—her self-imposed isolation and the working of too many hours or her presence in a country and work environment where all women were considered second-class citizens at best. The lack of professional respect due simply to the fact she was a woman compounded her frustrations about her work at Enpact. She'd been hired to modernize and develop the company's new drug division in order to meet the various regulations required by the hundred or more countries in which Enpact sold its products. In the first eight months, however, all her recommendations to management had been either ignored or rejected.

The one bright spot, she thought, was that Dr. Deepak Patel had been hired to take over the research department. Dr. Patel had an outstanding reputation throughout the scientific world and Barrett was excited and hopeful that management's resistance to change might stop when the two of them, working together, made recommendations. She knew Patel from an earlier experience and he'd treated her with respect for her professionalism on that occasion. She sat at her workbench in the laboratory and looked at her watch. It was four o'clock on a Saturday afternoon and she looked wistfully outside through the office window. She missed North Carolina. She missed her apartment there. Most of all, she missed her friends. She closed her eyes to fight back tears and took a deep breath to clear her head from the moldy smell of laboratory air that reinforced her sense of isolation. The money was excellent. At first she'd thought she could put up with the loneliness and the rejection, but lately she was having second thoughts, especially when her superiors were constantly rejecting her efforts.

"These results are really good," she said to herself in the empty laboratory. She had just tested a new generic product for a third time because she thought she'd made a mistake and tested the wrong product. These particular tests were important because the company had to show that the drug was the equivalent to the brand-name drug currently being marketed in the U.S. The Food and Drug Administration would only approve a generic drug for marketing if such equivalency were shown. Three times now, the tests on the product were identical to the American-made trade-name brand of the drug. She hadn't made a mistake. She removed a file for a different drug from the file cabinet in her office and located the equivalency tests for that drug.

Very interesting, she thought. The results for this drug were also identical to those of the American brand-name drug. These results were too good to be true. This was no mere coincidence. It couldn't happen by chance. She checked the company directory, found the extension she was looking for and dialed the number.

"May I please speak to Dr. Patel?"

"This is Dr. Patel. Who's calling?"

"This is Dr. Elizabeth Barrett. We met a year ago in Philadelphia at a drug conference. We were on the same panel discussing drug safety. I was really impressed by what you had to say. When I heard you were coming to work at Enpact, I was excited. I've been here for a little less than a year."

"I remember you from that panel," Patel responded. "Your presentation was impressive. I knew you were here and have been meaning to look you up, but I've been so busy."

"Actually, I've found some things that worry me. I'm in the building right now. Can we meet somewhere? I'd like to discuss my concerns with you."

"I'll come to your lab. I'll be right there."

# # #

Dr. Barrett showed Patel the test results on generic Lorital that she thought were "too perfect." She sat and waited as he reviewed the documents.

"You are absolutely right," Patel said. "There is no question in my mind that these tests were performed on brand-name Lorital and not our generic product. No question at all." He raised his eyebrows and looked at her. "These tests are fake. We gave the FDA these false test results to get approval of generic Lorital. What do we do about it?"

Barrett thought for a moment. "I was worried that I was misinterpreting these results. I fear that if I bring this to the attention of management, they'll disregard it. In the short time I've been here, they haven't listened to me or acknowledged any suggestion I've made. Not once. My experience here so far tells

33

me that this is the way all women are treated in India."

"Being a woman may be a factor," Patel responded, "but from what I've observed since I arrived, it may be more than that. There are a lot of problems here at this company, big problems. We need to look into this further, find out more."

Barrett liked Patel. He possessed a jolly appearance that put her at ease. His smile and expansive body build complimented his gentle disposition and thoughtful, careful manner of speaking. He could be trusted. Barrett spoke softly. "When did you start thinking there might be problems?"

"When I arrived I was surprised that my laboratory facility was so small. They'd led me to believe I was taking over a big research department. There were only eight people in the department and only three had scientific training. The lab equipment was shoddy and outdated. It was not a pleasant beginning."

"My experience was the same," Barrett said. "It just hasn't happened the way they told me it would."

"About three years ago," Patel said, "the head of sales at Orex asked me to present a talk on one of my research papers to that company's entire sales staff. I thought nothing of it at the time as I had made the same presentation at several medical meetings already. I had already published more than forty peer-reviewed papers on the effects of testosterone in various animals. In my talk, I compared Orex's reported adverse reactions of their brand name Lorital with those reported of generic Lorital. Generic Lorital had problems that the trade-name product didn't have. Serious problems like heart attacks and strokes in users were reported frequently and I questioned why this was happening. In both my research paper and the presentation, I speculated about various reasons that might be causing these problems. Shortly after my talk, the CEO of Enpact called and asked me to join their company as research director. I was flattered and impressed that they were interested in improving the safety of their products. They wanted, I was told, to understand why their generic drug caused these problems when the brand-name drug didn't. Promises were made to me, all false. Looking back, they hired me just to shut me up."

Barrett looked at him. "I've felt that same way since I've been here."

TOM BLEAKLEY

Chapter 4
October 2011

Katie arrived at the office at seven o'clock. Leslie had already seen to it that a nameplate bearing Katie's name was in place in the hallway outside the office. Katie stood and looked at her name. She wished her dad could have seen this. If he had still been alive, she knew exactly what he'd do. He'd bring his friends to downtown Detroit just to show them where his daughter worked as a lawyer. He would have just shown off the plaque and told them for the thousandth time how smart his daughter was. Visits to the hallway shrine would've become a part of his regular routine. She smiled, wiped away a tear, and entered the office.

Newton was sitting at his desk, a cup of coffee before him.

"Come in." He waved at her and gestured for her to sit down.

"Reporting for work, sir." She grinned and offered a mock salute. "Where do I start?"

"First, sit down and learn each client's file. They're all set out for you. You'll also take the interview of the new client. He's coming in today. The lawyer who sent him tells me the guy is only thirty-eight. He took the generic version of the drug Lorital for less than two months, had a heart attack, and hasn't been able to work since. We have his medical records so spend some time with them before you meet with him. If you have any questions just ask me."

"I'll get started. I hope it's not over my head."

"You wouldn't be here if I had any doubts about that. You'll do fine."

She walked out of Gary's office thinking she was pretty hot stuff. How many lawyers would ever get the chance to handle a case like this one during their entire careers, no less starting on something so big right out of the chute?

She went to the conference room and looked at the small stack of Lorital files on the table. Until the departing lawyer finished his last two weeks, she'd use the conference room as her office. She picked up the top file and read the summary of the interview of Sharon Albright. Two years earlier, Sharon's husband, Ralph, had died on the kitchen floor of the couple's home after he'd attacked her, broke several of her ribs, and punctured a lung. After this completely unexpected rampage, he'd fallen to the floor and remained conscious for only a few minutes before he closed his eyes and died. During that brief interval he'd murmured an apology and declared his love for her. An emergency rescue team arrived shortly thereafter and took the couple to the nearest hospital. Ralph was pronounced dead in the emergency room and Sharon was taken to the operating room where surgeons inflated her punctured lung and removed the rib fragment that caused the lung to collapse. Ralph's funeral was delayed several days until she was well enough to attend. An autopsy revealed that the cause of Ralph's death was a massive heart attack, an unusual finding in a thirty-nine-year old man with no previous medical history of any problems. Katie was moved to tears as she read the horrifying reaction of Sharon over the loss of her husband followed by her discovery three weeks later that she was pregnant. Katie's reaction was intensified because it brought back the memory of her father's death two weeks before she started law school. She sat back to collect herself, drew a big breath, and dried her eyes with a tissue.

She hadn't been prepared for this. She took another deep breath and resumed her review.

While sorting out Ralph's personal effects several weeks later, Sharon discovered a prescription bottle containing generic Lorital. She had no idea he'd been taking the drug. A nurse friend suggested that Ralph's taking of the "testosterone drug" might have caused his heart attack. When her doctor confirmed the possibility, Sharon's family lawyer referred her to the Newton firm. Katie put the file down and searched her purse for more tissues. She blotted the tears from her eyes and blew her nose. This job might be wrong for her, she thought, if this happened all the time. She picked up the file and continued reading. The medical records confirmed that the man had taken Lorital for three years prior to his death. Albright's doctor had prescribed the drug when he'd complained of fatigue and lack of interest in sex. He'd taken the drug daily without any apparent problems and, according to the doctor's medical chart, Ralph claimed it improved the way he felt about life. Two months before his death, he'd been switched at his medical insurer's insistence to the generic form of Lorital because it was "cheaper."

The file contained a story clipped from a newspaper about a study conducted by a Dr. Deepak Patel that reported that the generic form of Lorital caused cardiovascular problems in users that had not been reported with the brand-name product.

Katie set the file aside and moved on to the Hodgkin file, a variation of the Albright story. George Hodgkin was only fifty-three years old when he died suddenly after taking generic Lorital for three weeks after tests indicated a low "T" count. Katie had never heard of a "T" count and made a note to ask Gary about it.

Thelma Hodgkin's sister prodded Thelma to see a lawyer about the connection between generic Lorital and her husband's death after the sister read about the relationship in a newspaper article.

As she finished reading the file, Newton walked into the conference room.

"How is it going?" He noticed the redness of her eyes, her puffy face, and the discarded tissues on the table. "All these clients have a sad story. I can see you've discovered that."

Katie looked up, blinked. "I'm a mess right now. I've got to toughen up."

He sat down across from her, gestured toward the files on the table and smiled. "Some lawyers see dollar signs when they have a client who has suffered a tragedy. We don't do that here. We see human beings who need our help. We can't put people back together again, but we can help them by never forgetting what has happened to them or their loved ones. If, as lawyers, we lose the ability to empathize with our clients, we should move on to a different profession."

"How do you keep feelings from interfering? I see myself falling apart in front of a jury."

He smiled again. "A famous trial lawyer once said that every lawyer should be able to shed a tear for a client. It's a balancing act. The key is emotional detachment. It's a learning process. Over time you'll learn how to detach yourself emotionally, just like a surgeon cutting into a patient. But, seeing you sitting here with red eyes and sniffles tells me that you have the compassion necessary to become a very good lawyer."

After Newton left, Katie thought about what he'd said. She spent the rest of the morning reviewing the remaining files. She shed a few more tears, and the pile of tissues grew larger.

She reviewed the newest client's materials last. She looked over his the medical records and made some notes. She went to Newton's office and tapped on the door.

"Gary, I have a question about the new client, Mark Stenson."

"What is it?"

"It's been almost three years since his heart attack, but there's no real clear documentation of his taking generic Lorital. All the other cases are pretty clear-cut, but not his. I'll need to follow up on that. Do we file suit anyhow? If we don't file pretty soon the three-year statute of limitations may bar the claim, but it might turn out that he has no case."

"That's a good question, Katie. We encounter this issue often. We must first protect the client's legal interests and sometimes we file a lawsuit before we have sufficient information to make a judgment on the validity of a case. It could be the best case in the country, but if we miss the three-year deadline for filing, the case would be thrown out of court. We'll file this case, but make sure that the client understands we are doing it to simply to protect his interests. Once our medical experts review the case, it may turn out that in their opinion there is no validity to the claim and we will decline to represent the client's interests any further. If the client agrees, we dismiss the case. If he disagrees with our conclusions, he can get another lawyer who may be willing to help. In any event, if our experts say it's not a good case, we don't involve ourselves any further. The client needs to understand that. Got it?"

"Got it."

# # #

Leslie flashed a bright smile at the man who walked into the office lobby and approached her desk. She wondered if his scowl was permanent.

"Hi. Can I help you?"

He hesitated and blushed at the unexpected effect of her smile on him. "I have an appointment." He looked down at his feet. "I'm Mark Stenson."

She stood. "I'm Leslie. Follow me." She turned and moved away from her desk.

Her figure was enhanced by form-fitting yoga pants. Stenson couldn't take his eyes off her backside as she walked him back to the conference room.

"Have a seat. Someone will be with you in a minute. Would you like something to drink? Coffee, tea, water?"

He tried to respond. His mouth was too dry. He shook his head and sat down. He glanced at her as she left the room.

Minutes later, Katie entered the room. Stenson was sallow, soft, and more than a little overweight. His clothes were unkempt, his eyes were red, and there was an unpleasant sour odor about him. His scowl was the clincher. This wasn't going to be love at first sight.

He glared at her after she had introduced herself. "How old are you? How long have you been practicing law? What kind of medical background do you have?"

Katie was perplexed. She wasn't used to men responding to her in such a negative way. She didn't want to tell the guy this was her first day as a lawyer. That would really set him off. "I'm a new lawyer. I'm new with the firm. I have no medical background."

"Where is Dr. Newton? I thought I was going to see him."

She understood the negative reaction—he was hell-bent on seeing Newton, not some rookie. "Mr. Newton assigned your case to me. I'll be responsible for handling your case. I've reviewed your medical records and I have a few questions."

"My lawyer sent me to Dr. Newton. I want him to handle my case."

"Mr. Newton runs this law firm like a team, like he's the manager of a baseball team and I'm on that team."

"You're not listening to me. I want him to be my lawyer."

Katie gritted her teeth. "I understand you may be disappointed about not seeing Mr. Newton today, but I assure you that he knows about you and your case. I'll keep him informed about every single thing that happens as we progress to trial if we take your case. Mr. Newton will be your trial lawyer."

"What do you mean 'if' you take my case? My case is going to trial."

Be patient, she told herself. She took a deep breath. He's just having a bad day. "There are a couple of things you need to know. The first thing that we have to do is to determine whether or not you have a valid case. If we do, then we will accept your case."

"The lawyer who sent me told me I have a great case."

Newton had told her how some lawyers would promise a potential client the moon just so the client would hire them. After signing the clients up, they'd spend most of the time trying to settle the cases rather than bringing suit. In many areas of less-complex personal injury cases, such as auto-accident cases, this strategy would work, but it was much different in cases against the pharmaceutical industry. In most complex drug product cases, companies brought a scorched earth attitude toward lawsuits against them. The old adage, Gary had explained, was "millions for defense, nothing for the victim." When these lawyers found out that easy settlements were not going to happen, they'd send the cases to Newton. He had carefully explained to Katie that it was important not to bad-mouth the lawyers who did this, because they were a constant source of new business, the life-blood of their law firm. Many times, Newton had said, it would turn out that upon careful review, there was no case. The firm saw about thirty potential clients every month and took only two or three of these cases into litigation. Katie explained this to Stenson. "Our practice at this firm is to have a potential case evaluated by a medical professional before we agree to accept the case."

"Why would Dr. Newton agree to accept my case then? Why am I here? Why can't I see him?" He sat with his arms folded across his chest.

"Let's talk specifically about your case and maybe that will answer your questions." From his puzzled and angry look, Katie was certain Stenson wasn't hearing a word she'd said.

"And as I said earlier, you need to know that my lawyer said I had a good case," he snapped.

"The lawyer who referred you to us sent us your medical records," Katie continued. "I've looked at them and your heart attack was nearly three years ago. Michigan law requires the filing of a lawsuit within three years of the date of injury. This is what I recommend. We'll file suit on your behalf right away and this will protect your legal interest. When our medical experts review your case, they may tell us that you don't have a case. If we receive a negative review, it means that we won't handle your case. If that happens, you have several options: either you can dismiss your case or you can get another lawyer who might be willing to help you. I also notice that you are married so your wife will also be added to the case."

He shook his head and said, "I don't think you're listening to me. My lawyer said I had a good case. And…I don't want my wife involved in this. This is my case, not hers."

Katie had envisioned her first client interview going a lot easier. She took another deep breath. "In order to prove your case, it's necessary for us to present expert medical testimony about what happened to you and why it happened. Your other lawyer might think it's a good case, but a lawyer is not permitted under the law to give an opinion in court. The advantage of Dr. Newton being a doctor is that these cases are complicated and require handling and presentation by someone with the medical knowledge to do so. That's why your lawyer sent you here."

"And that is why I thought Dr. Newton was going to be my lawyer. Why in the hell should I be wasting my time with you? I want to see Dr. Newton or I'm walking out of here."

"Let me check and see if he's in. I'll be right back." Katie stood, walked out of the conference room, and went directly to Gary's office. He was on the phone. Katie mouthed her request silently: "I need to talk." He held up a finger. When the call ended, he said, "What's up? You look frazzled."

"I am. This new client is giving me a hard time. He says you're his lawyer and he doesn't want to waste his time with me. I need you to speak with him. I don't know how to handle this."

Gary stood. "Let's go. What's his name?"

"Stenson. Mark Stenson."

It took twenty minutes for Newton to mollify Stenson. He assured him that he'd be directly involved in the handling of his case. He stood and looked at the man. "Now, I understand that Ms. Hornsby has some questions, so I'll leave the two of you alone to get the basics out of the way."

Katie waited until Gary was gone. "Let's get started on those questions." She looked down at her notes. "When did you start taking generic Lorital?"

"You said you read my records. If you did, you'd know I started on trade Lorital first."

"Mr. Stenson, I did read your records and I do know that you started on trade Lorital first. I asked when you started on generic Lorital. When were you switched from the brand-name drug?"

"That's in the records"

"There's no mention of a switch to generic Lorital anywhere in your medical records."

"Goddamn insurance company insisted on the switch. They wouldn't pay for the trade name once the generic was available. I don't know when the switch happened."

It wasn't what he said but how he'd said it that was bugging her. Katie had a difficult time just looking at the guy. She struggled to avoid saying something she'd regret later. "Have you kept any of the bottles the drug came in?"

"When a bottle is done, I throw it away. Isn't that what I'm supposed to do?"

"Let's go back. When did you start on the real Lorital?"

"I thought you said you read the records."

"Let me put it another way then. Why did you start taking Lorital?" She forced herself to smile at him. His scowl deepened.

"Why does anybody start taking a drug? My doctor put me on it."

"But what was the reason for taking the drug?" Gary's assurances hadn't helped much. Stenson continued to aggravate her to no end. What was his problem?

"He said I was a good candidate for the drug."

"Did he say why you were a good candidate?"

"You'd have to ask him."

"Let's move to another topic. What is it that you claim Lorital did to you?"

"That should be in the records."

Katie bit her tongue. Her patience was waning. She wanted to tell him that she hadn't asked him what the fucking records said. Instead, she took a deep breath and slowly exhaled. "Mr. Stenson, if we accept your case, you'll need to tell your story to the lawyers for the other side when your deposition is taken. You'll also need to testify about what happened to you at trial. I know some of this information is contained in your medical records, but I'd rather hear it directly from you."

"I suffered a heart attack. I had to give up my job. I haven't worked in three years."

"Has any doctor told you that this was caused by Lorital?"

"My lawyer said you'd find a doctor who would say that."

"He did?"

"Yes. He said your firm had all the contacts to find doctors who testify."

"Does that mean that no doctor has told you that your heart

attack was caused by Lorital?"

"Not exactly. A couple of them raised their eyebrows."

"Do you remember the names of these doctors?"

"Should be in my medical records." He gestured toward the small stack of his medical records the referring lawyer had sent.

"There's nothing in your medical records about doctors raising their eyebrows. I'm asking what you know."

Stenson gave her a weird smile, like he'd just won some kind of battle between the two of them. "I don't like the tone of your voice. I'm just answering your questions. You don't have to get snippy with me. I don't know their names. They were two young doctors, residents, in the hospital. They both told me to stop the drug and never take it again."

She stared hard at him. This was an exercise in frustration and he'd pissed her off. "That's all the questions I have for now. I'll organize your medical records and have them reviewed by a doctor. As we discussed earlier, while we wait for the reviewing doctor's report I will file suit on your behalf. I'll send you a letter summarizing this interview."

She stood to let him know the interview was over.

# # #

After Stenson left, she went back into Gary's office.

He looked up. "How did it go?"

"It didn't get any better after you left. He's not real clear on the Lorital heart attack relationship. Apparently a doctor at the hospital told him never to take Lorital again when he was admitted for his heart attack." She hesitated. "He can be a real asshole."

48

"I'd gathered that already. Put a package together and we'll have it reviewed. If our reviewing doctor thinks it's a good case, we'll take it. By the way, I'm really pleased that you picked up on the statute of limitations concern on your first day."

"Statute of limitations issues are first-year law school stuff."

"Don't be modest. A lot of lawyers with a heck of a lot more experience than you would have missed it. Good work. Get busy and file his suit. Use the pleadings in the other cases as examples."

"Got it."

Gary sat back in his chair and smiled. "So...how is your first day going?"

"How much time do you have?" She winced and grinned back.

# # #

On his way out of the office, Stenson stopped at the front desk and stood in front of Leslie. She looked up at him.

"Is everything all right?" She flashed a smile.

"I...I need to use the restroom."

"Men's room is down the hallway to the right. Third door. It's locked." She rattled off the combination.

Leslie answered the phone fifteen minutes later. "Good afternoon. Law offices of Riley and Newton."

"This is Mark Stenson. I'm having a drink in the bar downstairs in your building. Would you like to join me?"

"Thank you for asking." She rolled her eyes. "But I can't leave work."

"What time do you get off? You can meet me then."

Leslie hesitated. "Our firm has a policy of not fraternizing with clients. I couldn't do that even if I wanted to. I'm sure you understand."

Stenson hung up without responding. Leslie looked at the phone in her hand and shrugged her shoulders. That was weird. The guy gave her the creeps.

Chapter 5
May 2011

Deepak Patel, as Enpact's director of research, had good access to all of the information he needed to look into the questions his meeting with Dr. Barrett had raised. He'd begun with a visit to an employee who worked in the office of regulatory affairs. He'd explained that the purpose of his visit was to find out how procedures in India differed from those in the U.S. He was surprised by what he heard.

"The bosses want results," the employee said. "We give them results. If something is white and it's supposed to be black, we just say it's black. It's as simple as that."

Patel struggled to maintain his composure. From his meeting with Dr. Barrett, he'd known the situation at Enpact was bad, but he didn't think it was as bad as this. "Can you give me any examples?"

The man took a drag on his cigarette. "The best example I can think of is what we do in Africa. Most of the countries in Africa have no regulations. There is no one to tell us what we can or cannot do, so we just do what the bosses want. Most of the stuff we sell in Africa is useless, because we don't put real drugs in the products. We just make cheap pills, sugar pills, and sell it as real drugs. Who is there to complain?" He stubbed his cigarette in an ashtray and lit another. "You should start with that and check it out. I don't think American drug companies sell useless drugs, but who knows. But a lot of companies here in India do. I know because I've worked for other companies. They're all the same. But, if you think you're going to change or make a big deal out of it, it won't happen because no one will believe you or want to believe you. They will also make you pay, as you Americans like to say, for rocking the boat."

Patel was distressed by this revelation. He stopped by Barrett's office and told her about the discussion. "Science is about knowing things," he said. "It's about determining what is true by following a rigid pattern of testing that leaves nothing to chance. My training, our training, in science requires no less than one hundred percent honesty. We've both been hired to help this company change and despite what the man said, I don't think we should back off."

Barrett nodded and replied, "At my prior company, nothing went untested or undocumented and all testing results were recorded in ink, no erasures were permitted, and everything was subject to auditing. Nothing was ever discarded. Nothing here comes close. How much more do we need before we can take our concerns to management?"

"I'll go back and look for more," Patel said, "because we should be as thorough as possible." And for the next few weeks he continued to discretely canvas the project managers that worked under him.

"What I am telling you is not something that is concealed," one of them told him. "It is common knowledge among upper management. Lying to regulators and backdating and forgery is commonplace."

Another manager related the information that workers in the manufacturing plants were ordered to substitute cheaper, lower-quality ingredients in place of better ingredients. The manager of the quality control unit told him, "By law, we're supposed to have batch production and control records. We don't keep them so I just make them up at the end of the month and submit them to the FDA." He added, "We don't have adequate laboratory resources, including the personnel or equipment, for conducting the testing we're supposed to be doing."

Patel also wanted to confirm, as was suggested by Barrett's testing, that it was standard practice at the company to use brand-name drugs in bio-equivalence tests to produce better results. Another manager explained how this was done. "Whenever we visit the U.S., we bring back samples of various drugs made by American companies. We use those samples to produce the test results that are submitted to the FDA for approval to market our generic drugs. The best way to do that is to simply test the real drug and submit the results. We never test bio-equivalence on our own drugs. What would be the point in that?"

Patel walked away from the interview and shook his head in disgust.

He met again with Barrett. The two put the information they'd received together and wrote a report that summarized their findings. They worked out a plan that they thought might change the way things were being done. Patel told Barrett, "I'll talk to a friend of mine at the FDA. He will know what to do."

Patel called his contact at the FDA in Washington; the man listened patiently before saying, "Send me your report. I'll see what can be done." Patel sent the report by overnight mail. Several weeks passed by. There was no response. He and Barrett were getting impatient. He called his contact again.

"It's in the works."

"How long?"

"Don't know. A lot of things are going on right now. You know how it works, Deepak. Any action requires a decision from someone well beyond my pay scale and only after the information has moved through the hierarchy, one slow step at a time. Just be patient."

"We don't have the time to be patient," he told the man. "People are dying."

# # #

Katie drafted Stenson's lawsuit and added his case to the other Lorital cases. She sent a letter to Stenson explaining what was being done and why. It was a rehash of everything she had told him at the time of the interview. She'd prepared a package of his medical records to be sent to the doctors Gary had recommended.

"Hartley and Emrich?"

Gary nodded. "Actually, I'm meeting them for drinks and dinner tonight. It would be great if you could go with me because you should meet them."

"Count me in."

That evening, Gary and Katie met with the two doctors at the Traffic Jam, a bar located near the central campus of Wayne State University close to downtown Detroit and near the area known as the Cass Corridor, a haven for derelicts, prostitutes, and pimps. Initially a dumpy hippy hangout, it'd become the go-to place for students and professors, cops, and a cadre of office workers from downtown.

Katie and Gary found Alex Hartley and Jan Emrich at a table in the back of the room. Gary made the introductions.

After they sat down, a young waiter approached and announced, "All beers are a dollar tonight."

Gary spoke. "We'll order later. Meanwhile, give us two of what they're drinking." He nodded toward Alex and Jan.

The waiter walked away. Hartley looked at Katie. "Gary's been doing a lot of bragging about you."

Emrich nodded, "And he didn't mention how beautiful you are."

Gary chuckled. "I hadn't noticed." This felt good to Katie. Since she had first walked through the door of the firm, neither he nor anyone else in the firm had commented on her looks. She'd been surprised, but pleased, at being accepted for other than her physical appearance.

Gary smiled. "It's her mind that intrigues me. I've never met another young lawyer who thinks things through as clearly as she does."

Katie blushed. The waiter arrived with their beers, giving her a moment to gather her thoughts. "That's enough about me. I'm interested in hearing about the two of you."

Alex held up his glass. "None of us would be together here if it wasn't for Bob Riley. Let's make a toast to him first and then we'll talk." The others raised their glasses. Alex looked up at the ceiling. "Bob, we're here at the Traffic Jam, the place you introduced us to. We're going to all have a couple of beers in your honor."

Katie wondered if that was a tear in Hartley's eye.

Gary interrupted her musings. "Alex is an internist and a pharmacologist right here in town. He treats a lot of patients who suffer from adverse reactions to drugs. He's the head of the local poison center as well. And he runs the second-year medical school course in pharmacology. Over the years, he's raised a lot of hell with the drug industry. If he thinks a drug is dangerous, he doesn't hesitate to speak his mind. He's my hero."

Hartley, in his mid-forties, was tall and thin and Katie found him handsome. His dark hair and deep brown eyes created an impression of sincerity that would make it impossible for someone not to trust him.

He smiled at Katie. "I did some research early in my career on a drug, DES. It was during my medical residency. We published the results and Bob Riley wound up with several cases involving the drug. I agreed to help him and it damn near cost me my career. The drug company that made DES accused me of scientific fraud and I was nearly drummed out of the medical profession. Riley came to my rescue and restored my faith in humanity…although I must admit I still hate and mistrust most lawyers, present company excluded of course."

The small group chuckled.

Alex continued, "Also, don't listen to your boss about this hero stuff. If anyone at this table is a hero, it's Jan."

Now Janet Emrich blushed. Katie thought she was beautiful - model-beautiful, blonde, trim and athletic-looking with a peach-colored complexion that set off her light blue eyes.

Gary looked at Katie. "Jan has a doctorate in pharmacology and knows more about the effects of drugs on the human body than anybody I've ever met."

Emrich poked Hartley in the ribs. "See. I told you he thinks I'm smarter than you." Everyone laughed.

"Ready to order?" The waiter who had returned with pen and pad in hand interrupted the reverie.

Gary held up four fingers. "Four more beers."

Hartley looked at Katie. "Our agreement with your firm is that Jan and I are willing to look at any case that comes into your office that has drug implications, either against a drug company or a doctor or both. If we think that the case is good, we will testify for you as experts. If we don't think it's a good case, you agree to not file the case, or if the case is already in suit for some reason, you agree to dismiss it."

Gary nodded. "They reject more than eighty percent of the cases they review for us."

Alex added, "We think it really adds to our credibility if we follow this practice. Juries tend to think that experts will say anything in favor of the lawyer paying them and those opinions can be bought. We've seen a lot of situations where that is exactly what happens. If a jury understands that we don't do that, that we reject a heck of a lot more cases than we agree to testify about, it makes our testimony more believable. The best part of our approach, though, is that doctors know that we will not be part of a case that has no merit. I give lectures to the Wayne County Medical Society and other groups throughout the state where I tell them exactly what I'm telling you. Doctors like to complain about frivolous medical suits and they appreciate knowing that there is someone out there trying to keep them from happening. No one likes to be sued but it is particularly grating when a case is brought that has no merit."

Katie nodded and looked at Jan.

"How did you happen to get mixed up with these guys?"

Emrich cleared her throat. "I'm a Bob Riley fan, too. I got involved in the Serenity cases just before he died. When we first met, I was the Serenity drug monitor at the FDA. To make a long story short, I was fired because I raised so much hell at the agency because my boss was hell-bent on ignoring safety issues that were coming up with the drug. I agreed to testify for Riley and Gary in the big Serenity case here in Detroit and I met this lug sitting next to me and found him kind of attractive." She gave Alex another gentle poke in the ribs with her elbow. "Bob Riley was instrumental in getting me a staff appointment in the department of pharmacology here at the medical school. As the fairy tale goes, we are now living happily ever after." She elbowed Alex again. "As long as he does what I tell him to do."

The four laughed. The waiter appeared with their beers and distributed them.

Jan looked at Katie. "Gary tells me you're a big baseball fan."

Katie nodded. "I'm a big fan of baseball...and the Tigers."

"Me too. We've got to catch a game some time. They're back in town next week and I've got two season tickets. This guy..."—she rolled her eyes at Alex—"isn't as crazy about the Tigers as I am. It would be great to go to a game with someone who is. I'll give you a call."

"That would be really nice. I'll wear my new Miguel Cabrera shirt."

Jan laughed. "I've got one too."

Chapter 6
June 2011

Judge Steven Green and his wife, Nancy, drove up the circular driveway of the world famous Oakland Hills golf course and left his golf bag at the club drop with a young man who pointed them to the clubhouse where the luncheon was being held.

Green surveyed the sumptuous surroundings. The Oakland Hills complex was stunning. He could learn to like this.

"This must be costing a pretty penny," said Nancy.

"I was just thinking the same thing."

"What did you do to get this invitation?"

Her tone irritated him. He hated it when she mocked him. He ignored the question but he'd asked himself the same thing: just what had he done to attract the attention of the Chief Justice of the Michigan Supreme Court? Before his appointment by the governor to the vacant seat on the Wayne County circuit court, Green had done nothing much to distinguish himself as a lawyer, except for his handling of a recent case involving the National Rifle Association. He'd also dabbled in local politics and had contributed generously to several politicians, including the governor, in the last election. He assumed it was the size of his donation to the governor's campaign that was the deciding factor...and maybe the NRA case.

The local branch of the NRA had retained him to represent their interests in a case involving a gun dealer from Ferndale, Michigan, who had sold a revolver to an underage kid. The kid shot and killed his teacher with the weapon. The teacher's family sued both the gun dealer and the NRA. At the time, Green had guessed the reason the NRA came to him was twofold: his membership in the organization and his law license. Not too many lawyers belonged to the NRA. He'd been successful in getting the case against both the NRA and the gun dealer dismissed on a technicality, which resulted in a fair amount of local publicity, some positive, some negative. He'd been invited to speak at several local functions about the topic. He'd been surprised when asked if he'd accept an appointment to fill the judicial vacancy, and even more surprised when he received the appointment.

Chief Justice Gerald Haley stood in the lobby of the clubhouse greeting arrivals. This was big time, Green thought. He and Nancy waited in the informal reception line to meet him. When it was their turn, the Chief Justice vigorously shook his hand. "Judge Green, how nice that you could make it on such short notice. You'll love this meeting as well as the golf. The speaker is fantastic. At some point today, I'd like a minute of your time. How about meeting after golf in the bar? There are a couple of people I want you to meet."

"It would be a pleasure, Your Honor."

"Cut the crap with the formalities, Steven. Call me Jerry."

"Thanks for inviting me...Jerry."

Haley turned toward Nancy and took her hand. "It's Nancy, isn't it? She nodded, surprised Haley knew her name. She thought he looked like a used car salesman. "There's a program scheduled for the wives that I know you're going to enjoy. My wife planned it. After golf, I'll need a little time with your husband. I hope you don't mind."

"Of course not. I'm used to waiting."

As they walked away, Green glared at Nancy. "Why did you have to say that?"

"What?"

"That you're used to waiting."

"Well, it's true. What's wrong with telling the truth?"

The edge in her voice irritated him. "If you're trying to pick a fight, I'm not falling for it. I'm here to have a good time and I suggest you try to do the same."

Nancy stopped and looked at him. His image meant everything to him. Since he'd become a judge, it was as if she and their three daughters didn't exist. She was sick and tired of the way he'd been treating her and the girls. "That sounds fair. You go off and play golf on the best golf course in the world while I attend some stupid class on how to cook a chicken or powder my nose. I didn't want to come here in the first place, and now the guy wants me to wait around while you drink with him. I'm not going to wait. I'll take the car and you can just take a cab when you're done drinking."

Green stood there, fists clenched, and struggled for control. He said nothing and they walked into the room where the meeting was being held and took seats in the back of the room

Chief Justice Haley stood at the podium. "Thank you all for coming today. We have a great day planned. After you hear from one of the best speakers in the country, we'll adjourn to the best golf course in the country and prove what lousy golfers we are."

The large group laughed. Nancy leaned toward Green and whispered, "You'd think this guy was the funniest comedian in the world. What a bunch of suck-ups."

Green grimaced and placed his index finger over his lips.

She whispered. "Don't tell me to be quiet."

Haley continued. "I'd like you to welcome our guest speaker, Oliver Brewster, who has an important topic he'd like to discuss. Mr. Brewster…"

Brewster stood and squared his shoulders, sucked in his gut and imagined that everyone in the audience, especially the ladies, noticed his powerful presence, his animal magnetism, and his imposing form. He was several inches taller than everyone in the room and it was rare, indeed, when anyone at any function ever matched his height. His banged-up right knee from football added to his allure, he thought. Women who wanted a man with meat on his bones got what they wanted with him. Nothing reminded him of what he'd achieved in his sixty-four years on this planet more than the lustful glances of young women, whenever there were any, in the largely male groups gathered to hear his diatribes about trial lawyers, the scourge of American society. His magnificent full head of chemically augmented red hair enhanced his flamboyant speaking style. Most men his age were bald, graying, or both, but not him. He scanned the audience. No young women present, but there were several no-less-attractive middle-aged women scattered among the group. He slowly exhaled while exploring the buttons of his shirt as it strained from the expansion of his swollen paunch. It wouldn't do if one popped open to reveal the bare skin of his abdomen. It'd happened once, so he'd make sure it didn't again.

He was all set. He stepped away from the microphone. "I don't need this damn thing. Can everyone hear me all right? Raise your hands if you can hear me."

He scanned the room. "All hands raised. Let's get started. I want to tell you about a dangerous crisis in America today.

Lawsuits are draining the lifeblood of our society. The number of lawsuits filed every day is getting out of control. Judges don't have time to do what they're supposed to be doing. Every little squabble between people becomes a lawsuit. Doctors can't make a medical decision without the fear of getting sued or losing their medical licenses. Medical malpractice insurance rates are driving doctors out of practice. If someone wants something that another person has, they hire a slimy lawyer who will try to get it. Speaking about lawyers, they have no scruples other than money. Getting money from other people has become their religion. Our founding fathers did not contemplate that lawyers would take over the damn country with television ads encouraging people to sue for this, sue for that.

"I'm here today to suggest a few things that we ordinary citizens can do about this blight on our society."

Brewster paused and looked around. He had everyone's attention.

"There are judges who condone this kind of thing. These judges encourage litigation because they themselves come from the ranks of greedy plaintiff lawyers who sue anytime and anybody at the drop of a hat. Plaintiff lawyers buy their lawyer friends their judgeships in the first place. It's a good deal for them. Back another plaintiff lawyer with big money when that lawyer runs for election as a judge and then reap the fruits of that backing because the judge rules constantly in favor of the lawyer's clients. It is bribery. It's a 'wash my back and I'll wash yours' arrangement. It's time for us ordinary citizens to stop it.

"I'm here as a representative of ALEC to tell you what we have been doing and what we would like to have you do to stand up and be counted. First, I'll tell you about ALEC, which is shorthand for the American Legislative Exchange Council. More than forty years ago, a small group of state legislators and conservative policy advocates with a vision met in Chicago. What resulted from that vision is a nonpartisan membership association for conservative state lawmakers who share a common belief in limited government, free markets, federalism, and individual liberty."

Nancy leaned over and whispered in her husband's ear. "Nonpartisan, my ass."

"Just sit there and shut up," Green replied.

She gave him a wan smile, lifted her hand toward his face, and pointed her middle finger at him. "I'm out of here. I'll see you at home...if you ever get there."

She stood and left the room. Green watched her until she was out of sight. She'd been acting strange. He'd tell her to go see a doctor but knew what she'd say. He turned his attention back to Brewster.

Brewster also noticed Nancy's exit. This didn't happen too often. Not too many women ever walked away from his presentations. It was usually the other way around. They'd swarm meetings to hear him speak, hanging on his every word in adulation. He sucked in his gut even more and continued his speech.

# # #

At the end of the golf round, Green walked into the men's grill and looked around. It had been a tough day on the golf course. The wind howled and the weather had been colder than predicted. It had rained hard for thirty minutes and Green's shirt was still wet.

He spotted Chief Justice Haley seated at a table across the room with the speaker from earlier in the day and another man. Haley stood, waved, and pulled over a chair from the adjoining table as Green approached. "Steve, sit here. Let me introduce Tim Holt and Oliver Brewster."

He shook hands with the two. Brewster was by far the largest of the three but he sensed that Holt was the dominant person in the small group. Holt's forced smile suggested power, a blended aura of arrogance and dignity.

Green smiled at Brewster. "I enjoyed your talk."

"Thanks," Brewster said. "I appreciate your comment. We're fighting a tough battle against a bunch of greedy plaintiff lawyers who look at big business as a bank stuffed with money with the vault wide open."

Holt looked at Green. "Is the weatha' always like this here in Deetroit?"

Green, noting the Southern accent, shook his head. "We have a lot of nice days. Today just wasn't one of them."

Haley leaned forward. "Tim is general counsel for Enpact. I understand you have a case involving Enpact in your courtroom? He fancies himself a Southern gentleman and can drink bourbon with the best of them."

Green was surprised at the mention of the Enpact lawsuit. He nodded while the others chuckled.

Haley looked at Green. "Anything going on in that case?"

Green was surprised. Why would the Chief Justice of the Michigan Supreme Court be interested in this case? Why would he even know about it? More important, should the two of them be discussing it in front of one of the parties? "There's a motion to dismiss pending…"

"The case reminds me of that gol' darn McDonald's coffee case," interjected Holt. "It's a piece of junk if there ever was one."

Brewster joined in. "We've got some new legislative proposals in Michigan to stop frivolous lawsuits. Have you heard about them? Hell, one of your legislators, a doctor, just introduced a bill to suspend plaintiff lawyers from practicing for ninety days if they lose a medical malpractice case. It's not going to pass but he's got a lot of publicity from the effort."

Green shook his head. He was uncomfortable about this conversation. And he was puzzled over the interest in the Enpact case. If the Chief Justice kept talking about the case, he didn't want to risk offending him, but would it be reasonable for him to decline discussing the case?

Brewster looked at Green. "ALEC was successful in getting your Michigan legislature to pass the law that bars drug-product lawsuits against FDA-approved drugs. The McCrery case clinched the deal. When that jury returned that big verdict on such flimsy evidence, something had to be done. That goddamn Bob Riley milked that case for all it was worth. Riley's dead now and your legislature's made certain it doesn't happen again. So far Michigan's the only state to do this. We're working hard in a dozen other states to get the same result. The drug industry needs protection from these nuisance suits."

"What did you say this morning, Oliver?" the Chief Justice interjected. "ALEC has seventy-three pieces of legislation pending around the country?"

Brewster smiled. "Actually, Mr. Chief Justice, seventy-three laws have already passed in the past year alone. There are several hundred others pending. The best known of these is the stand-your-ground law that's getting so much attention in Florida right now. Variations of it have passed in fifteen other states already." He turned to Green. "We got a lot of help on stand-your-ground from the NRA, and I know you've done some good things for them."

Green nodded. He couldn't just sit there and not respond. "I don't know if that particular Michigan law will come into play on the Enpact case." He looked at Holt. "The unique part of the case, as you know, is that your client is in India. I find myself asking if the case should be heard in Michigan. The issue of inconvenient forum has been raised and I don't remember when the motion is scheduled to be heard, but it's sometime soon."

"Do you have a gut feeling as to which way you're going?" asked Haley.

Green hesitated. "It seems unreasonable to force a company from India to defend itself in a Michigan courtroom for something that happened in India."

Green missed the slight nod between Holt and the Chief Justice. Holt spoke. "We raised that bidness with you first, Judge, because we're thinking the same way as you. But if you do decide against us, y'all be seeing a lot of me." He chuckled. "Now, tell me, any good golf courses around here other than Oakland Hills?"

"I belong to a small private club, Gowanie Golf Club, just north of Detroit. It's not Oakland Hills, buts it's a gem of a course—tight narrow fairways with small fast greens. Let me know when you're coming in and we'll go there. Come to think of it." Green smirked. "I might just deny your motion just so that you have to come back to town and give me a chance to give the money back I won today."

The four men laughed.

Green was relieved that he could steer the discussion away from the merits of the case. This was just harmless banter, he'd decided. "My wife and I were talking earlier. We'd like to join here." He gestured with his hand. "This really is a great golf course. Nice bar, too."

Holt laughed. "Hell, I'd never want you to dismiss the case. If you do, y'all can bring me here every time I come to town. Let the damn case take a couple years. We can do our bidness on the golf course." The four of them laughed again.

Brewster ordered another round. When it was served, he proposed a toast: "Here's to good friends, lousy golf weather, and the end of frivolous lawsuits." The four men tapped beer mugs.

Haley leaned toward Green and spoke softly. "I have a suggestion for you on this Enpact case."

Green sat and listened.

Chapter 7
October 2011

"Dad, tell me about the Albright case." Abigail Green took a bite of her hot dog and waited. She and her father were seated at the Lafayette Coney Island in downtown Detroit on a rainy Saturday.

"What do you want to know?"

"Some boys at school take the drug."

"The drug?"

"Yes. Lorital. They claim it makes them bigger and stronger."

"I don't know that much about the drug. I know it comes from India."

"It's a steroid, just like the ball players use. All the guys who say they use it say their faces break out in pimples. And they get mad and lose their tempers, get in fights. I read about it. It's called 'Roid Rage'."

Green pursed his lips. "I didn't know that. Sounds like a bad drug."

Abigail was proud of her father. He was a judge. Her father's new status elevated her own. As a junior in high school with good athletic skills and excellent grades, she was beginning to like who she was. She and her dad hadn't gotten along so well since she'd reached her teens. She'd question his authority at every opportunity. The two had fought when she had decided to become a vegetarian. He'd said she was impulsive and lacking in common sense. She'd responded by testing the limits of his authority and being especially irksome when he'd taken on the NRA case. She just couldn't stop ragging on him about why he was defending what happened to that schoolteacher. To her the issue was black and white. So when her father received his appointment to the bench, she'd backed off a bit because she enjoyed the spotlight in school for the first time. She'd also discovered what she wanted to do with her life. She wanted to study law, become a lawyer, and follow in her father's footsteps. She wanted to be a judge. Just like him.

Judge Green's usual routine was to go alone to his office on Saturday mornings. He liked the solitude of the courthouse on weekends, and there was always a pile of work requiring his attention. He'd found that he could accomplish more with no one around. Nancy had been on him lately because he wasn't spending enough time with his three daughters. When his oldest daughter, Abigail, had asked if she could go to his office with him on Saturdays, he'd been reluctant to interrupt his routine but agreed so as to avoid his wife's wrath.

Over the course of the first few weeks, he'd found that Abigail, rather than interfering, was helpful in organizing files and performing tasks that needed attention. Stella, his court clerk, would leave Abigail a variety of small jobs to do that kept her occupied while her father worked. She'd done these assignments faithfully and enthusiastically and also stayed out of his way. They'd established a routine of working a couple of hours followed by a visit to Coney Island restaurant where they'd each have a hot dog and fries. Green was surprised by how much he was enjoying his oldest daughter's presence. She was a bright kid.

Green looked at Abigail. She had mustard on her face so he

leaned over and wiped it off with his napkin. She looked so much like her mother. She acted like her, too. Most of the time she was a sweet lovable kid, but when something bothered her she'd let him know in no uncertain terms. She wore her dark brown hair long, well past her shoulders. Her green eyes served as a mirror to her moods that ranged from brooding intensity to ethereal playfulness. She was attractive, well liked at school, smart, and talented. She played oboe in the high school band and second singles on the varsity tennis team. She was the vice president of the student council. She'd recently made the transition from an awkward gawky adolescent to a blooming, beautiful young woman.

She took another bite of her hot dog and carefully wiped her chin.

"I read your Albright opinion. It was sitting on your credenza. Why are you going to throw the cases out?"

Green didn't want to talk about the case. And he sure as hell didn't want to tell her why he was going to dismiss the case. "I haven't actually dismissed it yet but I probably will after I listen to the lawyers argue."

"I thought you were supposed to listen to the lawyers argue first before you make up your mind."

Green hesitated. "Usually I do. But this case is clear-cut. Not much to think about."

"Could you deny the motion if you wanted? Let them go to trial instead?"

"I could. But the drug company would appeal."

"If you dismiss the case, can the people who were hurt by the drug appeal? They can, can't they?"

"That's true, they can. But they probably wouldn't. Appeals are

71

expensive. Most people can't afford to hire a lawyer to handle an appeal."

Abigail took a sip of her soft drink. "Why do you say that? I think they would appeal. All the people who were hurt suffered a lot. I read some of the stuff about them. I feel sorry for them. I don't see them giving up that easily. I know I wouldn't if it were me."

Green finished his hot dog, took a drink, and wiped his chin. "Want anything else? More Coke? Another hot dog?"

She shook her head. "Does it matter to you whether they suffered?"

"Of course it does, but…I have to follow the law. The drug company is in India. That's where it makes its drugs. India has its own laws and its own court system. The courts in the U.S. shouldn't have the responsibility of being the watchdog for the rest of the other countries in the world."

"I think that sucks."

"That's just the way it is."

Chapter 8
October 2011

Newton walked into Katie's office. "The motion on the Lorital cases is set for next Friday. I want you to go with me."

"Do you want me to do anything else?"

"We've done the brief. Review the pleadings in the case again to refresh your memory. I don't think the motion is going to be taken seriously by the judge."

"Will I be arguing it?"

Newton shook his head. "Just sitting and listening…and learning." He smiled.

# # #

The morning of the scheduled motion Leslie walked into Katie's office and grinned. "Your big moment has arrived. Gary called and he's running late. He's tied up in court in Oakland Country, so he wants you to go over and check in. Wait there for him. You should go over now. Check-in time is 8:30. Take the file."

The only time Katie had ever been in a courtroom was for her swearing-in ceremony, but at least she knew how to find the courthouse. She cleared security on the ground floor of the sixteen-story building and checked the directory for the location of Judge Green's courtroom. The tenth floor.

She stood at the bank of eight elevators and waited with the rapidly expanding crowd of lawyers and clients. When the next elevator arrived, Katie was jostled and pushed aside. By the time she recovered, the elevator was too full to enter. The experience was repeated again, but she made it on the third elevator by pushing back. All part of the learning process, she guessed.

Judge Green's courtroom was empty except for the clerk at the desk adjacent to the judge's bench. Katie checked her watch. She was ten minutes late.

"I'm late. The elevators were slow. I'm checking in on the Albright vs. Enpact motion."

The clerk grinned. "You're the first one here. Our elevators leave a lot to be desired. Your case will be called first. Let me know when your opponent arrives."

"I'm checking in for Gary Newton who's running late. He's going to handle the motion."

"Newton? Are you the new lawyer in his firm?"

"Yes."

"Congratulations. I heard he got himself a new lawyer. You're a lucky girl. Gary's a helluva lawyer. What's your name, honey?"

"Katie Hornsby."

"Nice meeting you. I'm Stella. Just let me know when Gary gets here. I'll put the file to the side."

Katie sat in the last row and watched as other lawyers checked in. Thirty minutes went by and no judge appeared. There were thirty-seven other lawyers also waiting. She had counted them. Twice. It was better than counting the 454 tiles on the ceiling again. Waiting was one thing Katie really didn't like. Another half hour went by until the judge came on the bench. The bailiff announced his arrival, called the room to order, and Stella called

74

the first case. Two hours later, Katie was the only one left. Where was Gary? Where was the other lawyer on the case?

Judge Green stood and looked at Katie. "I understand we're waiting for Mr. Newton. I'm going to take a break until he gets here. Just let the clerk know." He left through the door behind the bench.

Fifteen minutes went by and Gary walked into the courtroom. The clerk looked up. "Good morning, Mr. Newton. Would you like a minute to get settled?"

"I'm fine, Stella. Sorry about the delay."

"I'll tell the judge you're ready. I met your new lawyer. She's a beautiful girl."

Newton looked at Katie, who blushed. "I apologize for keeping you here so long."

Katie shrugged her shoulders and smiled. She whispered, "Speaking of long, did you know that the longest baseball game in the history of baseball was between the Milwaukee Brewers and the Chicago White Sox?"

Newton gave her a funny look. "Does waiting do this to you?"

"The longest baseball game, it happened on May 9, 1984, the game went twenty-five innings and lasted eight hours and six minutes. The game began on May 8 but according to the rules an inning couldn't begin after 12:59 AM so the players and fans had to come back the next day to watch the Chicago White Sox win 7-6 on a Harold Baines' home run in the twenty-fifth inning."

Newton stared at her. "You're funny."

"Do you know the longest baseball throw on record? A Canadian minor leaguer, who had a short stint in the majors from 1955 to 1957, still holds the record. He threw a baseball 445 feet and ten inches before hitting the ground and breaking the old record of 445 feet and one inch set in 1956 by Don Grate."

"Why don't we talk about the motion?"

"The thrower's name. Edward Gorbous. He was born on July 8, 1930. In Drumheller, Alberta."

Katie stopped her baseball spiel when she saw the look on Gary's face. "We're here to keep the judge from throwing out the cases. The issue is the safety of generic Lorital. The drug company, Enpact, makes and sells Lorital for the treatment of testosterone deficient men. It's an Indian company, and it makes the generic equivalent to Lorital which is still being sold and widely used. It has caused hundreds of deaths in users. Enpact has brought this motion to dismiss our cases because it will be too much of a burden for an Indian company to defend itself in Michigan..."

"Slow down. I know the history of the drug and why we're here. You need to speak more slowly. Now tell me what you think I should argue."

"It was the coffee. I shouldn't have had coffee this morning." Katie took a deep breath and continued, "Enpact put generic Lorital on the market on May 30, 2010 and, within two months, the drug killed more than two hundred men. We're here because we represent the families of ten generic Lorital users who died or suffered heart attacks or strokes."

Newton holds his hand up like a traffic cop.

"Katie, stop and breathe once in a while. Slow down. Let me tell you a little about our opponent in this case, Lester Hempstead. You will like him. He's the dean of the defense bar in the State of Michigan. His clients are drug and auto companies because of his trial skills. He's smart, savvy, and tough, but also a decent man.

He's developed a substantial national reputation winning case after case throughout the country and he's built his firm on that reputation. He now is the senior partner of a thirty-man firm of experienced trial lawyers. His firm has the top two floors of the Guardian Building, right across the street from our office."

The bailiff stood. "All rise. Court for the Honorable Steven Green is now back in session."

Green re-entered the courtroom from the door behind the bench and took his seat on the bench. Two other men emerged from the judge's private chambers behind him and followed him into the courtroom. They walked over to the other table.

Newton whispered to Katie, "The tall, distinguished looking man with a full head of silver-gray hair is Lester Hempstead, the attorney for Enpact I told you about. He acts tough but his bark is worse than his bite. I don't know the other guy."

The judge glanced at the clerk and nodded.

Stella called the case: "Albright versus Enpact."

Gary took his notes and approached the podium where the two men were standing. Katie remained seated.

"Good morning, Judge." Hempstead had a deep, pleasant baritone voice, Katie thought.

The judge smiled back. "Good morning, Mr. Hempstead. You have a motion?"

"Yes, Your Honor. This is a motion for summary judgment on behalf of my client, Enpact. I would like to introduce Mr. Timothy Holt, national counsel for Enpact from New York, who is here with me this morning."

Holt smiled at the judge. "Good mornin', Your Honor. Congratulations on your appointment to the bench."

Green's face beamed.

"Thank you, Mr. Holt, and welcome to Detroit. I trust you are enjoying your visit."

Newton turned and looked at Katie. He rolled his eyes and gestured for her to join him in front of the bench. He turned and looked at the judge. He had to end this love fest before the judge and the other two lawyers started high-fiving each other, or worse yet, kissing and hugging.

"Your Honor, Gary Newton and Katie Hornsby appearing on behalf of the plaintiffs."

Green looked over at Katie. "Hornsby? Like the ball player?"

Katie's face lit up. "Yes, Your Honor. Just like Roger Hornsby who batted .358 over his entire career with the Chicago Cubs from 1918 to 1937."

From the judge's look, Katie surmised that he wasn't interested in hearing about the man who was the best right-handed hitter to ever put on a baseball uniform. Although, she thought, the current Tiger star Miguel Cabrera was moving fast in that direction.

Green took a second glance at her before looking over at Hempstead. "Go ahead with your motion."

"Your Honor," Hempstead began, "this is a unique case which doesn't belong in this court in Detroit. In fact, it doesn't belong in any court in the State of Michigan or anywhere else in the United States. The reason is that my client, Enpact Pharmaceuticals, is a company founded and incorporated only in the country of India under the laws and regulations of the country of India. Its corporate offices and manufacturing facilities are located in India. Enpact makes none of its products in Michigan or anywhere else in the U.S. All of Enpact's employees live and work in India."

Katie was impressed with Hempstead. His demeanor fit well with his physical appearance. He was both dignified and respectful. Watching him in action, she understood why he'd been so successful. She glanced at Holt, who stood next to Hempstead. He was somewhere near Hempstead's age, but the passage of time had not been as kind to him. He was broad-shouldered and large, like a farmer in an expensive ill-fitting suit. His face was florid and featured what her dad would've said was a whiskey nose laced with prominent engorged blood vessels.

Hempstead continued, "In short, there is a totally insufficient basis for allowing the plaintiff's lawsuits to be heard in this court's jurisdiction when any and all of the alleged acts of wrongdoing, which we do not admit, occurred in India. All potential witnesses employed by Enpact are in India. Any business and production records numbering in the hundreds of thousands are located in India and it would result in a considerable burden and expense for Enpact to be required to come to this courtroom when the company is located, according to Google, 7,942 miles from here. The time, effort, and expense in managing a case in this forum for Enpact would be overwhelming. This case is a classic example of a lawsuit brought in an inconvenient forum and should be dismissed on that basis. On behalf of Enpact, I respectfully request that this case be dismissed with prejudice."

Green looked at Gary. "Counsel?"

Gary described the number of strokes, heart attacks, and deaths around the country caused by generic Lorital. The judge quickly interrupted him, holding up his hand like a traffic cop. "Please address the issue of inconvenient forum."

"Your Honor, I am going to get to that but there is some

79

foundation that you will need to keep in mind when deciding this motion. I have..."

The judge stopped him. "I asked you to discuss the issue of inconvenient forum. Please do so."

Newton was frustrated. "Judge, what I did not hear from Mr. Hempstead is what this case is all about. It's about an adulterated product that is being sold in the United States in violation of federal law. While Lorital may be made in India, and we don't know that for sure because all we have is a statement from Mr. Hempstead, Enpact has a very large presence in the U.S. Each of the plaintiffs in this case was injured by the defendant's product, which was sold in Michigan and caused injury in Michigan. In fact, as our brief points out, eighty-three percent of the prescription drugs used in this country are generic products and the defendant Enpact makes and sells forty percent of these generic drugs. In order to sell prescription drugs in the U.S. and Michigan, Enpact had to apply for and receive the approval of the Food and Drug Administration, which is, of course, located in this country. Enpact must likewise adhere to the law and the rules and the regulations of this country in selling its products. Also, there are some other pertinent facts that you must consider. To simplify, this case is about the feces of rats and mice and whole bodies of cockroaches found in the drugs sold in this country by Enpact. Even more important, the active ingredient in generic Lorital, testosterone, is present in varying dosages. While every package sold is supposed to have the same dosage, this is not the case. Some of the products sold here in the U.S. contain no testosterone whatsoever, some contain the correct amount of testosterone as stated on the label, and some have dangerously high levels of testosterone..."

"Stop. That's enough, counsel. You are bringing in facts that are not part of the consideration when the issue is inconvenience to the defendant. I told you to address the issue of inconvenient forum and you have failed to do so." He banged his gavel.

"Judge, I haven't finished…"

"Take a seat." The judge gestured toward the table.

Newton glared at the judge, and he and Katie returned to their seats.

Green cleared his throat, adjusted his glasses, and began to read from his already prepared opinion: "The defendant has brought this motion seeking dismissal of the pending cases on the basis that it would be inconvenient to defend itself in a forum nearly 8,000 miles from its location in the country of India and the court agrees with the defendant. It must be pointed out that Enpact has fully complied with all the requirements established by the Food and Drug Administration in the marketing of generic Lorital. This court has reviewed the documents submitted by the defendant in support of its motion and is convinced that defendant has fully complied with the law in all respects."

The judge sat back and looked hard at Newton for a moment. "I might add that the belittling attempt to introduce what I'll call 'cockroach' evidence has no bearing on this matter because what happens in India has no relevance to a drug that is approved for marketing in the U.S. by the FDA. Under Michigan law, which I must apply because these cases are brought in Michigan, a drug approved by the FDA is deemed to be safe as a matter of law and generic Lorital is one of those drugs. "

This may have been her first time in court, but Katie sensed that there was something very wrong about all this. She thought back to her ethics class in law school. A judge was supposed to avoid even an appearance of impropriety. Green's writing of a decision before hearing the argument of the other side was odd. It didn't pass the smell test. She also wondered about the judge's meeting with the two lawyers for the defendant just before the motion. They hadn't tried to hide the fact, but what other reason would they have for being in the judge's private chambers with him? She made a note to ask Gary about it.

Green looked at his notes and continued, "For the reasons I have stated, the motion is granted and the cases are dismissed."

Green glared at both Newton and Katie again, stood, and left the courtroom. The bailiff's belated "All rise" echoed throughout the room.

Chapter 9
October 2011

It took Drs. Elizabeth Barrett and Deepak Patel nearly four months to complete their investigation. Barrett called Patel and told him that she'd reviewed what he'd written and wanted to go over the report with him in person. They met and Barrett suggested some small changes. Patel worked on the report late that night. He read through the final version and was satisfied that it contained everything that needed to be said. He stood, stretched, and rubbed his eyes. He was weary. He turned out the lights in his lab, locked the door, and drove to his small apartment. The phone was ringing as he entered the front door. He guessed it was his wife or daughter calling from home. He missed them dearly and looked forward to talking with them.

"Dr. Patel, this is Siva Geer. We met a couple of years ago in Florida. We were both speakers on the same program."

"Of course I remember you. I still think about your remarkable presentation. How are you? What can I do for you?"

Geer was considered by many scientists to be a potential candidate for a Nobel Prize in medicine for his research on the molecular structures of various types of bacteria. His research had opened up a new era for the development of specific antibiotics for the treatment of infections caused by these organisms. Patel was flattered that he would receive a telephone call from such a distinguished scientist.

"I understand that you have come to India to work at Enpact, is that right?"

Patel had the feeling that this call was going to be more than just a cordial welcome. "Yes, that's right. I am the head of the department of scientific research. I've been here eight months now."

"I've tried for several days to speak with someone at your company, but no one returned my phone calls until this evening. A Dr. Barrett called me back and said for me to speak with you. She gave me your number."

"Is there something wrong?"

"Yes. I have terrible news. I've discovered that in the past two years more than seven hundred children have died from serious infections after being treated with Enpact's brand of ampicillin. All of these deaths occurred at Senegal Medical Hospital or its allied hospitals. A few months ago, I was contacted by the chief pathologist of the hospitals who asked me if I could look into the reasons for these deaths because they seemed to be part of a pattern and I agreed to do so. Ampicillin, as you know, is the first line antibiotic to be used in the treatment of any severe childhood infection. Ninety-five percent of these children received your company's drug, which was supposed to contain five hundred milligrams of ampicillin. When I looked at this alarming number of deaths, and saw that the high rate of ampicillin use was ineffective, I thought it must be some problem with the drug. So I requested samples of your product from each of the hospitals and I found that not one of the samples contained any ampicillin. Then I requested that an order be placed from your company for additional antibiotics, which I then also tested, and not one contained ampicillin. Enpact's ampicillin is fake. These fake drugs used on these poor children who needed antibiotic treatment caused their deaths."

Patel could scarcely breathe as he listened to Geer. Seven hundred children dead and our product killed them.

"These tests were all done within the past month," Geer continued, "and I rushed my writing so that the information can be made known as quickly as possible so that other medical institutions can avoid this terrible problem."

The more the man spoke, the deeper Patel slipped into despair.

"My friend, your company is in deep trouble," Geer asserted. "I know of your reputation for integrity and I know you will deal with this. This drug has to be removed from the market immediately. Your company must notify other hospitals immediately to stop using your so-called ampicillin."

Patel knew that this was much more than just making minor lab errors that made no difference in treatment outcome. This was solid evidence of fraud that was causing great harm to users of its drugs. It was criminal, no other word for it. Something had to be done.

"To say that I'm sorry is meaningless. I will make this known to them immediately. I will see that something is done."

Patel ended the call and sat for a long time at the table with his head in his hands. It was too late to try anything tonight. He thought about what he should do, how this should be handled. He went to bed and tried to sleep.

The next morning he was exhausted. He hadn't been able to sleep. Geer's phone call clinched his resolve. This couldn't wait any longer. He had to do something quickly to force the issue, not only on this ampicillin disaster but also on the entire drug product line. This was the twenty-first century, for God's sake, not the middle ages. He sat at his apartment in his small kitchen, stirred his cold cup of coffee and thought about the phone call. It was difficult for him to concentrate on anything other than the dead children, and what Enpact had done. He was sickened by his sense of shame at being involved with Enpact.

Chapter 10
October 2011

Back at the office, Gary looked at Katie. "I didn't expect this. I'm shocked by the judge's decision. He's flat-out wrong."

"What do we do now?" Katie asked.

Gary thought for a moment. "I'm going to call Hempstead and talk to him. There are only a handful of defense lawyers I trust and Hempstead is one of them. He doesn't play games. Judge Green's decision is wrong. Hempstead knows it, and it's probably worth a shot to see if we can reach an agreement with him to avoid an appeal. I'll call him."

Gary called Hempstead and Katie listened by speakerphone. "Lester, I'm thinking you feel the same way about Green's decision as I do. He's dead wrong. It's a stupid decision. I want you to think about agreeing to set aside the decision and restoring the cases to the docket. That would save us both a lot of time and effort, not to mention the costs involved for both sides in a lengthy appeal. Green doesn't realize it, but he'd be the laughing stock of Michigan courts when the word gets out about this stupid decision."

Silence on the other end of the line.

Newton pressed, "What do you think?"

"Gary, you met Tim Holt at the motion. He's the decision-maker. Personally, I think you're right and I've already told him the same thing. But he's adamant about pressing any advantage we have. Even if we ultimately lose on appeal."

Newton grimaced. "I'll go a step further. Let me offer something else. Tell Holt we'll drop our claim for punitive damages if he agrees to set aside the judge's ruling."

Another long pause. "I can try, but I tell you right now it's unlikely."

"All I can ask is that you try."

"I'll give him a call. Don't hold your breath."

After the call ended, Gary looked at Katie. "In Michigan, punitive damages can sometimes be awarded by a jury when the conduct of a defendant is egregious, but that is not the usual case in drug product litigation. Anything short of a company memo saying that the company deliberately intended to kill five thousand people by marketing a drug wouldn't meet the test for punitive damages. It's common practice for us lawyers to include everything possible in the pleadings when we file a lawsuit, but as a practical matter, claims for punitive damages are generally dropped before the trial begins. So, it's no big deal to agree to dismiss a claim for punitive damages this early in the game. But it does allow Hempstead to offer his client something in return for agreement on the judge's ruling. Understand?"

Katie nodded and spoke, "Can I ask a question?"

Gary nodded.

"The Michigan drug product liability law is in two parts. One part deals with misbranded labeling, the other with product adulteration. The judge used the wrong part. He considered the part that deals with misbranded drug labeling. He's confused that part from the other part that concerns adulterated drugs. Can he just disregard it like that? Can he do that?"

Gary rubbed his chin and thought for a moment. "Judges get

issues mixed up and do the wrong things all the time. That is why we have appellate courts, to straighten out the messes caused by trial judges. Generic Lorital is adulterated, and we don't claim that the drug is misbranded. We claim that Enpact is selling an adulterated product in this country and is violating the laws of this country involving adulteration. The issue of an inconvenient forum is a red herring. The judge should have given us the opportunity to develop facts to serve as the basis for our adulteration contention. He just blew off my comments about excessive testosterone dosage and belittled me about the cockroach thing. These are the very reasons that the drug is adulterated. If Hempstead doesn't agree to set aside the judge's decision, I predict the court of appeals will reverse Green and reinstate the cases. The problem is that it will take us a long time, probably a year or two. This phone call was worth a try, but it's a long shot. If it doesn't work, one way or another, we'll get these cases reinstated."

Katie spoke up. "Maybe next time he'll even wait until after argument before he writes his decision."

Gary smiled. "You noticed that too?"

"I was surprised. It was obvious he'd already made his mind up. When the judge walked into the courtroom, the two lawyers followed him right from his chambers. Is that right? The judge meeting with the two lawyers without us."

"You might expect that a judge would avoid any contact with just one side, but it happens all the time. I tried a case recently where the judge was a former partner of the defense lawyer. The two had lunch together every day of the trial. That judge assured me it wouldn't make any difference in how he handled the case. He was right. I won the case, but I was leery the whole time. As to

Judge Green writing out his decision beforehand, one would expect he would have at least allowed me to finish the argument."

Hempstead called back. The call had produced results. Hempstead agreed to present Judge Green with a conditional order of dismissal allowing the plaintiffs to conduct discovery for ninety days if they gave up a claim for punitive damages. Giving up punitive damages as a trade-off, Newton explained to Katie, wasn't a big deal since punitive damages were practically never awarded in Michigan anyway. "Most personal injury cases in the state are limited to compensatory damages by law and situations which call for punitive damages result from egregious criminal conduct well beyond what is seen in the ordinary civil negligence case. In my experience, even without claiming punitive damages, a jury will punish a defendant by awarding a larger sum of money when the defendant's conduct is really bad. Since we really haven't given up anything."

They now had ninety days to come up with something, a set of facts to change the judge's mind.

"Tonight, put a plan together for the next ninety days," Gary instructed Katie. "I'll do the same. We'll meet early tomorrow morning and compare notes, decide what to do. We also need to meet with our clients to bring them up to date. Besides, they need to meet the new super-star lawyer." He grinned. "Set them up for a meeting in our conference room in about two weeks."

Chapter 11
November 2011

Katie sat in her hotel room in Washington, D.C., attempting to focus on the next day. She'd made arrangements to review all the documents the FDA had on generic Lorital. The Freedom of Information Act required the government to produce whatever information and materials they had on demand. She knew there were more than a thousand documents but didn't know how many more. It would take at least one day to review them and make arrangements to have copies made. She planned a second day if necessary.

She thought about the ambitious plan she and Gary had to get as much done as possible over the ninety days. Gary had suggested she start by coming here to the FDA. Two weeks from now, she'd go to Enpact headquarters in India to review the company's in-house documents and take depositions of several key Enpact employees.

Her stomach growled, reminding her that she hadn't eaten since breakfast, so she went downstairs to the hotel restaurant. But it was too quiet there so she decided to order a sandwich at the adjacent bar, which was livelier with an after-work crowd. She took a seat at the far end of the bar and ordered a glass or merlot along with a sandwich. Shortly, a man sat in the seat next to hers. She watched as two attractive, young blondes at the other end of the bar worked a group of men standing around them. Katie wasn't close enough to hear the chatter, but she could guess what was being said by the too-obvious gestures of the girls. Their message was clear. If you wanted to talk to them, buy them drinks. Each had several in front of them.

"Excuse me. Would you like another drink?"

Katie turned to the man seated next to her. He'd spoken softly in a pleasant accent.

"Are you English?"

"No. I'm from India but I went to Oxford for five years. Stayed in England for a time after finishing."

Katie looked at her nearly empty wine glass. "Sure. I'd love another drink."

The man caught the eye of the bartender, held up two fingers, and gestured to the glasses in front of them. The bartender nodded.

"So tell me, what's a beautiful girl like you doing in a place like this?"

Oh, please, Katie thought, rolled her eyes. "You should fire the writer of your pickup lines."

He looked at her with a quizzical expression, giving her the chance to take a closer look at him. He was about twice her age, handsome, slim, and dressed in an expensive business suit. She liked his tie, a striking pattern of red on black, and glanced down at his shoes, polished to a high shine. She was drawn to his sparkling, deep-set brown eyes. His hair was longish and swept back in a fashionable style, giving him a movie-star look.

Katie usually enjoyed the give and take of bar talk, particularly with good-looking guys. She considered herself quite the expert on the subject of men in bars. She thought back to her father. When she was a kid, he'd take her to the local tavern to show off her prodigious memory for baseball trivia to his friends. A small group

SAFE NOWHERE

of his buddies would gather around and laugh heartily every time she'd spout a statistic or some obscure baseball detail. She'd look over at her dad and he'd always have his big smile. Now she'd get teary-eyed whenever she thought about him. He'd died the year before she started law school and she missed him badly.

"Hello. Anyone home?"

She looked over at the man. He must have asked a question. "I'm sorry. Did you say something?" She blinked, wiped a tear from her eye.

"Lost you for a minute there. Are you all right?"

"I'm fine. Just thinking about something. So what did you say?"

"I said I couldn't believe a beautiful woman like you would be here by herself."

She rolled her eyes again. "I haven't heard that line since I kicked the slats out of my cradle."

"Excuse me?"

"Never mind. Just one of my favorite expressions. What kind of work do you do?"

"I'm a lawyer. And you?"

"I'm a lawyer, too. I sue pharmaceutical companies. I'm a specialist in handling cases against the drug industry." She smiled as she thought about her interview with Newton. "Actually, I like to think of myself as a specialist in causing disruptive innovation in drug companies."

He gave her a strange look. He said nothing.

She extended her hand. "I'm Katie Hornsby. Like the baseball player."

He accepted her hand and shook it gently. "Richard Lion. Like

93

the beast."

They both laughed. He had a great smile.

"I'm a baseball nut, a Detroit Tiger fan."

"Yankee fan here," he said. "A through and true Yankee fan."

"Did you hear about the Yankee's triple play in April? It was unique because it took six throws to get the three outs."

He looked at Katie, shook his head, and shrugged.

"I can't help it. I like baseball trivia and because we're here in Washington, let me tell you a piece of Yankee trivia that also involves Washington. In the Broadway musical *Damn Yankees*, the story is really about the Washington Senators, who win the American League pennant race over your Yankees. My favorite song, 'You Gotta Have Heart,' comes from the play."

He said nothing, just sat there and looked at her, a curious expression on his face.

She was just getting warmed up. "How many ways can a batter get on base without making a hit?"

"What?"

"Try to answer the question. How many ways do you think:"

"You are an interesting person, Ms. Katie the baseball nut. I have no idea what the answer is."

"Just think about it." She took another sip of wine. The alcohol was having its intended effect. She looked at him. "What kind of law do you practice?"

"I don't actually practice law. I'm a consultant and I work as a lobbyist here in Washington for my clients. What is this disruptive innovation you mentioned?"

"It's a long story. What companies do you work for?"

"An American company and a couple of companies from

India."

"I'm here on a case against a drug company from India. You don't work for

Enpact, do you?"

"No, but I know about it. It is an industrial giant in India, very successful and highly reputable. I must admit that I think there are too many lawsuits in America as a result of your so-called system of justice."

"Houston. We have a problem."

"Houston?"

"It's a cliché. However, we do have a problem. I feel very strongly that lobbyists in Washington give too much money to politicians who do things that hurt a lot of ordinary people."

He looked somberly at her. "We disagree so we can't talk about this. We have to decide what we can talk about."

She smiled. "What do you suggest?" She looked at him closely.

"Why don't we go up to my suite? I'll tell you when we get there." He returned the smile. Such perfect teeth, she thought.

"You've got a good curve ball."

"Curve ball? I don't get it."

"It's a metaphor for your attempt to get me to your room, but it's not going to happen. I know how to hit a curve ball." She pointed her finger at the other end of the bar. "Maybe you want to go work on those two girls. Two for the price of one."

"I want to talk with you. I have no interest in them."

"I'll bet you say that to all the girls."

"All the girls?"

"Another cliché, probably my favorite."

"I'm enjoying talking with you. It's refreshing and you are so very beautiful."

"So talk. We don't need to go to your room to talk. Tell me how do you feel about the fact that big business bribes politicians to get what they want?" Katie stopped for a moment. Did she just say that?

"I don't buy that assumption."

"And I've got a bridge for sale."

"A bridge? You talk in circles."

"Never mind. So you really believe that lobbying and paying big money to influence politicians is ethical? Is this big business's attempted solution to avoid failure due to disruptive innovation?"

"I thought we agreed that subject was off limits."

"You said that. Not me. I'd like to know what your personal thoughts are about what you do for work, not what some giant corporation pays you to think."

"It doesn't matter what I personally think." He looked hard at Katie. "I think you've had too much to drink."

"I can understand why you don't want to talk about it. But my belief is that there are only two alternatives in this kind of situation. You are either part of the solution or part of the problem. Saying or doing nothing makes you part of the problem." What a motor mouth. She just couldn't stop. He was right. She'd had too much to drink.

He stood and she expected that he'd just walk away. She figured he was upset because she wouldn't go to his room.

He leaned closer. "I told you I'd rather not talk about it. Why don't you just leave it alone?"

"Hit a nerve, did I?"

"A nerve?"

"Another favorite expression. It means that you are going to think about this conversation and then try to do something about it."

She smiled, just to lighten the tension. It was time to back off. She could be such a bitch. He was apparently mollified because he sat back down. Fifteen minutes later, they stood in front of the hotel elevators. They shook hands and exchanged business cards. When the elevator door opened, she stepped in and waited for him to enter.

He mumbled and backed away. "I left something at the bar. Have a good night."

He was probably going to go back to hit on the two girls. Whether he did or not, she could care less.

TOM BLEAKLEY

Chapter 12
November 2011

Deepak Patel had become good friends with Vijay Gupta since his arrival at Enpact. Gupta had gone out of his way to make Patel feel welcome. He and his wife had invited him to dinner several times a week, and those pleasant evenings with the couple and their lively children had done much to ease the ache of loneliness that Patel felt so far away from home. Patel's wife and children had remained in the U.S. at their home in New Jersey, as it was agreed that both children would complete their high school education there. Patel had rented a hotel room about fifteen minutes from the gleaming headquarters of Enpact that served as a place to sleep and take his morning coffee. He was grateful for the generosity and friendship of the Guptas in opening their home to him. Their generosity and the fact that Gupta worked directly under him in Patel's department created an obligation for him, he thought, to let Gupta know what was going on. Geer's phone call last night was the final straw. He'd called Gupta early this morning and asked him to meet him before the workday began at his office. It was so early that the gardeners were still watering shrubs and cleaners were still polishing the lobby's tile floors when Gupta arrived. As always, he was punctual.

Gupta was alarmed by the sudden change in his friend. Patel's round face and deep-set eyes radiated a sadness that was new. He looked exhausted and Gupta noticed that the man's shoulders slumped as if he carried a too-heavy burden. They sat across from each other in the large conference room adjoining Patel's office.

Patel took a deep breath. "I am very discouraged and disheartened about events that have occurred."

Gupta leaned forward. "My friend, you do not look well."

"I didn't sleep last night. That's why I called you here. We need to talk. I can trust you."

"Of course. What can I do?"

"I need you to just listen for a few minutes. Help me decide what I must do, what action I should take."

Gupta nodded. "Go ahead."

"This company, our company, has committed terrible crimes. I came here to make things better. What I have discovered is that it is much worse than I could have ever imagined. Much worse…"

Gupta waited for him to continue.

"I received a terrible phone call last night from a distinguished scientist in this country." He summarized the conversation with Geer, concluding, "My guess is that most of the drugs made at Enpact are worthless or, worse yet, toxic. There is no data or research to support any claims that are made about most of the product line. What data or research we do have is taken or stolen from drugs of our competitors."

"You believe this Dr. Geer? You guess all of our drugs are worthless? Is there any proof? What makes you think this is so?"

"One of the project directors went to the States three weeks ago. As he was leaving to come back, they gave him a briefcase and asked him to deliver it to our laboratories here. The briefcase contained stock packages of several trade name drugs from other companies. But later that week I found out that the drugs he brought in were going to be tested and submitted to the FDA as if they were the test results of our own products."

"How do you know that? What proof do you have?"

"I spoke with the lab technician, the guy who runs the tests. He told me that it was routine policy to submit studies done on trade drugs from other companies as our own."

"He might have been joking."

"He wasn't joking. I insisted on finding out for myself whether he was telling the truth. I went into his laboratory and verified that the only testing we do is on the products of other companies. Dr. Barrett contacted me about the very same thing. We sat down and went over the tests that were submitted on generic Lorital. We did not do equivalency tests on our own products. I looked at the studies of several drugs, including Lorital. All of them were the same. Now that I've heard from Dr. Geer about his test results on our ampicillin and what it's done to those children, I am fully aware of the terrible consequences of this dangerous practice. We not only cheat and submit false data to gain approval of our products; we then make the drugs in a totally unacceptable manner. One of the project managers told me that what we sell in Africa is absolutely worthless and that our management knows about this and approves it. We sell almost forty percent of the generic drugs used in the U.S. Our generic Lorital sales in America alone are well over $2 billion and we have done no actual testing on the product. Before I came here, I did a study comparing generic Lorital with the trade-name drug. Ours was definitely more toxic and I could not explain why. One of the reasons I was hired was to improve the safety of not only Lorital but also Enpact's entire drug line. We have continued to receive reports of serious adverse reactions in users of our products and these reactions are not seen or reported with brand-name product. Our Lorital is a dangerous drug, but we don't have the slightest idea how dangerous it is."

"You aren't joking, are you?" Gupta knew he wasn't.

"My friend, this is not the kind of thing one jokes about."

"You say you need my help. Why?"

"This is a big company. I am new. Management is more likely to take this seriously if it's more than just me bringing it to their attention. There is strength in number. Dr. Barrett has agreed to do so with me. I would like you to join with us in approaching them as well."

Gupta sat back and thought. "What you've just told me is not new. These rumors have been circulating for a couple of years now. In the past, employees who have brought these rumors to the attention of our superiors have found themselves out of work."

"These are not rumors, my friend. They are true. I can prove it."

Gupta hesitated and then spoke carefully. "You have spent your professional life in America. Things are different here in India. There is an unwritten rule here in India that we just do what we want to do. If a problem occurs, there is nothing a couple of phone calls cannot fix. There is always someone who knows someone, who knows somebody else who can and will intervene to take care of problems. All it takes is a little money to make things go away. So business goes on as usual. This is India, not the U.S." Gupta stopped and looked at Patel. "And there's a problem for me personally. My friend, as you know, I have a wife and six children to feed at home. I am sorry but I must think of them. I cannot be of help to you."

Gupta stood and extended his hand. "A word of advice, though. Be very careful, my friend. Very careful."

# # #

After Gupta left, Patel sat at his desk and thought about Gupta's comments. He'd been right. The "business as usual" approach of Enpact was exactly how the company operated. With the new information about the children's deaths, he couldn't sit back and do nothing. He'd take care of this by himself. He wouldn't put other employees, including Barrett, at risk of losing their jobs, but the possible loss to him was of no concern. He picked up his report, and headed upstairs to the CEO's office. Patel could not put this off any longer. Immediate action was necessary.

"I want to see Mr. Singh now."

The attractive receptionist looked up at him. "Mr. Singh is busy." She looked at the calendar on her desk. "I can give you an appointment next Monday at four o'clock."

"I want to see him right now. Tell him that I'm here, and that it's an emergency."

She hesitated. "I'm afraid that is not possible."

"Please call right now or I'm just going to walk right in."

"He will be very angry." She shook her head.

Patel didn't hesitate. He walked past the receptionist into Singh's office without knocking. Singh was lying on a massage table. A young woman was giving him a massage.

Singh sat up. "Who are you? What are you doing here? Get out."

Patel stood and looked at the portly man as the masseuse

attempted to cover his naked body with a towel.

"I must speak with you...now."

"Get out of here. Get out or I'll have security take you out."

"Sir, I am Deepak Patel, your head of research. I have information for you that must be acted upon immediately."

"I don't care what you have...or who you are. Get out. I am busy."

Patel had no choice. "I am not leaving this room until you do me the courtesy of listening. I will turn my back while you get dressed, but I am not leaving. You need to hear what I have to say."

Patel turned away and folded his arms. Singh walked to his desk and yelled into his phone. "Call security. Get them up here right now."

Singh hung up and Patel turned around. Singh's large breasts hung over his pendulous abdomen, a pathetic comic caricature of a human body. He held a small towel in front of him.

"You are fired. Get out."

Patel fought to maintain his composure, "Mr. Singh, Enpact is in terrible trouble. We are responsible for the deaths of more than seven hundred children. The drug that caused these deaths must be removed from the market immediately. You must issue an order recalling the drug everywhere it's been sold. I'm surprised that the police are not already here to arrest you. You must do something. I have prepared a detailed report of other problems I have observed in the few months I've been here." He held the report up in his hand.

"I said get out."

Patel stepped forward and placed the report on the man's desk.

"I am leaving. You don't have to throw me out. I'm leaving this office and I'm leaving Enpact today. I can't be part of such a dishonest company. But for God's sake, please do something immediately about these dead children. Read this report and take the necessary steps to make your products safe."

Patel turned and left the room. He went back to his office and cleaned out his desk, nervously waited for security to remove him from the building. Nothing. No guards, no word from Singh's office, nothing. He sat and thought for a long time. The ampicillin issue had to be dealt with first. He composed an email on his laptop and sent it to the heads of all departments in the company. The message was clear and simple. Stop the production of ampicillin. Get the product already sold back from hospitals and wholesalers. Tell doctors to stop using Enpact's ampicillin. Warn people by radio or television to stop use of any such drug in their possession. He didn't care whether he'd been fired or not, whether he had the authority to act or not. It just needed to be done, so he did it.

He called Dr. Barrett and told her what he'd done.

"I received your email and have already instructed my people to follow your instructions exactly. I have also tried to schedule a meeting with Mr. Singh, but he refuses to see me. I am giving my notice, too. I can't be part of this place any longer. This is such a terrible thing. Those poor children..." She started crying and hung up the phone.

Patel finished packing and left the office. He spent another sleepless night wondering what his next step should be. What else could he do? This was an international crisis. Enpact's drugs were used throughout the world, including the U.S. The next morning, he booked his flight to return to the U.S. He looked at his watch. By this time tomorrow, he would be home.

He took the rest of the day and negotiated the terms of his departure with the company. The only thing the company really wanted was for him to leave his report behind, not to take it with him. He was given a generous severance check conditioned upon his acceptance of that condition. The company could keep the damn report, he thought, but nothing could prevent him from telling others what he knew. He wouldn't be leaving his brain or his personal knowledge behind.

Chapter 13
November 2011

After nine hours of looking at documents, Katie was hungry, tired, and needing a drink. It had been a rough day. She opted for the drink first so she headed to the bar.

She sat at the end of the bar and sipped her wine—her therapy and a gift to herself for having dealt all day with Lance Rebus, Jr., the young silk-stocking lawyer from Hempstead's firm who monitored her every move the entire day. All day long, she'd follow the same routine: pick up a document, read it, attach a paper clip if she wanted it copied. Sometimes she'd make a note on her laptop, then repeat the routine with the next document. Rebus Junior just sat there eyeing her. The room had been too small for the both of them and, to make matters worse, Rebus had eaten something with garlic for lunch so by the end of the day the room was hot, smelly, and humid. But, as she took a sip of her wine, she did admit to herself that Junior was kind of cute in his own dorky way.

She checked her phone for emails and felt a gentle tap on her shoulder. She looked up. It was Richard.

"You're back." His tone of voice suggested he was glad to see her. He slid onto the next stool.

"And you're back, too." She grinned. "There must be a magnet around here somewhere." She pretended to look under her seat.

"That's cute. You're a funny girl, Ms. Baseball."

She grinned again. "You just say that because you cannot

107

remember my name, Mr. Richard Lion."

"Yes I can. You're Katie Hornsby, the great-granddaughter of the greatest baseball player who ever lived."

His accent was so charming. "You've got the name right, but I'm not related to that Roger Hornsby."

He smiled. "I thought about your question all day."

"My question?"

"Yes. How many ways a batter can get on base without making a hit. A player can get on base by getting hit by a pitch, or the catcher drops a third strike."

She laughed and held up two fingers. "That's only two. You've got four more to go." They both laughed. He ordered drinks for both of them, then another round, and another. She never got around to eating dinner. The rest of the evening was a blur.

# # #

She woke with a start, confused about where she was. She was nude. She looked around the large room and saw her clothes folded neatly on a small couch against the wall. Where was she? How did she get here? Why wasn't she wearing her nightgown? She sat up and saw that she was on one side of a king-size bed and that someone had obviously slept on the other side. She had a splitting headache. She tried but couldn't remember how she got here. Her eyes hurt from the bright sunlight shining through the window.

Richard Lion walked into the room and she scrambled to cover herself with the bed sheet. He was fully dressed.

"Good morning. I thought I heard you moving around. Breakfast and hot coffee are waiting in the other room. I've got an early meeting. Please let yourself out. No rush. Can we have dinner tonight?"

She nodded. He walked over and kissed her on the lips. She wished she could remember last night, how she got here.

He left the suite and she lay still, tried to deal with her hangover, the splitting headache, and the question of what happened to bring her to this room. She crawled out of bed and took a long hot shower. She checked the time. She was already thirty minutes late for the document review. She dressed, same outfit with a few wrinkles, slurped some too-hot coffee, grabbed a croissant off the tray and headed out the door. Almost too late, she realized her laptop was still in the suite; she managed to stop the door before it shut. She took a deep breath. She would have had a tough time explaining at the front desk why they should let her into the suite when she was registered in another room.

She decided not to go back to her own room to change clothes. There was no time. Rebus Junior would just have to put up with her just the way she was.

TOM BLEAKLEY

Chapter 14
November 2011

"Goddammit, why can't you make the call? I've got a lot of irons in the fire. Besides, you know Haley a hell of a lot better than I do." Oliver Brewster took a large swallow of scotch and looked at Timothy Holt.

Holt shrugged. "Ah know him better than you, but every time I see him I'm asking a favor. Ah think he's getting tired of my requests."

Brewster downed his drink. "If I remember correctly, he's got three more years before he has to run for reelection. Hell, then he'll be sniffing around you for money like a dog in heat. Judges are politicians in robes and they're all alike. Remember, the favors run both ways. You sure as hell have given him enough money in the past to justify your asking him to help on this. Incidentally, I've also sent a letter to our friend Judge Green. I told him if he needs a sponsor to get into Oakland Hills, I could take care of that for him."

Holt sat forward. "Just call Haley and ask him to put pressure on Green to hold firm on his Enpact decision. He'll know what to do. We've got to have those Enpact cases stay dismissed. Green dismissed the cases and then turned around and gave Newton ninety days to conduct discovery. I don't know why he did that. These cases have got to go away. I got a phone call this morning tellin' me that Stanley Crumley is making noises about comin' into the case. That asshole would fuck up a wet dream. If we don't get

111

Newton's cases dismissed before Stanley jumps in, they'll be ads in every newspaper in the country drummin' up Lorital clients. Stanley will find some judge somewhere in the country to take the case. He forum shops all the goddamn time. Last big case was in Mississippi where all the judges are prob'ly on his payroll. We can't let that happen in this case."

Brewster looked at Holt and smiled. "Stanley's not such a bad guy. I've worked with him before. He's a sheep in wolf's clothing."

"You said it wrong. You mean a wolf in sheep's clothing."

"No. I'm saying it exactly the way I meant to say it. Let me tell you why."

Holt checked his watch. "I don' have time to listen to one of your stories. Tell me some other time. Call Haley and put some pressure on him. Remember, we give ALEC a hell of a lot of money too."

Holt tossed down the rest of his drink and left Brewster at the table by himself. Oliver sat there for a while, had another drink, and thought about what he would say to Haley. God, he loved this work.

# # #

Richard lifted his glass of wine and tapped it against Katie's. "Cheers. How was your day?"

They were at the Navy Club, a swanky, members-only restaurant four blocks from the White House, seated at a corner table away from other diners, at Richard's request. Katie, wide-eyed, looked around. She tried not to stare but it was almost too much to process. At a nearby table, the leader of the Senate was engaged in quiet conversation with the Speaker of the House. Several Congressmen stopped by their table to say hello to Richard. She found it difficult to speak when introduced so she just nodded and smiled. A Supreme Court Justice sat at another table and nodded toward Richard.

"I'm so star-struck I can hardly speak," she said. She took a sip if wine and collected her thoughts. "But my day went well. To be exact, I'll be going back to Detroit with 1,024 pages of documents in my brief case. At twenty cents a page, it wasn't cheap, but knowing what I got it'll be worth it."

"What did you find so interesting?"

This was what was so nice about Richard. He was interested in what she had to say. He knew how to listen.

"Orex Pharmaceuticals is a really big drug company here in the United States. I found some documents showing that Enpact and Orex are working together. The two companies share information and do a lot of things together. If I had to guess, I'd say they're part of the same corporation."

"Katie, I hate to be so ignorant, but why do these documents help your case?"

"Well, if there actually is some collusion or agreement between the two companies, it gives us more evidence to bolster our contention that Enpact has sufficient contacts in the United States."

"That's good, then. I'm happy for you."

"There's other good stuff, too, but I really am too tired to talk about it."

Richard looked at her. "We won't stay out late. I know you have an early flight. My day went well. I'm going to New York tomorrow."

She nodded. "I know so little about you."

"You look gorgeous in that outfit."

"Thank you. I love your tie." Clothes make the man, and the man makes the girl. She grinned at the thought.

"What's so funny?"

"Nothing. It's just so nice here. I'm enjoying this so much. So many famous people…and most of them know you. Thank you for bringing me here."

He reached for the bottle of wine and refilled her glass. She took a sip. It tasted good, liquid gold. But she shouldn't drink too much. She needed to keep her wits about her—it had taken almost the entire day, and many aspirin, to get rid of her headache from drinking too much the night before. She thought about how she'd searched for Richard on Google before she leaving her room this evening. She'd wanted to know more about this tall, dark, and handsome stranger. Her search came up empty. There were a lot of Richard Lions listed, but none of them were him.

"I don't even know where you live. What city do you live in?"

"I maintain an apartment in Manhattan. I travel so much that I'm rarely there. You'll have to come and visit me. I also come here to Washington a great deal of the time. You can come to visit me here, too."

She liked the way he smiled at her. For all she knew, he could be married. She didn't want to ask. Besides, after last night, the point was moot. That reminded her of something. "Thought any more about my question?"

He smiled. "As a matter of fact, yes. A batter can be walked by the pitcher or a catcher can interfere with the batter."

She giggled in response. "That's two more. Four down and two to go. And how was your day?"

"My day was excellent…almost as good as last night."

She blushed and took a large swallow of wine. She sat quietly, looking around the room.

Richard leaned toward her. "Is something wrong?"

She was still processing the "good as last night" comment. All day long, she had tried as hard as she could to remember the night before. She shook her head. "I'm just tired. Tell me more about you."

He leaned forward and took her hand. He drew small circles on the back of her hand with his index finger. His touch felt good. "What is it that you want to know?"

"Do you have an office? Where do you work?"

"I do not have an office. The companies I work with generally provide me space to work. I also work in my apartment a lot."

"Why do I get the feeling that you don't live in the apartment in New York?"

"I don't live there, but it's the closest thing to home for me. Whenever I have a break in my schedule, that's where I go."

"How do you know all these politicians?"

"My work calls for me to contact congressmen and senators and tell them about the needs of my clients. I am a registered lobbyist, but it's only a small part of what I do."

"Given the choice of anyone in the world, who would you want as a dinner guest?"

He stopped and looked at her for a moment, puzzled by the question.

"Why do you ask?"

"Just trying to learn things about you. Your job sounds so interesting. I'd have Justice Ruth Ginsburg. She's a pioneer on breaking legal ground for women. I'd prefer Miguel Cabrera, the Tigers star, but he doesn't speak English very well." Katie stopped. She was so tired that she was just rambling.

Richard said quietly, "I've never thought about it. I'd have to take some time before I could answer."

He reached into his jacket pocket and handed her a business card. It was different from the one he'd given her the other night. "These are my numbers in case you want to reach me."

The card listed a website as well as three phone numbers. It was an impressive looking card. She realized she was probably right about the first card he'd given her; it was for girls he'd meet while traveling.

"Do you have a family? Are they in the U.S.?"

"My parents are both alive and living in India. I have several brothers and sisters who live in India as well. I miss them terribly but I work so much that I hardly ever have the opportunity to visit them. I do love being in the States. I am happy here."

She tried unsuccessfully to stifle a yawn.

"Do you want to leave?"

"I'm really not hungry."

He grins. "I'm hungry, but not for food. We can eat later at the hotel if we want food. Let's go."

Unlike the night before, she remembered everything about the rest of the night. Everything.

Chapter 15
December 2011

"Dad, why is ALEC interested in your Lorital case? I saw the letter."

Green knew that Abigail must have gone through his desk. There was no other way she could have known about the letter. He had stashed it away carefully. He would never have left it out in plain sight.

He looked around the dinner table. It wasn't just Abigail who waited for his answer. All three daughters and Nancy had stopped eating and looked at him.

"It's a group of judges who meet and discuss things."

Nancy smirked. "Is the letter from that Brewster guy you played golf with?"

Green avoided looking at his wife. "Yes. He told me how much he enjoyed playing."

Abigail wouldn't leave it alone. "If the group is supposed to be just judges, why do they call it the American Legislative Exchange Council? I'm not stupid. Legislators are not judges."

"It's judges and legislators."

Nancy smirked again. "It's a group that hates trial lawyers who sue the drug industry, if you believe what Brewster had to say." She looked into Green's eyes. "Have you joined ALEC? From what I've heard they're pro-NRA. That should be right up your alley."

What is this, he thought, the inquisition? "I have not joined. I played golf with the guy. That's all."

"Dad. I read the letter. It said that he looked forward to your favorable ruling on Albright. I thought judges weren't supposed to discuss their rulings with others."

Green was miffed. "Where did you find that letter? I know it wasn't sitting out on my desk."

"I went through your desk to try to find some paper clips. It was right there in a drawer."

"You had no right to go snooping in my desk."

"I wasn't snooping in your desk. I told you, I was looking for papers clips."

Nancy's eyes narrowed and she focused on her husband. "Abigail has asked a question. I'd like to hear the answer. Is it all right for a judge to discuss his potential decision on a big case against a drug company with a high-ranking member of an organization dedicated to eliminating lawsuits against the industry? And...if it is all right, why are you afraid to even talk with your family about it? After all, we stand to lose as much as you do if it becomes public knowledge that you're hanging around with a bunch of nuts telling you what to do. Good-bye, Judge Green."

Abigail stood. "I looked up ALEC. Mom's right. It's a group backed by a bunch of millionaires and drug and tobacco companies. I didn't snoop in your desk, but even if I had you hanging around with people telling you what to do on your cases is a whole lot worse." She stood, burst into tears, and ran out of the room.

# # #

A week after her return from Washington, Katie and Gary met with the Lorital clients in the conference room. Newton called the meeting to order. "I appreciate you coming down today on such short notice. There is some information about your cases that is important for you to know, and we felt it was best to discuss this in a group setting, so that you are all on the same page. Before we get started, I'd like to introduce Katie Hornsby, our new associate, who is responsible for handling the day-to-day details of the Lorital litigation. She'll be telling you about what has happened. Let's go around the table and have everyone tell us their name. Sharon, why don't we start with you?"

Albright stood. "I'm Sharon Albright. My husband died of a heart attack after taking generic Lorital for nearly three years."

One by one, each of the remaining clients stood and gave their names and brief descriptions of their individual claims. Katie wrote down each name as they spoke. Mark Stenson went last and remained seated, arms folded across his chest. "I had a heart attack after taking generic Lorital for three weeks. I've been out of work since."

Newton nodded toward Katie. "Katie, bring us up-to-date on what's happened? Then, we'll answer questions."

Katie stood. "If you do have a question, please wait until I finish, because I may answer it in the meantime. There has been a negative turn of events, as Mr. Newton said, and we felt it was important to bring you all together so you could hear about the bad news from us. Our belief is that the judge may soon dismiss your cases. By the end of this meeting, we want you to understand what has happened and what we intend to do about it if that happens."

She looked around the room and everyone, except Mark Stinson, nodded in agreement. He glared at her. "I've heard that our case has already been dismissed. Is that true?"

"I'll give some background information to give you a better idea of what is going on."

"Well, is it dismissed or isn't it? Why did we have to come down here just to be told our case has been thrown out of court?"

"If you give me a few minutes, I can explain."

"Why can't you answer my simple question? Why are we wasting time here?"

"Mr. Stenson, let me finish my remarks and I will answer your question."

"I'd like the answer right now."

Jim Oliver, a tall, slender mid-sixtyish man who'd suffered a massive heart attack after two weeks on generic Lorital, stood slowly. "Let's listen to what our lawyer has to say." He and Stenson glared at each other. The rest of the clients nodded and murmured in agreement.

Katie continued. "The case is in front of circuit court judge Steven Green who was just recently appointed to the bench by the governor. Your lawsuits are against the drug company, Enpact, which is based in India. Enpact, of course, makes generic Lorital. We have identified this as the drug that caused your problems. The patent on brand name Lorital, sometimes called trade-name Lorital, was held by the American company Orex, and expired more than three years ago. Enpact jumped into the market with its generic form of the drug to take advantage of the huge market created by

Orex. Total sales of both brand- name and generic Lorital were over four billion dollars worldwide last year.

"It's been shown that there is a thirty percent increased risk of suffering a heart attack or stroke if someone is taking the generic form of the drug, rather than the brand-name. We know that Enpact makes its product in India and has very poor manufacturing standards. We know that with the Enpact product, the dosages of testosterone, which are supposed to be the same in every package, are wildly different. Some packages have more than three times the dosage of testosterone than stated on the package. Several scientists have correlated these abnormally high doses with heart attacks and strokes. Based on that information, your lawsuits were filed with the claim that you were each exposed to the high doses."

Katie paused. "Enpact claims that, because it is based in India, it cannot be held legally responsible in the United States. At this time, the judge has conditionally dismissed your cases. But he's given us ninety days to develop facts that may cause him to change his mind. We are twenty days into the ninety-day period right now. I just returned from Washington where I reviewed Enpact's new drug application. Among the thousands of documents I saw, there were several hundred that will be helpful in changing the judge's ruling. I brought these documents back with me and will use them to convince the judge that he was wrong in his original dismissal.

"Also, I'm headed to India next week to look at records at Enpact headquarters and take depositions of some key personnel."

Katie looked around the room. "That brings you up to date on where we are. We'll answer any questions."

A hand shot up. Katie nodded. "Mrs. Stoddard."

Laurie Stoddard, a petite woman of about fifty years of age, stood. She looked older. Her grief-lined face, unmasked by makeup, stood in sharp contrast to her youthful physique. "My husband died after taking generic Lorital for four months. How could the judge possibly dismiss our case?"

"Our position is that the judge is wrong because he used the wrong law, and also decided the facts of the case. Added to that, the facts he used were wrong. The Seventh Amendment of the Constitution gives you all the right to have a jury, instead of the judge, decide the facts in your cases. Instead, Judge Green wrongly used his version of the facts together with the wrong law in making his decision."

Another voice. "Why would the judge do that?"

"That's a good question. Before he was appointed to the bench, Green represented the National Rifle Association in a big case locally and won. As you may know, the NRA is a powerful political influence in our country and makes huge campaign contributions to elected officials who agree with its position on guns as well as other issues. We think that because of that connection, the governor rewarded Green with the appointment to the bench."

"So it's politics?"

"That's our interpretation. That's what we think."

Stenson spoke up loudly. "I liked the result in the NRA case," he said. "I hope we don't have to be gun control freaks to have you handle our cases properly."

Gary stood and nodded toward Katie. "I'll handle this one. Nothing of the sort is required. Ms. Hornsby didn't mention anything about political parties. Or gun control issues. Our position is very simple. We think that the law should be applied fairly to anyone who exercises their constitutional right to hold this company responsible for any damage caused by its drug. The basic principle behind the Seventh Amendment, as Katie said, is that it is the jury that determines the facts of a case, and not the judge. Whether or not someone is or is not in favor of gun control has nothing to do with this case."

Another hand went up. "What evidence is there of criminal conduct?"

Gary nodded toward Katie. "She'll take that one."

"That's another good question. Enpact violated federal criminal law in selling its generic product in America. The key word to remember is 'adulterated.' Federal law makes it a criminal offense if a drug company sells an adulterated drug. What that means is if a drug is made under unsanitary conditions or in a dosage other than as stated on its package insert, it is adulterated. There is evidence that generic Lorital was contaminated with rat and mice feces and had significantly different amounts of testosterone in some packages of the drug even though they all were supposed to be the same. In more than a third of tested packages, the doses were up to three times higher than could be safely taken. The generic drug has already killed more than one hundred people and a thousand others have suffered heart attacks or strokes."

Gary stood. "There is a high probability that abnormally high testosterone levels in the product you or your loved ones took caused the damage."

Stenson, arms folded, said, "It's only a guess that we took high doses, isn't it?"

Gary responded, "That's an evidentiary issue. The proof of cause will require circumstantial evidence. None of the damage seen with the generic product occurred with the dosage level in brand name Lorital. This is strong circumstantial evidence that excessive dosages in the generic version caused all your problems."

Stenson looked angry. "I don't buy that. It sounds to me that the judge was right when he dismissed our cases. Why waste our time and get our hopes up when you can't conclusively prove we all took a product with high doses?"

Gary answered the question. "Judge Green ignored the evidence and pretended it didn't exist. In doing so, he decided facts that a jury should be permitted to decide. It's a clear-cut violation of the Seventh Amendment."

Another hand was raised. "How long is this going to take?"

"If the judge changes his mind after the ninety-day period of discovery," said Gary, "we will go to trial within a year. If he doesn't change his mind, an appeal could take a couple of years."

Katie looked around the room. Everyone seemed satisfied, except Stenson whose arms were still crossed. "Thank you for coming," she said. "We wanted to keep you up-to-date and we thought there might be some publicity about the case and we wanted you to hear about it from us first."

# # #

Lester Hempstead sat behind his desk and looked at Lance Rebus, Jr., who sat across from him

Rebus' name was last on the letterhead and he'd joined the firm after he'd graduated from Harvard Law School magna cum laude and was admitted to the Michigan Bar at the same time as Katie.

"Newton wants to do some discovery at Enpact headquarters in India. He's sending that new girl lawyer. I'm sending you, kid. It'll be a good experience for you."

Rebus reddened. "Why me? I appreciate your confidence, but I'm just a rookie. There are lawyers in the firm that know a lot more than I do about drugs and legal procedure."

"What better way to get experience? Handling a deposition is no big deal. Besides, you're single and I don't want to send a married lawyer to India for a week, particularly during the holidays. I'll get too many complaints from the wives. Newton's new lawyer is going. Wait 'til you see her. She's a looker. Eye candy. That's another reason I don't want to send a married guy. If nothing else, it'll be fun to just sit there and look at her all day. Hell, I'd do it myself, but she'd raise my testosterone level to where I'd probably have a heart attack." He laughed. "So, you're going. It will be a good experience."

"I know what she looks like. I sat in the room with her for two days in Washington."

"I forgot about that. You've already met her. And you survived?" He grinned. "You must have a pretty damn good heart."

Rebus blushed again. "I'll do my best. You're right, though. She is pretty good-looking."

"I expect nothing less than your best. Now go home and pack your bags. You're leaving tomorrow morning. I've had my paralegal prepare some information to bring you up-to-date on the case. Just remember what it is all about. She'll be looking for information about our client we don't want her to know. Your job is to make her it difficult for her to find it."

He stood and shook hands with Rebus. "Have a nice trip and keep your zipper zipped."

Chapter 16
December 2011

The excitement of Katie's trip to India had worn off by the end of the long trip from Detroit to Delhi. Twenty-nine hours and forty minutes, three different planes, and two stops was too much of an ordeal to be cooped up in a coach seat even for someone her size. It was early morning when the plane touched down and she was tired as hell. Gary had given her the option of flying business class, but when she learned what it cost she'd opted for coach. Bad decision. She'd slept poorly during the flights and now had a full day ahead of her.

She waited curbside in front of the terminal for the hotel bus and thought about the upcoming day. God, she was tired. Big mistake to arrive on the same day the document examination was scheduled. She should have come yesterday. She fell asleep during the bus ride to the hotel and the driver gently shook her. "We're here. Welcome to Shangri-La, the finest hotel in India."

She made arrangements for a cab to take her from the hotel to Enpact headquarters in Gurgaon. She'd stashed her suitcase in her room and tried to close her eyes and rest for a few minutes. She couldn't relax because of the excitement of being in India and the worry of sleeping too long. The cab driver said it was a forty-five-minute ride but it turned out to be ninety minutes. During the drive, she saw peasant women alongside the side of the dusty highway patting cow dung into cakes to dry for use as fuel. Others washed cattle with vessels of muddy water. It was like moving through three centuries all at once, she thought. There was a lot of talk about poverty in America but nothing like this. As the cab reached the outskirts of Gurgaon, the contrast between poverty and wealth became more sharply defined. The landscape shifted to modern apartment buildings that stood in the midst of a well-manicured golf course so green it hurt her eyes. She watched as well-dressed women walked dozens of young children in maroon uniforms to school, no connection whatsoever to the suffering that existed but a short distance away. Gurgaon, according to the brochure in her hotel room, was a symbol of a rising new India.

The cab driver pointed ahead to an imposing high-rise building that towered above the surrounding office buildings. The corporate offices of Enpact, the world's third largest producer of generic drugs, trumped the other structures in both elegance and size. The building was surrounded by a moat reinforced by barbed wire, offering a general impression of a military building. The cab dropped her at the entrance and it took her thirty minutes to clear security after she identified herself at the reception desk. A large, burly, uniformed security guard walked her to a large conference room where thousands of documents were strewn haphazardly on a large table. A young man in a business suit was seated with his back to the door when she walked into the room. He stood and turned and she realized it was Lance Rebus, Jr.

"We meet again." She smiled.

He blushed and gestured for her to sit. "You have two days to review documents. On the third day, and the fourth day if you need it, you may conduct three depositions of employees. You can tell me tomorrow morning which three employees you want. Whatever documents you select during the first two days will be made available to you the morning of the third day. We'll use the same procedure we used in Washington when you were there. Every document in this room"—he gestured toward the large stacks—"has a stamped number at the bottom of the page. All you have to do is record the number of each document you want and it will be copied for you. Other than that, nothing will leave this room. I will accompany you wherever and whenever you are in the building during your visit. When you need a bathroom break, let me know and I'll call for a woman to accompany you."

"And what if I pee my pants before she gets here?"

Rebus looked at her and his face turned scarlet. He didn't know how to respond. Imagine that, Katie thought, a lawyer at a loss for words. Some people just have no sense of humor. He was cute when he blushed. She recalled that he'd blushed a lot when they were together in Washington.

"Let's get started." She sat down, opened her briefcase, took out her laptop, and started to work. She pulled the nearest stack of materials toward her and began her search. Her goal was to select any documents that might reasonably be used during trial. The rest of the day was a repeat of the Washington experience. It would have been better if Rebus was friendly, but at least this time he smelled nice. She wondered what kind of after-shave he wore.

# # #

Mark Stenson looked at Newton and ran his hands through his hair. He sat forward and placed his hands on his knees.

"I don't feel comfortable with Hornsby as my lawyer."

Newton stared at him. "Why's that?"

"She's too young."

"Too young? Ms. Hornsby is a well-educated, first-rate lawyer and probably the brightest person I've ever met."

"There are issues in my lawsuit I just don't feel comfortable talking about with her."

"Such as?"

"She asked me why I started taking Lorital."

"I don't understand. What's wrong with that?"

"I just don't feel comfortable talking about such personal things with someone so young…and with her being a girl. I'd rather have you as my lawyer, like I was supposed to."

"Let me get this straight. You asked us to file a lawsuit claiming that your life, including your health and sex life, has been ruined by generic Lorital, but you object to your own lawyer asking you about it, is that right?"

"It's not just because she's a lawyer, it's her."

"What about her? What is it about her that bothers you?"

Stenson smirked. "I'm surprised you have to ask that question. Do you ever take a good look at her?"

Gary ignored the innuendo. "Let me ask you: why did you start on the drug?"

"I was active until I hit my mid-thirties. Around that time, I lost the energy to work out in the gym, and even if I could manage to drag myself there my muscles didn't respond to the exercise like when I was younger. I was depressed, had little appetite, no energy. Nothing felt right so I saw my doctor. He tested me and my testosterone was too low so he prescribed Lorital. Right away, I felt energized and motivated. My mental clarity was restored, and I was interested in everything again. I had the energy to work out in the gym and was pleased with how my body responded to exercise. My depression was gone. I was doing great until my insurance company insisted that I switch to generic Lorital. Then, I had the heart attack. Nothing has been the same since."

If he'd closed his eyes, Newton would think Stenson was reading from a script.

"Including your sex life?"

Stenson looked down at his feet. He avoided eye contact. "Yes, but I didn't think I'd have to spill my guts about that to some sexy young girl."

"The fact that Ms. Hornsby is attractive has nothing to do with this. She's not a young girl but a full-grown woman who knows the issues in this litigation better than anyone."

"Hell, she's a new lawyer. She can't possibly know law or medicine any better than you. I came to you because you're a doctor and a lawyer. I thought you'd be handling my case."

"I oversee every case that comes into this office. Nothing goes on without my permission. My job is to make sure that my lawyers understand the medicine. I have done that in this case with her. But Ms. Hornsby is the one in this office who has responsibility for attending to the details of your case. And, she is going to keep doing that."

"I don't like it. I hired you to be my lawyer."

"Mr. Stenson, let me make it perfectly clear. Hornsby is going to handle your case. I don't know how many ways I can make that clear to you. I'm sorry if that bothers you. But it's not going to change. If that's a problem, you may want to consider retaining another law firm. I can give you the names of several lawyers in this town that might be of help to you. At the present, my firm is the only one handling this litigation, but one of those lawyers may be willing to take your case."

"She doesn't return my phone calls. I call and am told she will call back. She doesn't."

"When was the last time you spoke with her?"

"She called to ask some questions about two weeks ago. I didn't have the information about a couple of things so I told her I'd call back. I called two days ago. Nothing. Then I called again yesterday. Still no response. You say she's my lawyer, but she ignores my calls. That's why I came in today."

"She's in India all week working on your case. You know that the major defendant in your case is based in India, don't you?"

"They have telephones in India."

"You expect her to call you from India?"

"It would be nice to be kept up on what is happening."

"The meeting last week for you and the other clients was to bring you up-to-date. Other than her trip to India, nothing else has changed."

"I still don't want her as my lawyer. She's too young, too inexperienced. She makes me uncomfortable when she asks questions about my sex life. I don't like it. This is her first case, isn't it?"

Give it up, Newton thought. "As I said, if you want a different lawyer, I can recommend another law firm. But so long as you're a client of this firm in Enpact litigation, Hornsby, under my direct supervision, will be your lawyer."

Leslie told Newton that Stenson was still grumbling to himself when he walked out of the office. She also told him that Stenson had asked her to leave the office and have a drink with him for the second time.

# # #

Katie returned to her hotel room at the end of the first day of document review. She was tired and hungry; jet lag had kicked in big time. There was a nice restaurant in the lobby of the hotel but she didn't have the energy to put herself together to leave her room. She needed to eat and then sleep. She checked the menu for room service and placed an order. While she waited, she sat down at her laptop.

She logged onto Enpact's website and surfed through the various pages. She found just what she'd expected: a lot of hype about Enpact, how it was a leader in producing a large percentage of the generic drugs used throughout the world, blah, blah, blah. She'd nearly signed out of the website when she noticed a reference to business records. She clicked into the section and a warning flashed across her screen. "This information is intended for the exclusive use of Enpact employees. Enter your password to continue."

She really didn't intend to hack into the corporate files. She just wanted to see if she could. She was surprised it was so easy. She by-passed the password requirement by using a trick she'd learned from a law-school classmate, a computer geek.

Once she gained entry, she surfed through the various files until she found a large cache of materials from the research department. She scanned quickly, looking for anything that might pertain to the case. She sat up straight when she saw a detailed report written by two doctors, Deepak Patel and Elizabeth Barrett. The report was entitled "Generic Lorital Safety Concerns." She knew the report hadn't been included in the materials provided for her review in Washington. Nor had she'd run across this report today.

Enpact probably hadn't submitted it to the FDA, she realized. She'd carefully reviewed everything the FDA had on Enpact while in Washington and wouldn't have missed seeing it there. She read the report twice. It was a home run; spelling out in detail everything Enpact had done wrong in the marketing and production of generic Lorital. She made a note to request Patel and Barrett as two of the three employees whose depositions she'd want to take. She didn't want to loiter inside the company website and trigger any security alert that might be installed so she copied and saved the report on her laptop and signed off. She wiped out any trace of her presence on the site, another trick of the geek.

She asked herself how she could get this report into evidence. She couldn't just simply use the hacked report, because it needed to be verified. The best way would be if Patel or Barrett verified its authenticity. Another alternative was if Enpact had already produced the report among the vast array of documents they'd provided and she could find it, its authenticity would be no problem and she could use it during the depositions. She needed to find this report tomorrow if it was present among those documents. It would be like looking for a needle in a haystack. Without a way to verify its authenticity, the Enpact lawyers would know that she'd somehow obtained it improperly if she tried to use it. She'd need to get around this problem somehow.

She closed her laptop and smiled. Enpact really needed some help with its security system. She could have fixed it for them in a half hour, but then again that was their problem not hers. There was a knock at the door. Her food had arrived.

# # #

The next day Katie spent a frustrating eight hours looking for the Patel-Barrett report. She didn't find it. What she did find, however, were a few documents written by Dr. Barrett that suggested her discontent with some of the procedures employed by Enpact with regard to the handling of complaints from physicians whose patients experienced adverse reactions from Enpact drugs. One of these documents was a memorandum to the Board of Directors of Enpact suggesting a change in the practice of ignoring these complaints. Dr. Patel was copied in on a couple of Barrett's memos. At the end of the day, she told Rebus she wanted him to produce Barrett, Patel and Mr. Singh, the Enpact CEO, for depositions beginning the next day. She also told him she wanted copies of forty-five documents she'd selected over the two days to be provided to her at the beginning of the first deposition, as Rebus had agreed at the beginning of her document review.

"I can produce Barrett and Singh. Dr. Patel is no longer an employee. You'll have to pick someone else if you want a third deposition."

Katie thought for a moment. "Just bring whoever it is who's doing his job now."

TOM BLEAKLEY

Chapter 17
December 2011

Tim Holt and Everett Plimpf, IV shared a common love for Indian food. When they'd gone to India for the signing of the closing papers on the sale of Enpact, they'd stayed at the Mauray Sheraton Hotel in New Delhi that housed The Bukhara, hands down the finest Indian restaurant in the world. They'd been pleased at the opportunity to repeat the restaurant experience when they learned that Katie Hornsby was going to Enpact headquarters in India to conduct discovery.

Both men had ordered the house specialty. As Holt washed the remains of his meal down with a large swallow of Indian wine, he said, "Hell, I could eat this food for breakfast, lunch, and dinnah. I don' think I could ever get tarred of it."

"That makes two of us," Plimpf agreed. "So why does Hornsby want Barrett's deposition? How did she even know that Barrett existed?"

"I don' know that answer. I suspect she saw Barrett's name in some of the documents she reviewed. She wasn't supposed to see anything from either Barrett or Patel. I'll talk to Hempstead's young lawyer about that. Someone screwed up." Holt pointed to another platter sitting on the table. "Pass me that."

Plimpf finished his meal and wiped his lips with his napkin.

Holt watched him. "We keep eating like this, we're going to pack on the pounds."

"Not me." Plimpf shook his head and patted his six-pack abs.

"I'll just work out longer and harder. Have you been to the gym here? It's fantastic. Better than anything we have at home. You should try it."

Holt said, "Other than the food, why did you come over? We don't want this gal asking questions about why the Orex CEO is sitting in on Enpact depositions. Too risky. Think it over before you show up tomorrow. If ya'll remember, we jumped through hoops to distance ourselves from Enpact."

"She doesn't have to know who I am. I'll just sit in the corner and listen. It's important for me to know what we're dealing with here. I'll be invisible." He took a sip of wine. "Besides, I hear Hornsby's a fine looking woman."

"Y'all are hard to miss...and you're right. She's a good-looking gal."

"You worry too much. You're the only one there who'll know who I am. We act like we never saw each other before. It's simple. Now, what are we going to have for dessert?"

# # #

Today was a big day, the taking of her first depositions as a lawyer. She'd sat in and watched Gary a couple of times, but had never done the real thing herself. But she was too tired to feel nervous. The first witness of the day, Dr. Elizabeth Barrett, was already seated in the conference room when Katie arrived. Dr. Barrett looked as exhausted as Katie felt. There were eight other lawyers in the room, all lined up next to the witness at the table across from her. Rebus sat on one side of Barrett and Timothy Holt sat on the other. Neither of them bothered to introduce themselves, the other lawyers in the room, or Barrett. The setting was clearly intended to intimidate her. She was not going to allow their rudeness to affect her.

She looked over at Rebus. His name, Lance Rebus, Jr., was a perfect fit for the young man with his Ivy League look and his know-it-all, holier-than-thou attitude. His name on the letterhead of Hempstead's law firm was way down at the bottom of the listing, in the last row of the bleachers. She smiled at the thought. If he gave her a hard time, she'd call him Junior. That would knock him down a peg or two, cute or not.

Gary had arranged for an English-speaking court reporter through the U.S. embassy. The parties had agreed that, despite the depositions being taken in India, Michigan court rules regarding depositions would apply.

"Hi, I'm Maggie." The court reporter extended her hand to Katie. Katie introduced herself and requested expedited copies of the deposition transcripts. Maggie grinned. "I'll do better than that. I can send you an unedited transcript to your computer at the end of each day." She then walked around the room and quietly wrote down the names of those present. Maggie was attractive, Katie thought, and each man in the room took special notice of her when she spoke to them. Maggie stopped at a really handsome big guy, impeccably dressed in an expensive suit, seated at the far end of the conference table. Katie watched while Maggie and the guy looked at each other for a long moment. The chemistry between the two of them was palpable.

"Name?"

"I'm just an interested by-stander."

"I must list the names of everyone in attendance."

Katie saw the man wink and smile. "That's my name—Interested By-Stander." He smiled more broadly and winked again. "And maybe at the end of the day you'd like to have a drink with Mr. By-stander. Yes?"

He was flirting with Maggie, who stood there and blushed.

"That'd be very nice, Mr. By-Stander. Do you hyphenate your last name?

Their eyes met and the two shared another quick grin.

Maggie's face was still flushed when she returned to her seat.

Katie was pleased to find that the documents she'd selected over the first two days were provided for her use. One less thing to fight about. She scanned through them quickly. The Patel-Barrett report was not among the documents. She had to figure out a way to get the information from that report into the record without letting anyone know that she had the report.

She had the court reporter mark the documents that she'd use as exhibits. Then, the reporter swore in the witness and nodded to Katie that she was ready.

"Will you state your name?"

"Elizabeth Barrett. Dr. Elizabeth Barrett."

Katie knew from reading the hacked report that Barrett was an American physician working at Enpact in the clinical medicine division. She reminded herself that she couldn't mention that she'd seen the report. So far as she knew—she smiled at the thought—discovery in civil proceedings didn't include hacking into an opponent's database.

"It is my understanding you are employed by Enpact?"

"Yes. I am the director of clinical medicine."

"What are your duties at Enpact in that capacity?"

"My task is to develop information about the effectiveness and safety of Enpact products worldwide. In doing so, I supervise a staff of ten physicians, each of whom is responsible for acquiring that information within a specific portion of the planet."

There was no sense in beating around the bush. Katie went right to the reason she wanted Barrett's testimony. "In your work at Enpact, have you dealt with Dr. Deepak Patel?"

Barrett hesitated and looked at both Holt and Junior. Holt gave her a short nod. She turned and looked at Katie. "Yes"

"Has any of your work with Dr. Patel dealt with the safety of an Enpact product?"

She looked once again at both lawyers. Holt nodded.

"Yes."

"Will you identify the products that you have worked on with Dr. Patel that concerned safety issues?"

She hesitated once again. "There have been two products, generic ampicillin and generic Lorital."

"What were the safety concerns about the generic ampicillin?"

Rebus reacted. "I instruct the witness not to answer."

Katie resisted the urge to call him "Junior." He was probably younger than her and she wondered if he shaved yet. But, cute or not, he wasn't too young to not know the damn rules of discovery.

"What is the basis for your objection, counsel? As you know, the scope of discovery allows for generous latitude in the scope of what is discoverable. And as you know full well, this case is about the safety of an Enpact drug. The scope of discovery extends to the issue of how Enpact deals with safety issues in its product line."

Junior looked down at the table in front of him; he didn't or couldn't look at her. Maybe she had spinach stuck in her teeth?

141

She didn't know that Holt had scolded him that morning for producing documents containing Barrett or Patel's names

"My instruction to the witness stands. Move on to your next question."

Rebus and Holt swapped terse grins. It was clear that Holt was in charge of the defense team and Junior was his attack puppy. She nearly laughed out loud at the thought. The others in the room, save for the hot-looking guy at the other end of the conference table, paid obvious deference to Holt. He was swarthy and rugged-looking. His red face and whiskey nose suggested a life of hard living fueled by too much booze. A heart attack waiting to happen is what her father would always tell her about men who looked like this. A man's man that most women, including her, would not find appealing. She checked her notes and continued.

"Is it true that in your work with Dr. Patel involving generic ampicillin, the issue was whether or not the products sold to a large hospital chain here in India contained any ampicillin at all and that it was believed by respected outside researchers that the fact that your products were fake and contained no ampicillin which caused more than seven hundred children to die?"

The question was clumsy in its wording, she thought, but she wanted to provoke Junior. She wanted to see if she could make him actually look at her.

"Objection. The witness is instructed not to answer the question. I've already told you, counsel, that she will not answer any questions about generic ampicillin. Move on."

"Actually, counsel." Katie paused. "My question had only to do with the deaths of seven hundred children. It wasn't about ampicillin because your client failed to put ampicillin in the packages that were used to treat these unfortunate children. Maybe you should reconsider your improper objection."

It didn't work. He simply stared at the table in front of him. "My instruction stands."

Katie had watched Barrett as the exchange of barbs with Junior became more heated. She was fidgety, nervous as hell. She'd had a look of alarm on her face when Katie brought up the seven hundred dead children and it was obvious that she was close to crying. And the lawyers, too, were clearly anxious about keeping away from the subject of the children. She'd give it another try.

"Did you review any of the autopsy results on the seven hundred children to determine if, in fact, their lives could have been saved if they had received ampicillin rather than Enpact's fake product?"

"Objection. She will not answer that question. One more reference to ampicillin and I'll terminate the deposition. Move on."

Katie looked at Junior and smirked. "Counsel, perhaps you could favor me as well as the court with any legal basis you have for withholding evidence."

Junior looked at Holt and then at the desk in front of him. "I said move on."

Katie noticed that Holt had nodded toward the slick-looking guy who had flirted with the court reporter. Who was he, she wondered? He was definitely not a local and he was dressed in a suit that probably cost more than the rest of the suits in the room combined. She thought about taking a picture of him with her cell phone, knowing his identity might prove useful. There was already enough disruption going on, so she rejected the idea. Maybe there'd be an opportunity at some other time.

Katie sat for a moment, had another thought. Gary had emphasized that it was always important to make the record as complete as possible during a deposition. "I will make this statement for the record. Counsel for the defendant continues to make objections to the record about ampicillin and my questions regarding the deaths of seven hundred young children. It should be made clear that my questions in this regard are not about ampicillin because these seven hundred children died from not receiving the drug. Upon information and belief, the defendant in this litigation, Enpact, sold huge amounts of a product that was said to containing ampicillin but in fact was worthless. The bottom line of my statement is that my questions in this regard dealt not with the drug ampicillin, per se, but with the conduct of the defendant that is an issue in this litigation inasmuch as the defendant did the same thing with Lorital as it did with the fake ampicillin. Also, I reserve my right to have the court order these questions be answered and that the defendant be ordered to pay for all costs in order to do so, including my return air fare to India and the lodgings necessary to make that happen."

Katie checked her notes and continued. "Did you and Dr. Patel discuss concerns about the safety of generic Lorital?"

Barrett hesitated and then said, "Yes, we did."

"What were those concerns?"

More hesitation. Barrett had a furtive look. Her eyes darted back and forth among Junior, Holt, and Katie. She cleared her throat. "Dr. Patel had written a memo about the safety of generic Lorital and shared it with me. I told him my concerns and we spent time trying to figure out why our product was causing so much trouble when the trade- name product wasn't. I determined that our generic product was not bio-equivalent to the trade product. We put our various thoughts together and prepared a report that summarized all of our concerns." Her face reddened. She was close to tears again.

"Did you conduct bio-equivalent studies on the generic Lorital and compare the results with the trade-name Lorital?"

"Yes, I did."

"What were your findings?"

"As I said, I discovered that our generic product was not bio-equivalent to the trade product."

"Did you analyze the bio-equivalency studies submitted to the FDA by Enpact to obtain approval to market generic Lorital in the U.S.?"

"Objection. Asked and answered. Instruct the witness not to answer."

"Counsel," Katie asked sarcastically, "would you mind pointing out for me when Dr. Barrett answered that question, because I don't believe she did."

Junior looked at her, then quickly away. "My instruction stands. She will not answer that question."

"Maybe you are confused, counsel. Dr. Barrett and I are now dealing with the subject matter of this litigation. I want to make it absolutely clear on the record that you are obstructing my right to conduct discovery on a subject that is clearly within the scope of discovery with regard to the product that has killed or damaged hundreds of people worldwide, including my clients or their deceased loved ones. Now, I'll repeat my question and insist that Dr. Barrett answer it."

She looked at Barrett. "Doctor, did you analyze the bio-equivalency studies submitted to the FDA by Enpact to obtain approval to market generic Lorital in the United States?"

Junior looked hard at the table in front of him. "Objection. You are a slow learner, Miss Hornsby. I instructed the witness not to answer the question and I will repeat that same instruction. You can ask it as many times as you want, but she is not going to give an answer."

Surprise, surprise, she thought, Junior knew her name. But she was too angry to care. "You are totally wrong, counsel. When we get back to the States, I am going to seek sanctions against you for misconduct. As I stated earlier, I am going to request that you or your client pay for a return trip here for me to have Dr. Barrett answer that question as well as the previous questions you have improperly refused to let her answer."

Junior flashed a thin-lipped smile at the other lawyers. "I guess we'll all do what we have to do, counsel. Does this mean the deposition is over?"

"No, it's far from over. Dr. Barrett, you have been sitting here listening to your lawyer instruct you not answer certain questions. If you chose not to follow his instructions, would you be able to answer those questions?"

"Objection. Same instruction. You are badgering the witness."

"Dr. Barrett, do you feel like I'm badgering you?"

"Objection. Same instruction. Don't answer the question, Doctor."

Katie was frustrated. She looked down at her notes. She was too angry at the moment to think clearly. If she had a baseball bat in her hands right now, she'd wipe that silly-ass smirk off Junior's face.

"Doctor, where did you work prior to starting your job with Enpact?"

"I worked at Eli Lilly and Company at their headquarters in Indianapolis for ten years."

"What was your job title at Lilly?"

"I was a clinical research associate."

"What were your reasons for leaving Lilly and coming to work at Enpact?"

"Primarily financial. Enpact offered me a generous starting salary, a lot more than what I was making at Lilly. There'd been a freeze on salaries at Lilly for two years. It was also an opportunity for me to work with Dr. Patel, who has an outstanding international reputation."

"You are familiar with testing standards in the drug industry as a result of your work at Lilly?"

"Yes. It was my responsibility at Lilly to see that testing standards and procedures were followed at all times."

"In your work at Enpact, do you apply the same testing standards as in your work at Lilly?"

She hesitates. "I tried to..."

"Stop. Don't answer that question." Junior practically yelled at the witness.

"By qualifying your answer, you appear to suggest that some of your efforts in applying standards at Enpact have not been successful. Is that right?"

Barrett looked at Holt. "Do I answer that?"

Junior interceded. "The witness is instructed not to answer the question."

Katie was left with no choice now but to hit the witness where she knew it would hurt. "Doctor, do you feel any personal responsibility for the deaths of the seven hundred children who were given the fake ampicillin product?" This ought to shake things up, Katie thought. She had to let them know she didn't give up easily.

Barrett squirmed, looked at Katie. "No, I don't. I've only worked here for eight months."

Katie noticed tears in Barrett's eyes. "Do you think Enpact bears responsibility for the deaths of those seven hundred children who were given the fake ampicillin?"

Junior again. "The witness is instructed not to answer."

Katie was satisfied with that answer. "I'll take that as an admission, counsel. Doctor, you mentioned earlier that you had received a report that Dr. Patel wrote about the safety of Lorital and that the two of you prepared a more complete report. Did you also prepare a separate memo with regard to the concerns you expressed earlier about the generic Lorital's bio-equivalency testing?"

Barrett hesitates. "Yes, I did. And those concerns were also put in our joint report."

"And you also discussed these concerns with Dr. Patel, correct?"

"That's right."

"Have you brought either of those reports with you here today?"

"No. I was told not to bring anything with me. It's my understanding that everything has already been produced for you."

"And how did you learn this?"

"He told me." She gestured toward Junior.

Katie directed her next statement to him. "I'd like to see her report as well as the report she and Dr. Patel wrote."

Junior didn't look up. He spoke to the table in front of him. "I don't know what you're talking about. What documents?"

Katie bit her lip and smiled. "The documents that your client just described and said she talked about with you. Where are they?"

"They were in the materials that you were provided for inspection. Do you expect me to do your work for you?" There was no mistake—he had a look of fear in his eyes. He looked guilty as hell.

"Do you mean that they were among the thousands of documents you produced yesterday? What are you afraid of me finding out, counsel?"

He refused to establish eye contact with her. "Your problem, counsel. Not mine."

She looked back at the witness. "Dr. Barrett, is your office in this building?"

Barrett nodded. "Yes."

"Do you have a copy of your reports in your office?"

"Yes."

Katie sat back. "Counsel, we will delay the deposition until Dr. Barrett goes to her office and brings back a copy of her reports. Any problems with that?"

"If Dr. Barrett leaves this room, she will not return."

"What do you have to hide, counsel?"

"I'm not here to answer your questions. Proceed with your deposition."

"Asshole," Katie muttered under her breath.

"What did you call me?"

"Now you're hearing things."

"Just get on with your deposition. You're wasting time."

"Dr. Barrett, I request that you send a copy of your reports to the court reporter with an accompanying letter verifying the documents as yours and I request that the court reporter mark the documents as Dr. Barrett Group Exhibit 1 when they are received. Can you both do that?"

The court reporter nodded. Barrett said, "I can do that."

"Doctor, can you summarize the results as reported in the reports?

"First, I looked at the bio-equivalency studies of generic Lorital that my predecessors here at Enpact had submitted to the FDA. I compared those results with the tests conducted on the trade-name product. They were…identical."

"Is this usually seen in a generic product that is supposed to be the equivalent of a trade-name product?"

"No. Usually, some discrepancy or variation in the test results between the two are observed and…expected."

"Did you draw any conclusions because of the identical test results reported in both products?"

"Not at first, but it did raise some questions. My first thought was that the company tested the trade-name drug by mistake. I sought information from others at Enpact as to why this would be the case. They informed me…"

Junior interrupted. "Excuse me, Doctor, you have already answered her question. Do not volunteer information."

"What information did you receive about test results from other employees at Enpact?"

Junior jumped in again. "Objection. Calls for hearsay. Don't answer the question."

Junior was dead wrong about his continuous instructions to the witness to refuse to answer questions. She decided to ignore the objection again.

"Go ahead, Doctor, you may answer the question."

"Hold on. I instructed the witness to not answer the question. You can't do that."

"Well, counsel, your instruction is totally improper and you know it. The rules allow such questions on the basis that any inquiry reasonably calculated to lead to discoverable evidence is permissible, including questions involving hearsay. Unless you missed that piece of information in Evidence 101, you know that as well as I do. She is going to answer the question now, and I am going to sit here until she does."

"Do you have the question in mind, Doctor?"

Barrett looked at Rebus and waited for his reaction.

Katie pushed a bit. "Go ahead, Doctor, please answer the question."

Rebus sat there looking at the table in front of him, a flush moved up his cheeks. She gestured with her hand for Barrett to continue.

"Other employees, as well as Dr. Patel, told me that it was customary practice at Enpact to perform bio-equivalency testing on trade-name products and submit those test results to the FDA instead of testing our products. As I understand it, that has been the customary practice here at Enpact for several years."

"Stop right there. You are volunteering information. I move to strike the answer." Junior glared at Barrett.

Bingo, Katie thought. No wonder he didn't want her to answer.

"When did you last speak with Dr. Patel?"

"Within the past two weeks. I forget the date."

"Have you had any contact since he left Enpact?"

"Objection. Work product?"

Katie snapped at Junior and she was not smiling. "Work product? What kind of objection is that?"

He stared at the table. "Conversations between employees are covered by lawyer's work product."

"You're making that up. What do you call it? The Rebus Junior rule?"

Maggie stifled a laugh and smiled broadly at Katie. She stopped typing for a moment and held her hand over her mouth. Katie glanced around the room. No one else seemed to think it was funny.

Barrett interjected, "Dr. Patel is not an employee."

Rebus looked at her. "He was when the conversation took place, wasn't he?"

Barrett hesitated. Katie pressed on. "When did you say your last conversation took place?"

"More than a couple of days ago. I can't remember exactly."

"So between then and now Patel has left the company?

Barrett looked at Junior before she answered. "He quit. I don't know the date he quit."

"Why did he quit?"

Junior interrupted. "You'll have to ask Dr. Patel that question. How would Dr. Barrett know?"

"Do you know why Dr. Patel quit?"

Barrett looked at her. There was fear in her eyes. "You'll have to ask Dr. Patel."

"Do you know where he lives, where he is right now?"

"I heard that he went back to the States."

Katie checked her notes. "That's all the questions I have. Thank you for your time, Dr. Barrett."

Katie took the court reporter aside as the room slowly emptied. "Who is the nice-looking guy at the other end of the table?"

Maggie smiled. "He wouldn't give me his name. He told me he was an interested by-stander. Actually, he's a pretty interesting by-stander." She gave Katie a sly grin. "I may have an opportunity to find out who he is…later." The smile told Katie all she needed to know.

TOM BLEAKLEY

Chapter 18
December 2011

Katie felt good about the morning. It had been a good prelude to the next witness, Vijada Singh, the CEO and co-founder of Enpact. Before the deposition started, she'd sent an email to Gary and asked him to try to locate the whereabouts of Dr. Patel. Her dilemma was that she had the report stored on her laptop but couldn't use it. Unless she found a way to somehow establish its validity, it was useless. If Barrett did what she'd said she would, the report would be attached to her deposition. Given Junior's intransigence on the issue, however, she wouldn't be surprised if the report wasn't produced. Yogi Berra once said, "When you get to a fork in the road, take it." She'd taken one of the forks in this litigation, she thought, but couldn't tell anybody about it. There had to be another fork somewhere, somehow. She'd find it. She had to keep looking, trying. She'd get it into evidence somehow. One way or another.

Katie looked at the court reporter. "Please swear in the witness."

The court reporter raised her right hand and looked at the man sitting across the table from Katie. He raised his right hand. "Do you swear to tell the truth, the whole truth, and nothing but the truth so help you God."

"I do."

Katie took a deep breath and scanned the room. There were ten lawyers present now, two more than during the morning session.

Before the deposition started, the others had hovered around the witness like he was a rock star. The only one in the room who hadn't done so was the handsome guy in the expensive suit. He'd sat at the other end of the table and just watched.

The witness preened like a peacock. His greased black hair was too long. He was a comic version of Buddha, dressed in a business suit. There was a statue of Buddha in the lobby of her hotel and the similarity between the two made her smile. Unlike the statue, however, she couldn't imagine patting this guy's belly. Rebus and Holt sat on each side of him as they readied to begin the deposition.

Short and round, the man rested his forearms on his protruding stomach and looked at Katie through dark eyes half-hidden by drooping eyelids. He was already perspiring even though the deposition hadn't begun. "Sir, would you state your name and occupation?"

"My name is Vijada Singh and I am the CEO of Enpact Pharmaceuticals."

"How long have you been the CEO of Enpact?"

"Since my brother and I founded the company ten years ago." His English was clipped with an Indian accent and difficult for her to understand.

"Enpact makes and sells generic drugs for the American marketplace. Is this correct?"

"Yes. In fact, we sell our products to more than 150 countries throughout the world."

"Does Enpact sell generic Lorital in the United States?"

"Yes, of course."

"In order to sell generic Lorital in the U.S., did you receive the approval of the Food and Drug Administration?" It was necessary to ask obvious questions that provide basic information about Enpact because Gary told her that this deposition would be read to the jury at trial if Singh for some reason failed to appear.

"Yes, of course. It is always necessary to obtain approval from the FDA of any drug we wish to sell in the U.S."

"How did your company become interested in the development of generic Lorital?"

"Enpact is the world expert in generic products. By FDA regulations, the first company to file and gain approval of a generic product, after the trade-name product's patent expires, gets the exclusive right to the generic market for six months before other generic makers' products will be approved. We are the experts in doing this. This is how we came to the making of generic Lorital."

Singh apparently thought that something he'd said was funny; he chuckled and his team of lawyers joined in. Their response reminded Katie of the canned laughter of a TV game show. What a bunch of suck-ups. She scanned the room quickly. The only ones who weren't laughing were Holt and the slick guy at the other end of the table.

She looked back at Singh. "Tell me about the generic market in the U.S. for Enpact's line of products."

"We are the leader in that field. In the U.S., Enpact has about forty percent of the generic market place. It is a big market as more than eighty percent of all prescription drugs used in the U.S. are generic. We were the first foreign generics manufacturer to sell drugs in the U.S. because we can meet the demand of supplying this huge market. We also sell our products in more than 150 countries and we have more than fourteen thousand employees scattered worldwide."

She felt like she was interviewing a walking talking advertising robot with tortured English delivered in a quick staccato rhythm.

"Do you promote generic Lorital in the U.S.?"

"I am uncertain what you mean by promote."

"Does Enpact advertise generic Lorital by way of television commercials or promotional brochures to doctors or the public?"

"I understand now. No. Orex, the brand-name manufacturer does that. We let Orex do that."

"When you say 'we let Orex do that,' can you clarify what you mean?" Katie noted out of the corner of her eye that Holt and the guy at the other end of the table shared a quick glance.

"Orex has done a wonderful job of building a substantial market for Lorital and it continues to both promote and sell Lorital since its patent expired five years ago, as I mentioned earlier. As you know, the healthcare industry in the U.S. is very cost-conscious so there is a tremendous market for lower-cost generic products. That includes generic Lorital. We benefit greatly from the continued Orex promotion of its trade-name Lorital."

"Are there other companies in the U.S. that sell generic Lorital?"

"No. A few have tried. But they cannot match our pricing structure. We own the marketplace for generic Lorital."

This deposition was going better than she'd expected. She wondered for a moment why Junior was so quiet this afternoon.

"Why is generic Lorital used?"

"You'll have to ask the doctors. I just make Lorital. I don't prescribe it. I can't. I am not a doctor."

"Let's switch topics. Can you describe for me how Enpact goes about the process of obtaining FDA approval of a generic drug?"

"We must demonstrate to the FDA that our generic products are the bio-equivalent of the trade-name product."

"When you say 'bio-equivalent,' what do you mean?"

"Each company that makes a drug has its own way of doing things. As a result, the end product for each company may not be exactly the same formulation or composition as the trade name-product, but so long as it contains the exact amount of the active ingredient, it is considered to be the bio-equivalent by the FDA. Generic Lorital is a good example. Our tablet is green and Orex's is white. We use different additives than Orex. We submit test results to the FDA to show them that our product contains the same active ingredient of the trade-name product. Once the FDA sees our test results, they approve the drug. It is as simple as that."

"Who does the testing at Enpact?"

"Our testing laboratories around the world. We employ the finest scientists in the world. No other generic manufacturer comes close to the excellence of our work."

Katie bit her lip. She'd the reports of both Patel and Barrett. This guy was lying through his teeth. "When were the tests for generic Lorital conducted?"

"I don't know the answer to that, my friend. You'll have to ask the lawyers."

So now she was his friend. She resisted the urge to react to the characterization. "Do you know Dr. Elizabeth Barrett?"

"Yes, a very fine lady, a wonderful scientist. The best in the world."

"Do you know that she testified this morning about the testing of generic Lorital?"

"Yes. The lawyers told me that."

"Did they tell you what she said about the testing of generic Lorital?"

Junior reacted quickly. "Counsel, this question is improper and I respectfully request that Mr. Singh not answer it."

Now she understood why Junior had been quiet. The "respectfully request" statement told her he was afraid of Singh.

"I'll rephrase the question. Given Dr. Barrett's sterling reputation, would you consider anything that she has to say about the testing of an Enpact product to be worthy of your consideration?"

"Yes, most certainly. That's why I hired her. Her advice and opinions are very valuable."

"Given the fact that you personally know nothing about the testing of generic Lorital, would you defer to Dr. Barrett on that subject?"

Singh hesitated. "I don't know. I would have to know more about what she said to know if I would agree with her or not." He laughed. "I guess you'll have to ask the lawyers whether or not I agree."

She looked around the room. No one smiled. "Have you made any inquiries within Enpact about what tests were done on generic Lorital to obtain FDA approval?"

"Me personally? No, it does not fit my job description." He chuckled. The choir responded in unison. Singh looked around and smiled at them. He enjoyed the spotlight. Despite the fact that she knew what role he played in setting up the inferior standards at Enpact, he had a likable way.

"Sir, Dr. Barrett made the following statement under oath.

Quote, 'Other employees, as well as Dr. Patel, told me that it was customary practice at Enpact to perform bio-equivalence testing on trade-name products and submit those test results to the FDA rather than tests done on our products. As I understand it, that has been the customary practice here at Enpact for several years.' End of quote. Is Dr. Barrett's description of the customary testing practice at Enpact accurate?"

"I don't believe she would make such a statement. We are honorable people in this company. Dr. Patel is no longer with the company. He cannot be trusted to say anything nice about us."

"Let's talk about Dr. Patel. You say he cannot be trusted. Why do you say that?"

"He has an axe to grind. We hired him because we thought he had an outstanding reputation. That turned out not to be true. When he presented his resume to us, it contained a list of the research studies he'd done. We hired an outstanding independent scientist to evaluate this research. All his studies suffer from serious flaws. He made statistical errors to justify his findings and when this independent scientist corrected the errors, there was no scientific value to any of his work. He was a fraud. He is a fraud. We should not have hired him in the first place. That's why I fired him."

The heads of the group bobbed up and down in unison, a certain musicality to the rhythm. Three Blind Mice came to her mind. She smiled at the thought.

"What is the name of this 'independent' scientist who evaluated Dr. Patel's work?"

"Objection, work product. Mr. Singh, I once more respectfully request that you not answer the question." Junior looked down at the table in front of him, but pointed his finger at her. "And do not use that tone of voice when you are speaking to Mr. Singh."

Singh looked at Junior. "I will do what you tell me. I will not answer the question."

"When did you hire this so-called 'independent scientist' to evaluate Patel's work?"

"Objection. I'm warning you, counsel. If you continue to speak disrespectfully to Mr. Singh, I will terminate this deposition." Junior looked at Singh. "Sir, please do not answer this question."

She looked at Junior. "You have created a new rule of law—the tone violation. Can you provide me with the case law or some rule of evidence that says a tone violation is a proper objection?"

Junior responded to the table in front of him. "I'm not here to answer your questions. Move on."

She was frustrated by the constant interference.

"Have you read Dr. Patel's report on the issue of the safety of generic Lorital?"

"No. I know of no such report."

"Is it not true, Mr. Singh, that the FDA has stopped the importation of more than twenty of your drug products in the past five years?"

Singh looked at her and smiled. "I do not think you are speaking disrespectfully to me. I think you are just doing your job. I do not know the exact number but, yes, they have stopped some of our products from being sold in America. It should be noted during the same time the FDA approved more than eighty of our products. I don't think you can find an American company with that approval percentage."

He smiled at her. "You are too young to know about the thalidomide drug which caused tens of thousands of birth defects

SAFE NOWHERE

throughout the world when pregnant women took the drug. Your FDA just recently approved that drug for marketing in the United States. I don't think you should hold the FDA out as a shining example of how to do things right. It makes mistakes all the time."

She'd never admit it but she'd started to like this guy. During preparation for his deposition, she'd read that he was somewhat of a recluse. He let other people do the talking for Enpact. It was his practice to decline all interviews; he was a mystery man who, together with his brother, built a multi-billion dollar business in ten years. He intrigued her and he'd started to open up. She didn't want him to stop. The problem was to keep Junior and his mindless objections out of the mix. Her instinct was to use a "get more flies with honey" approach. She'd have to stop thinking about the terrible things Enpact had done and just ask open-ended questions to keep him talking. She flashed her best smile. A little positive stroking of the man's ego wouldn't hurt if it kept him talking.

"Mr. Singh, you mentioned other Enpact drugs. How much of the generic American market does Enpact have?"

"I don't have the exact figures on that, but upwards of forty percent of all generic drugs sold in America come from us. We sell billions of dollars of drugs each year…I thought I mentioned that already."

"I can tell that, as the founder of Enpact, you are proud of the company." She'd join the suck-up brigade, but at least she had a good reason.

Singh's face beamed. "I am as proud of Enpact as I am of my eight children."

Junior shifted in his chair. Katie knew he'd interrupt this cozy chat in a heartbeat. Singh and she were getting along so well.

163

Singh smiled broadly. "Do you know what I think? I think it would be very nice if you and my lawyers all have dinner at my home with me tonight. What do you think?"

She looked at Junior. He didn't know how to respond to Singh's suggestion, and she wasn't going to let him off the hook. "That would be nice."

Junior stammered and looked at Singh. "Can we talk about this later?" he mumbled. "I am sure Miss Hornsby has other things to do this evening."

When in doubt, keep running and go for that extra base, her father always said. "I'm free tonight. Dinner sounds lovely."

"I'll send a car. Tell the receptionist where you are staying. We will eat at eight o-clock."

She checked her notes. Singh had endorsed the expertise of Dr. Barrett, which was significant because it solidified the case against Enpact. His attempt to belittle Patel was insulting. From what she knew about Patel, from reading his hacked report, Singh's accusations were wrong. It really didn't matter. Either way it would play to her advantage. If Patel was a fraud, he'd be Enpact's fraud, not hers. If he were a stand-up guy who helped their cases, he'd be the ultimate insider who'd blown the whistle on Enpact's wrongdoing. A win-win situation. She saw no reason to go any further with Singh's deposition.

"Thank you for your time, Mr. Singh. That's all the questions I have. I look forward to this evening."

Chapter 19
December 2011

Katie discovered that she and Junior were staying at the same hotel when she went down to the lobby to wait for Singh's car and found Rebus waiting in the lobby. He checked his watch, gave her a nervous glance, and looked away as she approached. He was wearing the same suit he'd worn all day but had changed his shirt and tie. He looked different, though. Nice, not as stern looking.

"We meet again." Katie smiled.

Rebus looked down at his feet and mumbled an unintelligible response. She picked a spot to wait a short distance away from him and said nothing. The evening's social event had clearly started off on the wrong foot. A chauffeur arrived in a Mercedes limousine and the two sat in the back seat. She was surprised by how much she enjoyed Junior's discomfort, and she also liked the aroma of his aftershave. The ride took forty-five minutes and they'd said nothing to each other. She had swapped her business attire for something a little more chic—a nice silk blouse that revealed a little cleavage and a dark skirt, shorter than she'd wear in a courtroom. She'd completed her outfit with stiletto-heeled shoes, not quite hooker-heels but calculated to catch the eye. As far as she could tell, the combination wasn't working on Junior. He worked hard to avoid any eye contact. Every time their eyes met inadvertently, he'd blush.

The chauffeur drove up a tree-lined driveway that ascended into a lush swell of lawn. At the top of the hill, the driveway made an expansive loop in front of the house. The driver swung around and stopped near the front door and waited while they got out.

The house was breathtaking, a palace in the middle of nowhere. She felt a catch in her throat as she and Junior stood at the front door and looked around. Rows of trees created an elegant refined setting that accentuated the home's beauty.

Rebus rang the bell. An attractive Indian woman answered the door. She was young, about Katie's age, either Singh's trophy wife or his daughter; she wore a stylish black dress that revealed ample cleavage and long legs. Katie noted that the hemline of the dress was shorter than hers. She had second wife written all over her.

The young woman opened the door wide and gestured them inside, yelling, "Dad, the others are here."

That answers that question, Katie mused.

Singh emerged from a nearby room and ushered them into a large dark wood-paneled room, the library she'd guess. Three sides of the room were lined with bookcases filled with books from floor to ceiling. The remaining wall contained a large window that overlooked an expansive swimming pool and the rapidly fading sun, a magnificent sunset that took Katie's breath away. The slick powerful-looking guy who'd sat quietly at the other end of the conference table all day stood at the picture window and looked out. Maggie, the court reporter, stood next to him. He turned and introduced himself. "I'm Ev. And you've both met Maggie."

Katie said, "Ev? Just Ev?"

Mr. Slick smiled. "Just Ev."

She wondered for a moment about the propriety of the court reporter being present in a social situation like this. She shook both of their hands. "Hi, Maggie."

The daughter kissed her father on the cheek. "I'm going out. Have a nice dinner."

Singh waited until his daughter left the room and closed the door. "I wish she wouldn't wear such clothes when she goes out. My daughter, she is single. A modern woman. Most Indian women are married by the time they reach twenty-five. They are also much more modest than my daughter." He shrugged his shoulders. "What can a father do? First a drink, then we eat."

Junior had a beer; Katie and Maggie sipped on the martinis Singh had prepared. 'Ev' and Singh drank scotch.

Singh looked at Katie. "How do you like India? Are you enjoying your stay?"

"The contrast between the rich and the poor is very stark. I'm surprised to see that contrast so vividly everywhere I look."

Singh took a long, slow sip of his drink. "This is simply our system. Those of us who are successful need to act protectively. We get our own water from tankers; we have our own security guards; we have our own diesel generator sets generating our own electricity; we send our children abroad to study; we go to private hospitals; we live in gated communities. All of this is necessary for us to function effectively, to live happily, and to be safe. The poor will try to take these things from us if they can."

"Is there much here in the way of charitable giving?"

"I cannot speak for others, but as for myself and my family, for all practical purposes, unless we protect ourselves, we cannot live in India and anything we might care to do would be a drop in the bucket, as you Americans like to say. But the rich do have problems. We have to travel on public roads in order to get to work and, of course, to the airport. And these roads are hellish. I have a chauffeur, and I can use my iPad as I sit in the backseat of my car. But I hate the endless delays. That is why at all the cocktail parties of the rich, the conversation gets to the topic of bad roads and impossible traffic. Complaining about the heavy traffic is part of who we are."

He held up his glass. "This is a cocktail party and that is why I am complaining about the roads. They are very bad." He laughed.

The group stood and finished their drinks and the polite chitchat ended. "It is just going to be the five of us," Singh said. "Everyone in the family has something going on."

He led them into a large dining room that Katie could only describe as sumptuous. She didn't know much about art but the paintings on each wall of the room looked familiar and expensive.

"The paintings are magnificent," she said.

"Are you a connoisseur?"

"No, not at all. But these are beautiful."

"Thank you. This is a Modigliani." He gestured toward the head of the room. Ev steered Maggie over to the painting and she studied it closely while he studied her. "And on this wall, a couple by Picasso," Singh continued. "These two artists didn't like each other very much but I keep them in the same room so they have to get along." He chuckled and pointed across the room. "On the other wall, is my very favorite, a Monet."

They moved to the end of a long table in the middle of the room set for five places. Singh watched Katie closely as he held her chair. He then took the seat at the head of the table. Ev and Maggie sat across the table and Rebus sat on her right. He hadn't so much as glanced at Katie.

A tuxedo-clad servant entered the room with two bottles of

wine, one red, and one white. Singh selected the red. "While we're waiting for dinner, why don't you tell us about yourself?" Singh asked Katie.

She took a sip of the wine. It was delicious. She pointed at Rebus. "Him first." She grinned and looked at Ev and Maggie. "Or one of them."

Singh grinned back. "No. You first. How does it come about that you are a lawyer? You could have been a big-time model on Madison Avenue in New York."

She'd been asked this question before, many times. In law school, some of her classmates would admit they were in law school because their fathers were lawyers and others were simply undecided about their careers. Most made a comment about money, as if a law degree was the real-life equivalent of grabbing the brass ring. But, her story was different. As a young girl, she'd watched the film "To Kill a Mockingbird" and had immediately become taken with the idea of becoming a layer, a trial lawyer, who would take on the power structures that beat down the disadvantaged members of society. Her goal, kept secret from her father who hated all lawyers for no apparent reason, was to prove that a member of the so-called weaker sex could change society for the better by providing and ensuring justice for the downtrodden and disadvantaged members of society. Since she'd started with the Newton firm, the goal had become who she was and her dream of taking on privileged corporations, banks and professionals who flaunted their power by standing solidly in the way of justice for all was an every-present part of her reality. The piggish CEO of Enpact seated at the head of the table stood for everything she was against. He wouldn't understand what it meant for her to be on this quest. Her thoughts drifted briefly to Richard, who'd understood how she felt when she'd explained it to him. All this slob seated in front of her thought about was that she was a woman who should surrender herself sexually to him because he was rich and powerful. If she tried to explain, her words would be wasted.

She shrugged. "I thought about it but I like pizza too much." She glanced quickly over at Rebus to see if he was taking notes. He wasn't. He appeared to be as uncomfortable as she felt. "Actually, that's a lie. I've never wanted to be anything but a lawyer and I certainly never wanted to be a model eating lettuce three times a day with a carrot for dessert." The small group laughed. All except Rebus.

Singh smiled. "I don't think you've eaten too much pizza."

She didn't like the way Singh looked at her, his eyes focused on her chest. She took another sip of wine. She also didn't like Ev. No last name and his lustful looks at Maggie seemed to fuel Singh's attention on her. She wished she hadn't jumped so eagerly at the dinner invitation. She'd need to talk with Gary about whether it was appropriate for a court reporter to mingle with one of the parties to a deposition. Except it was probably going to be a little more than just mingling if what was going on across the table was any indication.

Who the hell was this Ev anyway? Why was he sitting in on the depositions? Why was he so reluctant to identify himself? Why was he here tonight? Since she'd arrived at Singh's home, Ev had been watching her carefully. She could feel his eyes on her, but other than the brief introduction, he hadn't said a thing to her. His silence was rude. She tried to establish eye contact with Singh, but his eyes were still fixed on her chest. She looked quickly at Ev who pretended not to notice. Maggie was oblivious. The girl couldn't take her eyes off of Ev. She was glad Rebus was here. My chaperone, my hero. She smiled to herself.

"I love being a lawyer. In the United States the rule of law is what guides the entire country. People make fun of lawyers but we are important. We are sworn to uphold the law when we are admitted to practice."

"That's good, for you to love your work. I love my work, too." Singh reached for his glass of wine and took a long slow sip, never taking his eyes off her chest. "We can all go for a swim after dinner."

Maggie piped in. "That would be nice."

Katie ignored the comment. She hoped that Rebus would start talking. She also wished that she hadn't worn such a short skirt. Even Ev had stopped staring in Maggie's eyes to quickly glance several times at her legs when they'd stood in the library.

She looked up at the Modigliani. "When did you start collecting art?"

Singh stared at her with his hooded dark eyes. He was mentally undressing her. The only thing on his mind was sex. This was really getting creepy. Another quick glance at Ev. He and Maggie had their own thing going, staring at each other.

Singh pressed further. "We were talking about you, not Modigliani. Tell me more about you." He reached for the wine bottle and filled her glass. Singh didn't even know Rebus was in the room, and so far he'd said nothing to Ev or Maggie. She didn't like looking at Singh but he liked looking at her. Ev liked looking at Maggie and Maggie liked looking at him. Rebus didn't like looking at anyone. The very definition of a three-ring circus, she thought and smiled ruefully.

"I'm twenty-five years old…about the same age as your daughter."

She needed to steer the topic of conversation away from her.

"Your country is very much different than mine. The ride from New Delhi to Gurgaon was fascinating." She looked over at Rebus. She had to bring him into this conversation.

"Do you think so, too?"

He mumbled something unintelligible.

She said, "I didn't hear what you said."

His face reddened. "I said I hadn't noticed."

Ev commented, "You're right. The ride is fascinating." He looked her right in the eyes and Katie felt her cheeks redden. He turned his attention back to Maggie.

So much for small talk, Katie thought. There was an awkward silence. Singh continued to look at her like she was a piece of meat, while Junior stared at the table in front of him. Ev and Maggie had gone back to their examination of the Modigliani and each other. What the hell, she thought, did Junior see that was so fascinating on the table in front of him? She was desperate. She needed to move this conversation along, and she needed Junior to do more than just sit there. Maybe if she took a different approach, Singh would take his eyes off her chest. Maybe Ev or Maggie would stop staring at each other and would actually speak. Maybe the moon was made of green cheese. She smiled to herself at the thought.

The tuxedoed server interrupted the scintillating conversation. He served the five of them and they ate without speaking. She was surprised at the amount of food Singh put away. He tried to pour her more wine but she put her hand over her glass. Maggie eagerly accepted. Singh ignored Junior and Ev and finished the bottle himself. She'd had enough but it was good wine. It reminded her of that nice dinner she and Richard had. She finished and pushed her plate away, looked over at Rebus.

"Do you go to many baseball games? Any baseball fans here?"

Why did he have such a hard time looking at her? It's rude to not look at someone when you speak to him or her. She considered reminding him of that simple rule of courtesy, but right now she needed him on her side.

"I grew up in Chicago. I'm a Cubs fan. I've been a Cubs fan all my life."

She was surprised. She glanced quickly at the rest of the group. No one paid any attention to the baseball talk. But Rebus being a baseball fan gave her a foothold to liven the conversation. "Roger Hornsby is my favorite Cub player. He holds the Cubs record for the most runs scored in a single season. He scored 156 times in 1929 and also hit .380 that year."

Rebus looked at her.

"Are you related to Roger Hornsby?"

Singh interrupted, "Who is this Roger Hornsby?" As he spoke, his eyes once again raked over her.

She experienced a flashback to the same unpleasant reaction she'd felt when she was fourteen years old and a foul-mouth, alcohol-breathing carnie at a midway booth ogled her while trying to guess her weight. Then there was that high school teacher and the same reaction. Dad always said to pay attention to the red flags these types of situations raised. With Singh's eyes roaming over her body, a large red flag waved back and forth. It made her feel dirty. It gave her the creeps. She shuddered and turned back to Rebus.

"Roger Hornsby was the best right-handed hitter baseball has ever seen. He captured seven batting titles—including six in a row—topping .400 three times. His .424 mark in 1924 is a National League record for the twentieth century and his career average of .359 is the highest ever in the National League. He was called 'The Rajah' by the press and was a two-time MVP and Triple Crown winner."

Singh interrupted, "I know nothing about baseball. Cricket is the biggest sport in India. Cricket and football. What the rest of the world calls football, Americans call soccer."

"Were you born and raised in India?" She was determined to get his mind to focus on something else.

He nodded. "But I did go to Oxford in England. I majored in economics. They also play soccer and cricket there."

Katie turned and interrupted Ev and Maggie's' star-gazing. "And where are you from, Ev?"

"I'm just a guest of Mr. Singh's. Don't mind me." He nodded in Katie's direction but kept his eyes on Maggie.

His accent sounded Brooklynese, she thought. Like the old Dodger manager, Leo Durocher. There was no question; he was American.

Rebus went back to staring at his glass of wine. She was surprised when he looked up again and said, "Roger Hornsby is my favorite player too. I had his baseball card as a kid."

"So did I. As a kid, I thought we might be related. We're not."

This was enough baseball talk for Singh. For the next hour, he told stories of his college days. She had no choice but to listen and occasionally nod, grateful that his attention had swung from her to himself. Singh opened a second bottle of wine and she fought to stay awake while he, Ev and Maggie drank the entire bottle. Singh kept talking. She stifled a yawn and looked at Rebus. He was fighting the same battle. Other than his brief mention of the Cubs and his Roger Hornsby baseball card, he'd been unconscious the entire evening and now he looked as tired as she felt.

"Are you ready for that swim now?" Singh stared at her with a greater intensity than before.

"I am." Maggie said excitedly.

Big help you are, Katie thought. "I have no swim suit."

"My daughter is about your size." He held his hands out in front of him in a gesture that could only be meant to compare the size of her chest with his daughter's. "You could wear one of hers."

What an asshole. She bit her tongue to prevent her from saying it aloud. "I'm really tired. I have jet lag. Tomorrow is a busy day and I need to get some sleep."

"A nice swim will relax you and help you sleep easier."

The creep factor was building again. She had no intention of letting him see her in a swimsuit. She looked at Junior and Ev. Help me out here. Someone do something, say something.

Nothing.

Maggie stood. "I'm going to change." She looked down at Ev. "Are you going to swim?" He nodded. She said, "I'll be right back."

Katie had to get out of here. She pushed away from the table and stood. "You've been such a gracious host. I don't want to spoil the evening but I do have to get back to my hotel. I need a good night's sleep."

"Some more wine? An after-dinner drink?"

Singh hadn't listened. He continued to stare at her.

"No thank you. I've had my limit."

"You have time for one more drink."

"I really must go."

"You can spend the night. I have several spare bedrooms. It is a long drive back to your hotel."

"I have work to do. Everything that needs to be done is back in my hotel room." This game was now in extra innings; she needed a relief pitcher and the other three were no help whatsoever. Maggie returned in a brief bikini and she and Ev went outside to the pool.

Singh relented but sulked after calling for the car. He was a man used to getting his own way, and because it wasn't going his way now, he pouted like a spoiled child. When the car arrived, Singh walked them out and held the door for her, but ignored Rebus. Singh stared at her legs as Katie slid into the car and said a terse goodnight.

She and Rebus rode in silence back to the hotel. She occasionally shuddered when she thought about Singh's behavior.

She and Rebus rode up the hotel elevator together. When the door opened at the sixth floor, she stepped out, but Rebus kept it from shutting with his hand. He said, "I'm sorry about what happened tonight, about what he put you through." He mumbled a quick goodnight and the door closed.

She stood and stared at the closed door. She'd been surprised. Rebus, the Chicago Cubs fan, understood what she'd gone through and apologized for it.

She checked the time as she entered her room. It was not a

good time to call Richard; it would be either too early or too late back home. She wasn't sure which. She fell asleep thinking about Tinkers to Evers to Chance, the best double play combination in the history of baseball. The trio played for the Cubs in the glory days back in the early 1900s. They beat the Tigers in the World Series in back to back years during that era.

She awoke in the middle of the night in a cold sweat. It had come back. She hadn't had the terrible dream in a long time. She knew that the night's experience with Singh had triggered a memory that she had tried hard to forget. She shivered when she thought about the similar experience with the high-school teacher a long time ago. She got out of bed and drank a glass of cold water and checked her laptop for emails. There were two waiting. The first was from Gary. He'd found Dr. Patel who agreed to meet with her when she returned to the States. The second one was from Richard. "I miss you and can't wait to see you. Travel safely."

She typed a reply. "Look forward to seeing you, too." She added a happy face and punched the send key. She smiled and went back to bed, closed her eyes and hoped that she'd sleep the rest of the night.

TOM BLEAKLEY

Chapter 20
December 2011

The last day in India and Katie intended to make the most of it. She was relieved that the experience with Singh—the spoiled, perverted dirty old man—was over. The experience left a bitter taste in her mouth.

All parties were present and accounted for, except for Ev. Apparently, he had something better to do.

She took Maggie aside. "Any luck with Mr. By-stander?"

"Do you mean, did I get lucky or did I find out who he is?" The answer is yes to just one of those questions." She smiled. "I'll let you guess which one."

She then assured Katie that the deposition transcripts would be sent to her office within the week. Meanwhile, she handed her a flash drive that contained an unedited version of yesterday's depositions that Katie downloaded on her laptop.

Since Patel was unavailable, Vijay Gupta, the second-in-command in Patel's department, replaced him. She knew nothing about Gupta and didn't recall having seen his name on any documents during her review.

Maggie administered the oath and Katie began.

"Would you please state your name?"

"My name is Vijay Gupta." The witness had a strong clipped accent, which Katie found difficult to understand.

"It is my understanding that you are employed by Enpact. What is your job status?"

"I am the assistant director of research."

"What are your responsibilities as assistant director of research?"

Gupta was nervous. His eyes darted around the room. He avoided looking at Katie. He searched his coat pocket and removed a pack of cigarettes, which he placed on the table in front of him. He looked at Junior. "There is no ashtray."

Junior looked down the line of lawyers at the table and gestured with a nod of his head toward Gupta. One of them stood and brought an ashtray from the credenza and placed it in front of Gupta. Katie noticed that his hands shook when he lit a cigarette. He inhaled deeply and blew the smoke directly at her.

"Your question again…?"

Katie waved the smoke away. "What are your responsibilities as the assistant director of research at Enpact?"

"I am responsible for coordinating all of the scientific research and testing done on Enpact products and reporting results to the director of the department."

"Who is the director of your department?"

"That position is vacant at the moment."

"Who was the last director of the department?"

"Dr. Patel."

"When did Dr. Patel leave the company?"

He paused and took a deep drag on his cigarette. He expelled the cloud of smoke slowly in her direction again. "I'm unsure of the date. Perhaps several weeks ago."

"So you have only been the acting head of the department of research at Enpact for the past few weeks?"

"Yes.'

"Do you know why Dr. Patel left the company?"

Gupta looked at Junior. "Do I answer that?"

Junior nodded. "If you can."

"There are rumors why Dr. Patel left the company. I cannot verify those rumors, so I do not know why he left." Gupta glanced at Holt who nodded slightly. Gupta visibly relaxed.

"What are those rumors?"

"Objection." Junior almost yelled. "I instruct the witness not to answer the question. By definition, rumors are unverified hearsay."

Katie hadn't missed the exchange between Holt and Gupta. She understood what was going on and Junior's eagerness to shut down this area of inquiry confirmed her suspicion. These past two minutes had been carefully rehearsed. Patel was a problem to Enpact and they wanted to get her off the subject.

"Did you ever speak with Dr. Patel about the reason he left Enpact?"

"Objection. Same instruction. The witness will not answer the question."

Junior was testy this morning. Maybe he was upset that Singh hadn't asked him if he'd wanted to go for a swim the night before. She smiled at the thought. But she knew it was more than that. Something was going on here.

"Are you and Dr. Patel personal friends?"

A look of panic appeared on his face. He looked at Junior for help.

"Not exactly."

This was like pulling teeth. "Not exactly?" Katie said. "What does that mean?

"Objection. You're badgering the witness, counsel."

Badgering the witness? Not exactly a friend? What is going on here?

Katie stared at Gupta for a moment. "Let me switch topics for a moment, but we will get back to the subject of your...friendship with Dr. Patel. What is your educational background?"

"I have a degree in science from American University."

"Any particular area of science?"

"No. Just science."

"You are not a doctor?"

"No."

"What kind of doctor is Dr. Patel?"

"He has a doctorate degree in embryology. As I understand, he is also a licensed physician in the United States."

"He's not a doctor who treats people then, is that right?"

"He could treat people if he wanted, but he does not treat people. He is a research doctor."

"What kind of research is done by you or others in the department of research?"

"It is as the name suggests. Scientific research."

"Can you be more specific about the kind of scientific research your department conducts?"

"We conduct scientific research on the amount of ingredients we place in our products, to discover things that will make our products better. We conduct testing on our own products."

"Can you be more specific than that? Can you give me an example of scientific research that has been done by your department?"

"Our scientific research is a trade secret. If I tell you about specific research projects, you could sell the information to others.

That cannot be permitted. I am sorry."

"I just want an example of scientific research your department has performed. I'm not looking for any trade secrets."

"I've said all I can say about our research."

"Tell me about your testing then. What kind of testing do you do?

"Our testing is our research. It means exactly what it says. We test our drugs."

Katie had had it with his dancing around her questions and she was fed up with Junior's interference. Junior can't have all the fun. She was going to push this guy as far as she could. "What is the purpose of testing your drugs?"

"I think it's self-explanatory. Do you understand what the word testing means?"

"My understanding of the word is fine. I am asking the questions here and you used the word testing first. What is the purpose of Enpact testing its drugs?"

"Objection. You are arguing with the witness."

She looked at Junior and he stared down at his coffee cup. "I am not arguing with the witness. I'm just trying to understand what this man has to hide when we are discussing such simple concepts."

She frowned and glared at Gupta. "These are simple questions, Mr. Gupta. If you do not understand a simple word, a word like 'testing' or a question that I ask, please let me know and I will see if I can explain it to you so that you can understand it. Now, I will repeat my question for the third time. What is the purpose of Enpact testing its drugs?"

Junior piped up. "There's that nasty tone in your voice again.

You will not badger the witness. One more time and this deposition will be terminated."

She was not going to respond to Junior. His objection was bullshit and they both knew it. She looked at Gupta and waited for his response.

"We test our drugs to determine what is in them."

"I don't understand. Your company makes its own drugs, is that correct?"

"Yes."

"If your company makes its own drugs, why does it have to test the drugs to find out what's in them?"

"Because we must prove to the Food and Drug Administration in your country that the drug is equivalent to the trade-name product. We do that by testing our drugs and submitting the test results to that agency."

"Are you telling me that every time you whip up a batch of your drugs, you must submit the test results to the FDA?"

"No, we only submit test results one time to obtain approval by the FDA to sell the drug in America as the generic equivalent of a trade-name product. Once we obtain that approval, there is no further requirement to submit test results."

"Let me ask, how many employees are in the department of clinical research and testing?"

"Research."

"I'm not certain why you just said that."

"You said department of clinical research and testing. There is no such department. There is a department of research."

"Let me rephrase the question. How many employees are there in the department of research?"

"Three here in India. I am unsure of the number in the rest of the world."

"Three? Does that include you?"

"Yes. As I said, I am the assistant director of the department."

"Who else is in the department?"

"As I said, two other people."

She really should have been a dentist, she thought. This was like pulling teeth. "What do these two other people do?"

"One is a laboratory technician and one is the laboratory secretary."

"With respect to the testing of drugs, which one of the three of you actually performs the tests?"

"The laboratory assistant."

"What is his or her scientific background?"

"It's Mr. Sabeen. He is a chemist by education and training. He is well qualified to perform testing on drugs."

A thought occurred to her. "Has the number of employees in the department of research changed since Dr. Patel left?"

"Yes."

"In what way?"

"Five employees left along with Dr. Patel. We had nine employees including Dr. Patel and me before he left."

She thought for a moment. "As I understand your earlier testimony, you would have us believe that you do not know the reason why all these people left your department, is that correct?"

"Yes. As I said, there are rumors, but one never knows."

"Other than having the title of assistant director, do you have any specific job responsibilities within the department?"

"My job is to coordinate the activities of the employees within the department."

"You perform no testing yourself, is that correct?"

"Yes, that is correct."

"So I take it that your job is to tell the laboratory assistant what to do?"

"Yes. That is correct."

"The three-person setup you have described was the way your department was set up before Dr. Patel arrived, and you have returned to that setup since he left, is that right?"

"Not exactly. We had more people before Dr. Patel came here. We had a couple of scientists who conducted testing and research."

"Can you give me their names?"

"No. I do not remember them." Gupta looked briefly at Holt who nodded.

"Let's use the example of generic Lorital. If your department's job is to submit test results to the FDA for generic Lorital, do you tell the laboratory assistant to test Lorital or generic Lorital?"

"Actually, I told the laboratory assistant to test both drugs so that we had a basis for comparison."

"Once the tests on both Lorital and generic Lorital had been completed, was it part of your job to determine which drug's results will be sent to the FDA top establish bio-equivalency?

"Our test results are turned over to management. What they do with the test results is their decision, not mine."

"In the case of generic Lorital, who specifically would you have given the test results to in management?"

"If I remember correctly, this occurred before Dr. Patel came to Enpact. I would have given the test results to the man Dr. Patel replaced. I don't recall his name, but he left the position of director of research about two to three months before Dr. Patel started here."

"Do you remember anything about the man? Was he a scientist?"

"Actually, I don't remember."

She didn't like his use of "actually." She remembered reading that people who answered questions by starting with the word "actually" were probably lying. It suggested to her that she was missing something.

"Are the records for the test results given to the FDA on generic Lorital stored in your department?"

"Yes, the test results for both the real Lorital and generic Lorital are stored in my department."

"When the test results for generic Lorital were submitted to the FDA, who in the company would have signed the letter of transmittal?"

"Actually, I don't know that information. It would not be someone in my department."

There's that word again, she thought. "Have you read Dr. Patel's report?"

"I am sure I have read some reports by Dr. Patel. Do you have a specific report in mind?"

She hesitated. She didn't want to describe the report that they'd kept from her, even though she'd already seen it. "I understand that Patel's report may have something to do about submitting test results from trade- name products rather than your generic products for the purpose of getting FDA approval."

"Actually, I know of no such report."

That word again. She took a deep breath. He was lying and she was getting nowhere. Her only hope for obtaining some real answers now was talking to Dr. Patel. She scanned her notes. India was a long way from home and this was the last opportunity she'd have to ask questions. Nothing came to mind.

"That's all the questions I have. Thank you, Mr. Gupta."

Chapter 21
February 2012

The time approached for Judge Steven Green's hearing of the renewed motion to dismiss Enpact's cases, and things were rapidly deteriorating for him at home. Abigail wouldn't leave the subject of his pending decision alone. Nancy joined her oldest daughter in her tirades against him. Green went into a shell, stopped talking, and stayed away most evenings until late at night. He'd come home, a strong odor of alcohol on his breath, and plop himself on the couch in the middle of the living room.

The youngest of the three daughters, Megan, looked over at his empty chair one night at dinner.

"I feel sorry for Daddy."

Abigail rebuked her. "Don't talk like that. He's an asshole."

"Abigail, don't use that word." Her mother shook her head. "I know you're upset about your father, but you can't go around swearing like that."

Abigail stood and put her hands on her hips. "Not only is he an asshole, he's hurting a lot of people just because he has power. Just because he's a big-shot judge. All of a sudden when he becomes a judge he's got so-called friends telling him to do all kinds of things. Just to save them from having to pay for killing people. You see how he treats us, don't you? Well, that's the same way he treats others. He's a hypocrite."

Megan gave her big sister a dirty look. "He's not what you said. He's our father. You shouldn't call him that." She burst out crying, pushed away from the table, and ran upstairs.

Madison, the middle daughter, sat there and sulked. She'd retreated into her own little shell as things gradually deteriorated around the Green household.

# # #

Green looked in the oven. It was late and he was hungry. The oven was empty. He opened the door of the refrigerator. Nothing. He walked into the living room where his wife was seated reading a book.

"Dammit, Nancy, I pay for the food around here. The least you could do is have some dinner ready for me."

"You expect me to guess when you're coming home rather than staying out drinking all night?"

"You have a real attitude lately. I don't even know who you are anymore."

Nancy laughed. "Bingo. I think you hit the nail on the head. Except that you're talking about the wrong person, Mr. Big Shot."

"I don't have the slightest idea what's going on in this house."

"You know exactly what we're upset about. We've finally seen who you really are."

"What the hell are you talking about?"

"You're doing something you damn well know you're not supposed to do. And you're making us pay for it. Abigail is right. A drug company is buying you off."

"Have you got a boyfriend? Is that it?"

Nancy laughed again. "You really don't have the slightest idea, do you? That's the way you look at things. When something bad happens, it's always someone else's fault. Sit down and talk to your daughters. They'll tell you. We've begged you to think about what you're doing with this Enpact thing, but all you've done is yell and scream at us. I don't know who you are anymore, the girls don't either, and you're oblivious. And it's going to be a hell of a lot worse when word gets out about what's you're doing. You better get used to being alone. We're sure as hell not going to visit you in jail"

"I'm not going to any goddamn prison. Did you tell the kids that I was? You're more screwed up than I thought."

"You broke Abigail's heart when you stopped taking her to your office."

The argument with his wife caused Green several sleepless nights. While he shaved one morning, a possible solution came to mind.

He placed the call when he arrived at the courthouse. "This is Judge Green. My daughter, Abigail, is a student in Mr. Stephen's government class. I'd like to invite the class to attend a court session. Will you have Mr. Stephens call me today? If he approves, we'll set something up."

When Stephens returned the call, he was delighted. He told Green, "I'll talk to Abigail and I know she'll be thrilled. She can check with you about a date and we'll arrange a trip. Thanks so much. Abigail is so proud of you and it's so generous and kind of you to think of us."

At the end of the call, Green sat back in his chair. This was good. This should take care of this nastiness his family had directed at him. Abigail had been totally unreasonable. Nancy had jumped on her bandwagon. Having Abigail's class come to his courtroom would get the two of them off his back.

# # #

Mr. Stephens told Abigail about her dad's generous offer. "What day of the week do you think would be best?"

She answered without hesitation. "Friday is his motion day. I know he has a really important motion coming up. It'd be great if we were there to hear the lawyers argue. I know a little about the case and I can tell the class about it beforehand. It's set to be heard a week from Friday."

When she got home that afternoon, Abigail called Stella and arranged the visit. "Can we keep it a secret from my dad? I'd like to surprise him."

Stella laughed. "Mum's the word, honey. See you a week from Friday."

Chapter 22
February 2012

Katie liked Dr. Patel the moment she spotted him walking toward her in the baggage claim area of the airport. He was distinguished looking, grey hair clipped short with a matching goatee, a rotund physique that made Katie think of Santa Claus, and he appeared to be about sixty years old. He smiled warmly when they shook hands.

"So nice to meet you, Katie. I've never been to Detroit. I've heard so many interesting things about the city. Now I will see for myself."

"You'll find things are much better than what you read in the newspapers."

They walked to the short-term parking lot and retrieved her car. On the way downtown, she asked, "Have you eaten? I don't want you to work on an empty stomach."

"I could use some lunch."

"Do you like Greek food? We have a wonderful Greek Town."

"That sounds wonderful. I do like Greek food. It is very much like Indian food, although not so spicy."

She should have known better than to take him to the Pegasus but simply didn't think about it until it was too late. After they were seated, Lester Hempstead and Lance Rebus, Jr. walked into the restaurant. Rebus spotted her and walked over to their table. Katie whispered to Patel, "The guy approaching the table is a lawyer for Enpact. I'm not going to tell him who you are."

"Hi, Katie. Welcome back to Detroit."

They must have replaced his batteries when he got back from India, she thought. He walks, he talks...

"Thank you, and the same to you."

Rebus stood there and looked at her, then at Patel. He was waiting to be introduced. She'd just let the fastball go by without swinging. She asked him, "Did you have a good trip back?"

He hesitated and swallowed. His face reddened. "The trip was fine. Have a nice lunch, Katie."

As he walked away, Patel smiled. "The young man is smitten."

She blushed. "He might be smitten but not with me. We were together in India for a week and other than his constant objections during my depositions, he didn't say two words to me. We both heard good things about you every day we were there. I didn't introduce you because I didn't want him to know who you are."

"I understand. I prefer that Enpact not know about this meeting as well."

After lunch they went to her office and she told him about the Enpact cases.

Patel looked at her. "What is it that you wish to know?"

"I've got a list of questions a mile long."

"Ask me anything you like. I'll answer what I can."

"Tell me how you happened to be working at Enpact."

"It is a simple story. Are you familiar with Orex? It is the company that makes brand-name Lorital."

Katie nodded.

Patel described the series of events that led both to his hiring and leaving the company

"When did you start thinking there might be a problem at Enpact?"

"Almost as soon as I got there. I should have asked more questions before I agreed to take the job. They led me to believe I was going to be taking over a big research department and that I could make it bigger and better. The laboratory facility was much smaller than I thought it would be. There were only eight people in the department when I got there. Only three of the people had any type of scientific training. The lab equipment was shoddy and most of it was outdated. It was not a very pleasant beginning. I feel guilty because the money they were paying me blurred my objectivity, the money and the promises. I thought things were going to get a lot better, but they didn't."

Katie rummaged through her briefcase and pulled out a well-marked copy of Dr. Barrett's deposition. "Listen to this, for a moment." She read him an excerpt of Barrett's testimony. "Other employees, as well as Dr. Patel, told me that it was customary practice at Enpact to perform bio-equivalency testing on trade-name products and submit those test results to the FDA rather than tests done on our products. As I understand it, that has been the customary practice here at Enpact for several years."

She looked up. "Was that the customary practice at Enpact?"

Patel's expression was grim. "Katie, it's true, but it's only the tip of the iceberg. There is more important information about Enpact than these fake equivalency tests. Much more."

She raised her hand. "Hold on. Let me bring Mr. Newton in before we go any further. I know he'd like to hear what you have to say."

She left the conference room and walked into Gary's office.

195

Jan Emrich was with him. "Dr. Patel is in the conference room and he's got some things to say that you should hear."

"Let's all go. Jan, do you have the time to spare?"

"I'm free all afternoon."

They walked into the conference room and Katie made the introductions. Emrich smiled at Patel as they sat down. "I heard your presentation at the FDA on testosterone. It was fascinating."

"That was several years ago," Patel said. "How did you happen to be there?"

"I was at the FDA for a few years and one of my responsibilities was monitoring the rate of adverse reactions reported on hormonal drugs. The presentation of your research at that meeting was most helpful."

"You are not with the FDA now?"

She shook her head. "I'm teaching pharmacology at the medical school here in town. Do you mind if I listen to what you have to say about Lorital?"

"No. Not at all."

"Dr. Emrich is one of the experts we've retained in the Enpact litigation," Gary explained to Patel. "We have had a longstanding and excellent relationship with her on matters that involve drugs and the FDA."

Katie began, "Dr. Patel just told me that it was the customary practice at Enpact to submit tests to the FDA performed on trade-name products as proof of bio-equivalence for the approval of its generic products."

Emrich's eyes lit up. "Seriously?"

Patel nodded. "I am most serious. As I told Katie, this is only the tip of the iceberg."

"What else is there?" Emrich asked.

Patel told them about the seven hundred children that died because of Enpact's fake antibiotic. He became teary-eyed as he described what happened. "That was the final straw. When I found out about these children, I went to Enpact's CEO, Mr. Singh. I tried to tell him what was happening. He didn't want to hear it. He fired me on the spot, but it didn't matter. I had already made up my mind to quit. I had prepared a report in collaboration with another doctor at the company before I confronted Singh. I sent a copy of the report to the FDA before I left."

Emrich asked, "Dr. Patel, who are you dealing with at the FDA?"

"Ted Collins."

Emrich shook her head. "I know Collins. He does whatever the drug companies tell him to do. Other than that, he's lazy as hell. Is there anyone else you can contact at the FDA? Collins will do nothing about your report."

Katie jumped into the conversation. "Speaking of your report, do you have it with you?"

Patel shrugged. "I do, but let me ask first for some legal advice. When I left Enpact, I signed an agreement to not take anything with me when I left. Because I prepared the report together with Dr. Barrett, I considered it ours, so I've kept a copy. I had sent it to the FDA because it was the right thing to do. I know Enpact considers it to be a corporate document because we prepared it while I was working for them. So, I'm not so sure that I can share it with you."

Katie looked at Gary. "Gary has a lot more experience with these kinds of issues. What do you think?"

"Did they give you anything in return for signing this agreement?" Gary asked Patel.

"They gave me six months' severance pay because of the signed agreement. They told that me if I didn't sign the agreement, I would only get one month's pay."

Gary looked at Katie. "I think Dr. Patel is right to be concerned. The only way around this is to submit a request to the FDA under the Freedom of Information Act for their copy of the report. The problem is that it will take forever for them to respond and we don't have that kind of time. But submit the request anyway. One never knows. Miracles do happen. For right now, however, I think it's best that to avoid discussing the report as such." He looked at Patel. "They could make your life pretty miserable if they find out you breached the agreement. There's nothing to prevent us from talking with you about what you did and what you found, but if you share the report with us, you'd have problems."

"I understand." Patel nodded.

Gary continued. "Are you willing to testify about your Enpact experience in our case?"

"Most definitely," Patel answered. "I'll do whatever it takes to stop them from hurting more people."

Jan Emrich spoke. "I've been sitting here thinking about your report, Dr. Patel. I have an idea about how we can get our hands on it. I have a couple of former colleagues at the FDA who I know can be trusted. Let me make a call and talk to one of them."

# # #

Holt, Brewster, and Plimpf sat at a table in Per Se in midtown Manhattan. Each man had just finished the nine-course meal, reputed to be the most expensive dinner in New York.

Holt patted his stomach. "Hangin' round with you guys, I've put on eight pounds. But it sure has been nice. I've never eaten so well in my life."

Plimpf sipped on his coffee. "Something keeps me awake at night."

"What's wrong?"

Plimpf spoke slowly and carefully, looked at Holt. "We're squarely in the middle of a conflict between Orex and Enpact. We didn't realize what a shoddy outfit Enpact was before we got into this litigation. Did you know about their so-called bio-equivalence testing before we signed the deal? Did anyone from Enpact tell you what they did to get approval of their drugs in the States?"

Holt shook his head. "No, they didn't. I was as surprised as you to find out. Y'all would think the FDA wouldn't allow drugs like them Enpact makes on the market."

Plimpf ran his hands through his hair. "Hornsby's made several insinuations that she knows about our deal with Enpact: from her questions in India and the reference during her oral argument. We can't let this come out. Our stock would be worthless if the relationship becomes public information. There are two options as I see it. One, we sue Enpact for failing to disclose material information to us. Two, we find a way to shut the girl up. The first option jeopardizes my status as Orex's CEO. My dad and all his cronies on the board will be whistling 'We told you so.' They'll throw me off the board. Can't let that happen. The only viable option, then, is to shut the girl up."

"You thinking of trying to buy her off? You think that would stop Newton?"

"I wish it were that easy. I don't think she'd fall for it. We've got to put her down and keep her down. Newton's smart enough to know that he'd be next if he didn't back away."

Holt was quiet for a moment. He looked at Brewster. "Oliver. You're kind of' famous for taking care of things like this. Have any suggestions?"

No one, for a moment, said anything.

Holt broke the silence. "Whatever we do, we've got to do it fast. How in the hell did she get her hands on Patel's report? She has sure been a pain in the ass." Holt looked at the other two men. "There's no way she got the report while she was in India. No way whatsoever. I made sure of that. Hell, I almost fainted when she started sniffin' around with Barrett. There's not a doubt in my mind that she has it."

Brewster broke his silence. He frowned. "What can I do? Better yet, tell me why I should do something about this?"

Plimpf rapped his knuckles on the table. "This is the way I see it—it's as important for ALEC as it is for us. I agree that If Orex's relationship with Enpact gets out, it will be a disaster for the company and me. But if Patel's report is made public, the whole damn industry will suffer. The entire industry spends a fortune every year building the trust that serves as the foundation of our industry. If people stop trusting us, they stop taking our drugs. They stop taking our drugs, we stop making money. It's as simple as that. Oliver, you've got to understand that there's a hell of a lot more at stake than just what happens to our company if the plaintiffs get this information out to the public. We need to find out how she made the connection between Enpact and Orex and how she got her hands on that damn report, but doing something to stop her about both of these issues is a hell of a lot more important."

Brewster hesitated for a moment and looked directly at Plimpf. "It's too bad your company bought Enpact in the first place. That Singh is a slime ball and I wouldn't trust him as far as I could throw him. His brother isn't much better, but at least he knows how to handle his money. Singh thinks Enpact is a toy. You should get his ass out of there."

Plimpf shrugged. "That's beside the point right now. We need to pull out all stops on this."

"Let me think about it for a couple of days," Brewster said. "What about Patel? What's the deal with him? Did he give her the report?"

"No," Holt answered. "He wasn't in India when she was there. Right now he's in Detroit spending a couple of days with her. It's the first time they've met. There's no indication that they ever talked before. Patel also sent his report to the FDA. We paid him big money as part of his severance with Enpact and one of the conditions was to turn over anything that had to do with his work at Enpact. He violated that agreement by keeping the report, no less sending it to the FDA. Our FDA contacts have agreed to bury it. It's never going to see the light of day from them. We can't go after Patel in court and claim that he's violated the confidentiality agreement because it'll make us look like we bribed him to keep his mouth shut. He's probably going to be Hornsby's expert witness. He's a loose cannon. Any suggestions? About either Patel or the girl?"

Brewster hesitated. "I'll work on that, do what I can. Get me an update on both of them. I'll see that it's taken care of."

"What are you going to do?"

"You don't need to know. You don't want to know. The more distance we keep between ourselves on this one, the better off we'll both be. Just get me whatever you have on the two of them."

"Is tomorrow all right?"

"Sure."

Plimpf signaled to the waiter, interjected, "Got room for dessert? I'm going to have a Calvados, an apple brandy from Normandy. Try it, guys. You'll love it."

Chapter 23
February 2012

The ninety-day period to complete discovery on the Enpact jurisdictional issue was nearly over. Katie had spent weeks poring through the deposition testimony from India as well as the documents she'd obtained from India and Washington. She'd put together a compelling argument and was convinced that Judge Green would change his mind when he heard the evidence. She and Gary spent the entire afternoon before the scheduled motion reviewing the materials and discussing various approaches that might appeal to Green.

Gary concluded the session, "I'm impressed with what you've done. I really don't see how he can decide against us. I want you to argue the motion. You have a much better grasp of the facts than I can possibly assimilate before tomorrow morning."

Katie was thrilled by Gary's suggestion. For the past two months, she'd thought about nothing but the pending motion and what she'd say if she was doing the argument. Now she was getting the opportunity. She'd spent the rest of the evening getting ready.

The next morning, when he and Katie arrived early in the courtroom, Gary was surprised to see that it was already filled with lawyers, news reporters, and regular court watchers. Hempstead, Rebus, and Holt were already seated and other lawyers from Hempstead's firm hovered around them. He noticed a group of high-school students seated in the first two rows. He hoped the packed room wouldn't intimidate Katie.

"Does the large crowd bother you?" he whispered.

She smiled and whispered back, "Buy me some peanuts and crackerjacks. This feels like opening day at Tiger stadium. I'm fine. Excited, but fine"

Judge Green entered the courtroom.

"All rise." Stella announced his arrival. Green sat down and looked around the courtroom. He was surprised to see his daughter and her class sitting in the first few rows. He didn't remember scheduling the class visit for today. Abigail hadn't mentioned it to him at dinner the night before. He forced a smile on his face.

"Before we begin, I'd like to welcome Mr. Stephens and his government class from Westland High School. They're here to observe the proceedings. At the end of the session, I'll answer any questions the class may have."

He looked over at Newton. "Mr. Newton. Let's hear what you have to say."

Gary stood. "Your Honor, Ms. Hornsby will present our argument."

Katie stood and approached the podium. "Good morning, Your Honor. There is one word I respectfully submit that defines the required contact with the State of Michigan such as to defeat this motion to dismiss based on the defendant's assertion of inconvenient forum. That word is 'footprint.'"

"Footprint?" asked Green.

Katie responded. "Yes, Your Honor. Footprint. I think the term is most appropriate when one considers the massive amount of drugs, all subject to FDA regulations and American law, sold by Enpact and used in this country. As my brief points out, the place of the injury is the controlling factor in considering a motion on the issue of inconvenient forum. All of the damages caused by this drug occurred here in Michigan, the plaintiffs bought the drug in Michigan, and they all took the drug in Michigan. Every person in Michigan has the right, under the Seventh Amendments of both the federal and Michigan constitutions, to a civil trial by jury. The claim of inconvenient forum is a red herring in that context. It doesn't matter where a drug is made. It is where it is used, and, in the context of this litigation, where it causes harm, that are the most significant factors in weighing the issue of inconvenient forum. To deprive plaintiffs of their constitutionally-guaranteed right to seek redress against Enpact on this red-herring claim would be wrong on its face."

Abigail watched the lawyers carefully. Katie Hornsby intrigued her. Abigail's enthusiasm for becoming a judge had waned since the problems between her and her father had started, but she had the grades, Mr. Stephens told her, to do whatever she wanted. Sitting there, watching and listening to Hornsby, Abigail became excited again about the prospect of becoming a lawyer. She watched Katie's every move. The lawyer spoke clearly and slowly. She knew lots about the drug she was talking about. She knew how to argue. Abigail hoped her dad would let Hornsby also answer some questions when he met with her class.

Green acted distracted and Katie was surprised that he didn't appear impressed by the horror story of Enpact's manufacturing processes and its submission of false information to the FDA. Any reasonable person would be horrified but Green acted bored, as if the weather was being discussed.

After she finished, Green stood. "I'm not going to reverse my earlier ruling," he announced. "The motion for dismissal is granted." He avoided looking at Katie. He also avoided looking at his daughter. He turned to leave the courtroom.

It took a moment for Katie to register what Green had said. She couldn't believe it. She resisted the urge to say something she might regret. "Your Honor, for the record can you at least state, as the law requires, the facts that you've used in making your ruling?"

It appeared that Green hadn't heard the question. Either that, Katie thought, or he'd deliberately ignored it. He walked out of the courtroom without saying a word.

The room was silent for a few moments. Everyone present had expected more. Gary looked at Katie and shook his head. "It's not your fault. He's wrong. Dead wrong."

As the courtroom slowly emptied, Katie packed her briefcase. When she finished, the only others remaining were the kids from the high school class and their teacher. Katie turned and looked at the teacher. "If there are any questions your class has, I'd be happy to answer them."

"We're waiting for Judge Green to speak to the class," said Mr. Stephens, who turned and looked at the students. "Does anyone have any questions for the lawyer?"

Abigail stood. "I do! Yes. Ma'am, I'd like to understand more about the inconvenient forum question. Did the drug company actually do all those things you told the judge?"

Katie looked at Gary, then at Abigail, and nodded. "Yes, it did. There's also a whole bunch of things I didn't mention in court. I just gave the highlights. Before we argue a motion like this, we file a written brief with all the good stuff that we think supports our position. For example, in this case I presented evidence we'd obtained before the motion that Enpact sells forty percent of the generic prescription drugs sold and used in the U.S. That's a fact I didn't talk about much in my argument, because it is a big part of my written brief. That's why I asked the judge if he could tell me for the record which facts he'd relied on in making his decision. I think his decision is wrong and I think he was wrong about not telling me what facts he used. It will be necessary for us to appeal to a higher court to try and get the decision reversed."

Another student raised her hand. "Do you think being a lawyer is a good career for a girl?"

"I think being a lawyer is a wonderful opportunity for a young woman to have an impact on our society. There are so many issues in our country right now that involve women that most men..." Katie paused and looked at Gary. "...except for my boss, don't seem to understand very well."

Gary laughed and stood. "I agree with Ms. Hornsby. The practice of law is like the practice of life. Most men don't understand women, and it is an exciting time for young women to be entering the legal field."

Mr. Stephens asked, "Any other questions?"

A boy in the second row stood, a big grin on his face. "Do you date younger guys?"

The class burst out in laughter and Katie grinned. "I wait until they're out of high school, but sometimes...I make an exception."

The class laughed again.

Katie and Gary left the courtroom and walked toward the elevators. Abigail came up behind them. "Ma'am, I think you dropped this when you were packing your bag." She tendered a white unmarked envelope to Katie.

"Thank you so much, but I don't think it's mine. Maybe you

should give it to the court clerk."

Abigail persisted. "I think it's yours. I saw it drop off the table." The two young women stood and looked at each other. "It's probably real important for your case," Abigail continued. "Please take it."

"Thank you." Katie took the envelope and extended her hand. "I'm Katie Hornsby. You asked the question about the facts of our case, didn't you?"

Abigail's face was scarlet. She shook Katie's hand. "Yes, ma'am. I'm Abigail Green. The judge is my father. Please, whatever you do, don't tell him I gave this to you." She turned and walked quickly back into the courtroom.

Chapter 24
February 2012

Katie had forgotten the envelope until she unpacked her briefcase in her office. She picked it up and turned it over, looked for some identifying mark. Nothing. Green's daughter was upset when she'd handed it to her. Katie wondered for a moment if she should notify the judge about the incident, but the girl had made it clear that she didn't want her father to know. She opened the envelope and removed a copy of a letter from Oliver Brewster, an official of ALEC, to Judge Green. Katie read the letter several times. Either she was terribly naïve or this letter was dynamite. Dated a month earlier, it clearly indicated that Green and ALEC's Brewster had discussed the Enpact motion and had reached an agreement on how it was to be decided.

She walked into Gary's office and dropped the letter in front of him. "This is what Green's daughter handed me in the hallway."

Gary read the letter and whistled. "This is a smoking gun. Why would she give this to you? She must know how terrible her father would look if this became public. We should think seriously about notifying her father."

Katie shook her head. "We can't do that. The girl asked me not to. There must be some way we can use this information without implicating her."

Gary ran his hands through his hair. "Let's just sit on it for now. ALEC is a powerful organization, and if they're interested in our case, we know there's some big money behind it. Maybe they've bribed Green, have something on him. On the other hand, he might be an ideologue. He represented the NRA in that big case. One way or another, he's marching to ALEC's tune. We've got to look into this relationship, but first we've got to deal with what Green's done to our cases. We have to appeal. We have no choice."

Katie pursed her lips. "What are our chances of winning in the court of appeals?"

Gary thought for a moment. "It depends on the panel we get. A panel of three judges is assigned at random. There are twenty-four judges sitting in the court of appeals and eighteen are conservatives. In a blind draw, the odds are we'll wind up with a panel with two of the conservatives. If we're lucky we could get two Democrats. So we have to decide on an approach that's going to appeal to their thinking. That should be easy. Conservatives like to hear about our Founding Fathers and how concerned the writers of our Constitution were about individual rights. They love to talk about that stuff. Our position is right up their alley."

Katie looked perplexed. "And I thought that judges were supposed to be neutral about politics."

"That's being naïve, Katie. Judges are politicians in robes. Lawyers have to always consider the politics of the judges sitting on their cases. It wasn't always this way, but in the past ten years things have changed. Green is a politician who has simply done what the people who put him in office want him to do. In this case, ALEC and big money corporations are his people. 'Don't bite the hand that feeds you' is the rule for judges like him. The tell-tale sign of judge who act that way is found in that their written opinions—clumsy and tortured illogical reasoning coupled with a result in favor of those who paid the most to get them elected. Green's decision in this case is a classic example. The only real surprise here is that we have actual proof now in this letter."

"I was certain that Green would change his mind when he heard the evidence," Katie said. "Is there anything we can do to speed up the process?"

"I was just asking myself the same question, Katie. Have you heard of mandamus?"

"Mandamus?"

"Yes. I've been tossing an idea around for a long time. I think this may be the ideal time to try it. Mandamus is making someone do something they don't want to do. It's the opposite of injunction, which is stopping someone from doing things they want to do. To stop something from happening, we ask a court to issue an injunction. Movie stars get injunctions, for example, to stop stalkers from getting too close. Mandamus, instead of ordering someone to stop doing something, is intended to make someone do something, particularly government officials. For example, if a mayor of a small town refuses to release money to be spent on improving a road, a court can issue a writ of mandamus ordering the mayor to release the money."

"I don't understand. How can we use it here?"

"There are a few things about Green's decision that make me think a writ of mandamus might work. Basically, his decision is both terrible and stupid. He totally ignored our facts. In deciding a motion to dismiss; a judge must use the facts offered by the party arguing against the motion. That's the basic rule he needed to follow. His decision is also a violation of the Seventh Amendment, which gives an injured party the constitutional right to have jurors decide facts, not judges. Let me put it this way. His decision is so bad that an appellate court will just look at his opinion with these errors and send the cases back to him ordering him to use the proper law and leave the fact-finding to a jury. The advantage of using mandamus rather than a lengthy appeal here is that we can get a mandamus hearing immediately."

Katie mused. "You sound pretty confident of the outcome of an appeal."

"We won't know is whether any of the three judges on the panel are also under the influence of ALEC. If that's the case, we would lose."

Katie knew nothing about the concept of mandamus. She'd never heard of it; nor had it been discussed in any of her law school classes. It wasn't a topic on the bar exam, either. She'd been lucky. If it had been, she wouldn't have had such a high score.

Gary continued, "The average time from the filing of an ordinary appeal to oral arguments is nineteen months. It takes about six months after oral argument for the court to issue an opinion. We're looking at a little more than two years if we do the usual appeal process. Mandamus is in the category of appeals called 'extraordinary writs' due to the recognition that there are some issues that should be decided quickly for a variety of reasons. If we file a motion for writ of mandamus, it'll be heard within two weeks. I think we should do it. Even if our mandamus motion is denied, we still can appeal. In other words, we get two bites at the apple. It's a no-lose situation."

Gary was excited. He couldn't sit still. He stood and paced back and forth across the room. "Katie, the more I think about it, the more I like it. Do some research on mandamus and draft a motion. You have to be polite and not call Green an idiot. The judges on the court of appeals will figure that out all by themselves. The panel will appreciate your restraint. I also think the appeals court will enjoy the novelty of our approach. So get busy. Drop everything else and get to work."

Katie walked out of Gary's office with a renewed sense of hope.

# # #

This was the worst. Green stomped out of the house after Abigail brought up the hearing on the motion at dinner. She had a lot of nerve talking to him like that. Who the hell did she think she was?

It all started when she had asked, "Why didn't you tell the lawyers the facts you relied on in throwing the case out? The lawyer asked you and, instead, you just got up and walked out."

"I'd rather not talk about it." Green refused to establish eye contact with her.

"You embarrassed me when you didn't come back and talk to my class. You told us you would, and you didn't." She didn't leave it alone. "If you want to know what I think, just acting like that made you look guilty, like you're trying to hide something."

"There are a lot of things you don't understand."

"I understand the difference between right and wrong and I think you handled it wrong, and you know you handled it wrong."

"Don't talk to me in that tone of voice, young lady."

Abigail stood and took her plate to the sink. "I'm not hungry. Don't YOU talk to me like I'm an imbecile. I'm not stupid."

"Don't you raise your voice to me!"

"You're so damn concerned about me yelling at you, you don't care about people dying from a drug made by a company that sells forty per cent of the drugs used in this country." She paused to catch her breath. "I say that's a big FUCKING deal." She left the kitchen and slammed her bedroom door so hard the house shook.

Green looked around the table. His other two daughters avoided eye contact. Nancy stared at him with a thin-lipped grin. "It's not funny," he pleaded with her. "She shouldn't talk like that, particularly not to me."

"What's bothering you is that she's right, and you know it."

"You don't know anything about it either."

"We've been through all this before. Abigail's terribly disappointed. She thought you'd do the right thing. You make a big deal out of inviting her class to your courtroom and then you ignore them and walk out without talking to them. That's important to a sixteen-year-old girl."

Green stood abruptly. "I don't have to take this crap. I don't have to answer to anybody about what I do on the bench, particularly to a sixteen-year- old. I'm the judge here. It's none of her business. It's none of your business. The sooner you all realize that, the sooner things will get back to normal around here. I'm going out."

He slammed the door to the garage on his way out. The house shook again.

# # #

Green hated that he'd resorted to sitting on a bar stool most evenings since Abigail started ragging him about the damn Enpact case. Nancy's attitude and support of Abigail were making things worse, much worse. Now his attempt to smooth things over by inviting her class to his courtroom had made things worse yet. He was caught in a vise, squeezed from two sides. Chief Justice Haley, on one side, had made it clear what was expected of him and why. His wife and Abigail applied pressure from the other side. Tonight was terrible. Abigail was right. He should have met with her class. He'd been afraid that she might confront him in front of her class and try to make him look like an ass. This was terrible. He was afraid of his own damn daughter, his own flesh and blood.

Lately he'd been going to this old tavern in Roseville because no one there would know him. He could stew in his melancholy without the fear of being recognized. Watching Tiger spring training on the old TV above the bar wasn't exactly the kind of thing he liked to do, but it did help to temporarily relieve the overwhelming black hole of despair that had enveloped him ever since Gerald Haley and Oliver Brewster had entered his life.

He'd just ordered his third drink when a man approached.

"Aren't you Judge Green?" The heavyset man smirked. "Can I buy you a drink?"

Green turned and looked at him. "Do I know you?"

"I was a juror in your courtroom a couple of months ago. You don't remember?"

Green threw a twenty-dollar bill on the bar and excused

himself. He walked in the direction of the men's room but kept on going out the back door. He sat in his car and wiped sweat from his face, waited until his breathing returned to normal. Damn! He couldn't go back to this dump again. Was there any place he could go and not feel the pressure of being a judge?

Chapter 25
March 2012

Katie labored over the mandamus motion. It was like preparing for the bar exam all over again. She finished the assignment late at night the fifth day after she'd begun. She sat in her office and reviewed what she hoped was the final draft of the motion and made several small corrections. Satisfied that everything was in order, she sent the materials to the printer. She rubbed her bloodshot eyes and sat back. She hoped Gary would be pleased with her effort.

She looked at her watch. She hadn't realized how late it was and didn't feel like walking in the dark three blocks to the parking lot. It would be after four o'clock in the morning before she'd get home and it was colder than hell outside. Gary had a couch in his office and she'd crash there. She walked into his office, kicked off her shoes, and stretched out on the couch. She drifted off to sleep thinking about mandamus.

She opened her eyes. It was still dark. A blanket was tucked around her. Her mouth was dry. She sat up, stretched, and found her shoes. She wandered out of Gary's office. Light was coming from the conference room; Gary was sitting at the table reading her mandamus motion. He looked up and smiled. "Katie. This is terrific. You nailed it. Absolutely nailed it."

# # #

A month went by. Since the mandamus motion was filed, Katie hadn't had the time to give it much thought because she'd been catching up on other work. She was in the conference room interviewing a potential medical malpractice client when Gary walked came to the door.

"Excuse me for interrupting. Katie, can I speak to you for a minute?"

The two stood in the hallway. "Good news," Gary said. "I just received word by phone from the court of appeals. They granted our mandamus motion. We're back in business. They're sending the cases back to Green for trial."

He stepped forward and hugged her. "Terrific work."

"It was your idea."

"But you put it into words in a way I never could have. You're hot stuff, Katie. Set up another meeting with the Lorital clients so we can tell them in person. This is really big."

"I'll finish this interview and get right on it."

Her mind drifted as she sat down and continued the client interview. She thought about calling Richard. He'd be thrilled. He was so supportive, so patient and supportive.

# # #

Timothy Holt was at breakfast when his cell phone rang. It was Oliver Brewster calling from ALEC headquarters.

"Mornin', Oliver."

"Tim, sorry to bother you so early. I just heard from our friend about a disturbing ruling yesterday on Albright in the court of appeals. Apparently the panel granted the mandamus petition and the file is being sent back to Judge Green. Chief Justice Haley suggests that if you kick it upstairs to his court before it goes back, he'll take care of it. Thought you'd just like to know."

"I'll get somethin' in his hands by this afternoon."

Holt checked his watch. Hempstead's office wasn't open yet. It was too early. He checked his contact list and speed-dialed Hempstead's personal number.

"I have something that needs your immediate attention."

After Holt's explanation, Hempstead responded, "I've already told you what I think about Green's decision. It stinks. A first-year law student could have done better. It's a big mistake to take this to the Supremes."

"Jus' do it. If you want our business."

When the call with Hempstead ended, Holt checked his contact list again, placed another call.

# # #

The phone call from Holt put the Chief Justice into action. He contacted three of the justices personally and arranged for lunch in his chambers. The small group gathered at noon.

"What's up, Chief?"

Haley looked over at Justice Anthony Scalici. "You know I don't like to be called that. Why do you do it? It irritates the hell out of me."

Scalici grinned and looked at the others. "Someone has to pull your chain now and then. We don't want you getting too big for your britches."

Justice Robert Thomason looked at his watch. "I didn't give up an important lunch date to listen to you two guys bicker. What's going on?"

Haley looked at each man before he spoke. "I need your help. An emergency appeal is on its way to us and we need to hear the case immediately."

Scalici smirked. "Is this another one of your big money deals?"

Haley looked at Scalici. "What's your point?

"C'mon, Chief, we're not dumb. This is the third time in the last two years you've asked for the same thing. The other two times involved big money. It's fair to assume this is the same."

Haley spoke carefully. "The case that's coming in is important. There are some underlying principles at stake that I know the four of us agree upon. We've worked hard to maintain a good climate for business in our state. Big verdicts drive business out of our state. This issue is fundamental to what we believe and why each of us was elected to the court. That's why I need your help, and I need it today."

At 2 p.m. that afternoon, a messenger hand-delivered seven copies of a Motion for Emergency Consideration to the Supreme Court on the matter of Albright, et al vs. Enpact.

Four justices, including the Chief Justice, granted the motion to hear the case an hour later.

# # #

Haley called Timothy Holt. "It's a done deal."

"Ya'll did it?"

"You owe me one. I had to do some serious arm-twisting."

"Tell me 'bout it."

"Our sessions are secret. Good thing for you, I might add."

"Ah'll be in town next week. Free anytime for dinnah?"

"There's likely to be some spin on this so it's probably best we aren't seen in public together. People might get some funny ideas." He laughed heartily.

"Buy our stock."

"I'm way ahead of you. I bought before the order went out."

"Hope it's not in your name."

"Do you think I'm stupid?"

A fake boisterous laugh. "Can never tell 'bout someone who four putts inside ten feet."

"That third putt was a gimme. You should have given it to me."

"Not for the amount of money we was playin' for. Besides, ah nevah saw anyone ever take four putts from inside of ten feet before."

They both laughed.

Chapter 26
April 2012

When Katie called Richard and told him about the mandamus victory, he'd invited her to celebrate the weekend with him in New York. When she arrived, she was delighted to find that they were going to spend the weekend at the bridal suite of the Regency Hotel, the nicest suite in the hotel. Richard had explained that some decorating was being done on his apartment and he didn't want to expose her to paint fumes. He'd also arranged for the best seats in the house for *The Producer* after they'd had dinner at 21.

Later that night, they lay in bed. She surprised him and asked, "Do we have a future?"

Katie had given her question considerable thought. She wondered if asking Richard would provoke a crisis in the relationship. She studied his face as she waited for his response. Throughout the entire time they'd spent together, there hadn't been a clue or mention as to his thinking on the subject. Slowly, a slight grin formed on his face. He rubbed his chin. "Let me see. We go out for a romantic dinner, to the best Broadway show in town, you wear a sexy dress that drives me crazy, you ply me with wine and then take me to bed. We spend a couple of hours that leave me gasping for air—by the way, I like the way you administer mouth-to-mouth administration—and then you ask if we have a future. That's what you were talking about, right?"

He laughed aloud and she punched him in the shoulder. Despite the seriousness of the question to her, she couldn't help but laugh along with him.

"That's not fair. You're making fun of me. I'm trying to be serious and you're making jokes."

He laughed harder. "How many of these high-intensity sessions do you think it'll take to kill me?"

She smacked him again on the shoulder. "I just may decide to kill you outright if you don't answer my question."

He embraced her in his arms. "At least I'd die a happy man."

She rested her head on his chest, waited a long moment. "You don't want to answer my question, do you?"

"You want me to look into a crystal ball and predict the future?"

"You'd make a great hockey goalie."

"What does that mean?"

"Never mind. Forget that I asked."

Richard lifted her head and looked in her eyes. "I say let's enjoy the time we spend together. You don't know much about Indian culture. In our families, outsiders are treated poorly. My parents would have a difficult time accepting you."

Katie sat up abruptly, pulled up the sheet to cover her. "I get it. We don't have a future unless I agree to keep screwing you on the side while you get yourself an Indian wife to keep your parents happy." She stood and wrapped the sheet around her. "Who knows? You probably already have a wife back in India." She turned and walked into the bathroom, slamming the door behind her.

Richard waited a moment. He walked to the bathroom door and taped softly. "Katie. I have no wife. I want our relationship to grow stronger and stronger. Please come out and let me tell you I love you right to your face."

Katie's mind was in a swirl. She sat on the edge of the toilet and took several deep breaths. She replayed the last few minutes in her mind. Damn. She wished she hadn't asked that question. She loved him. She really wanted him to love her back. The reality of having no future together stung. In so many ways, he'd shown her that he really cared for her. Now, here he was on the other side of the door proclaiming his love for her. She couldn't be stupid about this. Things can change.

She stood. "I'll be out in a minute. I need to wash my face."

"Unlock the door, Katie. I want to hold you in my arms."

She did, and he did. She was thrilled.

# # #

Early the next week, Gary walked into Katie's office and held up a court order. "The Supreme Court just granted an emergency motion by Enpact to hear Albright."

"That's strange. What does this mean?"

"I'll call Hempstead and find out." He picked up his phone, but thought for a moment before dialing. "I don't think it was Hempstead's idea to take the issue to the Supreme Court. The opinion of the court of appeals was solid in its reasoning and it's clear that Judge Green was wrong and his ruling should have been reversed. It takes four justices to agree to hear a case in the Supreme Court and it's troubling to think that four of the justices would want to take this case. Somebody's got some friends in high places. You're right, Katie. This is strange." He dialed Hempstead's private number.

Hempstead answered. "I know why you're calling. I'm as surprised as you. I was under marching orders to file the motion."

Gary looked at Katie as he spoke into the phone. "This means that four judges are already on board. All they need is another vote and our illustrious Supreme Court will become the laughing stock of the country."

"For once, Gary, we're in agreement," Hempstead responded. "That comment is off the record by the way. There is something going on here that I don't understand. I just do what I'm told to do, but I didn't think there was a chance in hell that the court would agree to hear it."

# # #

Katie went right back to work on a brief for the Supreme Court that was similar, but not identical, to the court of appeals effort. Each court in the appellate chain had different rules and guidelines to be followed and it was necessary to follow each court's procedure exactly or the brief would be rejected. It took two weeks and she finished her revision just before dinnertime. She needed some people contact so she wandered out to the reception area, but Leslie was gone for the day. She checked the time. She hadn't spoken to Richard over the two weeks. Maybe she could catch him now, so she went back to her office and placed the call.

"Richard, I'm calling to just say hello."

"I've missed you, Katie. I've been in India."

"I've missed you too."

"A lot going on with your big case?"

"I can't begin to tell you. The case is now going to the

Michigan Supreme Court."

"I thought it was going back to Judge Green."

Katie liked the fact that Richard always listened to what she had to say. "That's what I thought, too, but the defendant applied to the Supreme Court and they've agreed to hear the case. My boss says that it's a perfect example of bad cases making bad law."

Richard paused for a moment, said softly. "I'd like to see you. What would you think about coming back to New York this weekend?"

"That would be awesome," Katie said, feeling a pleasant flutter in her stomach. "I could use a break."

"I'll set it up," Richard said in a soothing voice.

"I'll be there."

"I'll make flight arrangements for you and pick you up at the airport."

Katie smiled when the phone call ended. Since the squabble over their future the last time, she'd been concerned that she might never see him again.

# # #

Leslie smiled the next day when Katie told her about the upcoming weekend. "You've got a special guy. I'm jealous as hell. You sure you don't want to take me along?"

Katie laughed. "I wouldn't dare let Richard see you. He'd drop me like a hot potato and sweep you off your feet."

Leslie grinned. "I'd like to know your secret. Other than being smart, beautiful, sexy, and nice, you must have some special tricks you've never told me about."

Katie smiled coyly. "Nice girls don't kiss and tell."

Leslie laughed. "My guess is there's a whole lot more than kissing going on." The two of them laughed. "Can you clone him for me? Does he have a brother?"

# # #

Katie was perplexed when Richard told her they were going to spend the weekend again in a midtown hotel. He'd met her flight at the Newark airport and they were on their way to Manhattan. Their cab had just crossed the George Washington Bridge before he'd mentioned the hotel.

"I thought we'd be staying at your apartment this time."

"My roommate has people in from Europe. He didn't tell me they were coming, or else I would have picked another weekend."

"You have a roommate?"

"I thought I told you. Yes, an old friend who travels as much as I do. Neither one of us is in town often enough to justify the big expense alone, so we share the place. It works out well."

Richard reached over and took her hand. "I'm so happy you're here. Let's not let this ruin our weekend. I've booked the honeymoon suite again. You'll love it…just like last time."

After checking in, they went to a small Italian restaurant in the East Village. The dozen or so tables were candlelit and Katie reveled in the familiar smell of garlic and basil. Richard held his wine glass up. "Here's to three days of bliss."

They touched glasses and she looked at him. She liked his eyes best—dark and mysterious. They both took long sips of wine. He set his glass down and leaned toward her. "You look tired. That case is taking a lot out of you."

"I've never argued in the Supreme Court. It took two weeks to finish the brief. I've been burning the midnight oil, staying up too late." She smiled. "But I'm not too tired now."

"How is your preparation coming along?"

She leaned forward and placed her index finger on his lips. "Shush. No more talk about my case. We'll have time later to talk. I'm famished. Let's eat and get out of here."

TOM BLEAKLEY

Chapter 27
May 2012

The mandamus motion on Albright v. Enpact was up for discussion. Chief Justice Gerald Haley was seated at the head of the conference table adjacent to his office. He looked around at the other eight justices. Oral argument was set for the next week but it was largely a formality. This meeting today was when the court decided the probable outcome. It was highly unlikely that anything said during oral arguments would cause anyone on the court to change their mind.

Haley knew he had four solid votes, including his own, to reverse the decision of the court of appeals, but he needed five. He was uncertain about Bryan Canady, the usual swing vote. If Canady went along with the four of them, Haley would choose him to write the opinion. If Canady went over to the other side, the old geezer Richard Phelan, the senior justice, would probably take the writing assignment himself. Haley couldn't let that happen. The liberal assholes on the court, led by Phelan, always overreached in their efforts to save the world and this case was too important.

He cleared his throat. "Let's consider what this case is really about. The principal defendant is Enpact, a drug company in India. The issue before us is inconvenient forum, and it is clear from the record that the drug at issue was made in India by this Indian company, subject to the rules and regulations of the government of India. We must consider the implications of allowing this litigation to continue here in the U.S. To do so is to tell the government of one of the largest countries in the world that it doesn't know what the hell it's doing. The political ramifications are obvious, and I do not need to spell them out for you. On that basis I suggest that this mandamus order be dismissed and the case thrown out right now on our own motion. Added to this is the extraordinary financial burden on Enpact in having to defend itself in an American court. The strongest reason for throwing this case out is that businesses are leaving Michigan every day because they are tired of the unions, tired of workers' compensation claims, and fed up with high taxes. One of the important principles of our court should be to help maintain a business environment that doesn't drive business away from the state." Haley paused. "To save some time, let's vote right now on the issue of reversing the court of appeals and outright dismissal of the case."

Justice Phelan spoke sharply. "Mr. Chief Justice. Your suggestion, as you call it, is highly unusual and totally improper. Save time? What's the rush? There's no need to try to ram this past us without any discussion. You're right that the issue of inconvenient forum is before us, but I apparently need to remind you, as well as Judge Green, that there are court rules in place that must be followed, simple rules like using the proper facts or not making up facts to support a political agenda. It…"

Haley's face reddened—he interrupted Phelan. "Perhaps you didn't hear me, Mr. Justice. I called for a vote." He looked around the table. "Those in favor of my recommendation, raise your hand." Four hands shot up, including that of the Chief Justice.

"Against?"

Five hands were in the air, including that of the swing vote, Justice Canady.

Haley snapped. "I'd like to hear from those of you who don't support this recommendation. Please keep in mind that if we do uphold the ruling of the court of appeals, this case will probably be back in front of us two or three years from now on the issue of inconvenient forum." He looked at Canady. "Bryan, why don't you tell us what you think?"

Justice Canady cleared his throat. "I agree with Justice Phelan. I should also point out that the respondent's brief has clearly described the extent of Enpact's marketing of its products in the U.S. There's also a suggestion of a collaboration with the American company Orex. Mr. Chief Justice, it would be highly imprudent to dismiss on the basis of inconvenient forum when Enpact is selling more than one third of all the prescription drugs being used in the U.S. To put it even more bluntly, it would be stupid."

There was complete silence in the room. The Chief Justice's ears turned scarlet red. The two most junior justices, the newest members of the Court, shared a grin at Haley's obvious discomfiture.

Canady continued, "But, rather than short-cut our normal procedure, why don't we allow the senior justice to offer his views first? As we all know, our protocol calls for each of us—in order from most to least senior—to state the basis on which each would decide the case, and then take a vote. There's nothing so pressing about this motion that justifies the setting aside of our usual routine. If there is, I'd like to hear it."

Canady nodded toward Phelan who was sitting next to the Chief Justice. Phelan looked around at his colleagues. "Let's cut right to the chase. Judge Green fucked this case up bad. I don't understand what the big hurry was in getting this case before us, but if we approve what Green did, every judge in the state will get the message loud and clear that our rules of civil procedure and the Constitution of the United States don't count. We'll have a bunch of cowboys on our hands. They'll expect us to bail them out on any crappy decisions they make. Your comment, Chief Justice, on our supposed obligation to create and maintain a business environment is offensive to me. We are not the Chamber of Commerce. We are the Supreme Court of the State of Michigan. This court has swung far to the right in favor of big business in nearly every case over the past eight years. This crap of rewarding big money in return for their campaign contributions is nothing but the conservatives on this court kissing ass to these interests…and it has got to stop."

The youngest member of the court, Justice Mary Sodenberg, interjected, "Tell us how you really feel, Mr. Justice." The four conservatives sat stone-faced while the rest of the group laughed.

Phelan looked around at the other members of the court. "Sitting here, I'm fighting the urge to give my standard lecture on the Seventh Amendment right to civil trial by jury. People are entitled to have their cases heard by a jury. It is a guaranteed right. It is as simple as that, just like our state constitution says, and just like the goddamn Seventh Amendment to the U.S. Constitution says. Green's ruling makes a hash of it. It's such a terrible opinion because he didn't even get the facts right. A high school sophomore could've done a better job. I'm not pointing any fingers, but some of us in this room spend a lot of time talking about everything our forefathers believed in, and then spend even more time ignoring it. So, Chief Justice Haley, if you don't want us to waste any more time on this, let our vote stand now or take the case off the docket and let the court of appeal's opinion stand. That takes the fucking politics out of the case. We can also send a letter of admonishment to Judge Green telling him not to fuck up again. Enough is enough."

The room erupted in a mixed chorus of shouts loud enough to be heard through the thick walls of the conference room.

Haley stood. "Quiet." He glared at Canady and then at Phelan. "Who do you choose to write the opinion?"

Phelan grinned. "Justice Canady."

"The mandamus issue requires quick action," Haley snapped. "All opinions, both the majority and any dissents, must be completed by the day of oral argument. If no one changes their mind, the opinion will be issued one week after the conclusion of arguments. This meeting is adjourned."

Haley stomped out of the room followed by the three conservative justices. The remaining justices sat there stunned.

Canady said quietly, "I'll have my draft opinion ready by next Tuesday."

Chapter 28
June 2012

Katie sat in the courtroom of the Michigan Supreme Court. There were two cases on the docket before hers. The setting was quiet and dignified—even somber, she thought. She leaned over and whispered to Gary, "This is nothing like the carnival atmosphere of Judge Green's courtroom." Gary nodded in agreement.

The nine justices were seated on an elevated bench across the front of the room according to seniority; Chief Justice Gerald Haley in the center and the other justices on alternating sides, with the most senior justice, Richard Phelan, on Haley's immediate right.

As the arguments in the second case wrapped up, Gary nudged her with his elbow and whispered, "Don't start with any baseball statistics."

It took a moment for her to realize that he was kidding. She returned a quick smile. Since her return from her visit to New York with Richard, she and Gary had spent a great deal of time together. He'd listen patiently for hours on end as she practiced her intended argument. He'd acted as devil's advocate, pointed out holes or inconsistencies in her approach, and gently chided her when she'd say something stupid. Except he never made her feel stupid. He'd tell her that she was bright, smart, intelligent, and make her feel good about herself in the same way her father always had. She'd learned so much from Gary already. He'd been a cheerleader and a mentor. She'd been so lucky to stumble across Leslie standing in the hallway on the first day of her job search. So much had happened since that day more than four years ago.

When their case was called, Donald Veritelli approached the podium. Gary and Katie had both been surprised when Veritelli filed his appearance in the case. He was a veteran of this Court on both sides of the bench. Veritelli had argued cases before the Michigan Supreme Court for a long time. He was a former Assistant Attorney General of Michigan where his main duties included presenting the state's position on matters before the court. He'd spent a brief two-year stint years ago on the Court itself as an interim appointment after the death of one of the justices. In short, Veritelli was no stranger to the place. His confident and easy manner was evident in his casual, yet dignified, demeanor as he began his argument.

Katie experienced a surge of anxiety and questioned Gary's judgment in letting her argue the case. She had to focus on why she was here but found it amazingly difficult. Breathe deeply. Breathe slowly, she told herself. Gary glanced at her and sensed her discomfort. He leaned over, pattered her hand and whispered, "You're going to do great."

Veritelli began. "Good morning, Chief Justice. Good morning, Justices. The issue before the court this morning is simple. Was the court of appeals wrong in reversing the trial court's order of dismissal when that court determined there was no basis in fact or law for the suit? Let me begin…"

Veritelli recited an uninterrupted and lengthy version of Enpact's view of the history of the motion. He then reiterated Enpact's assertion. "As I said, this is a simple issue. There is no precedent, whatsoever, and no facts or law to justify forcing a foreign company to come into a Michigan court and defend itself for its actions totally within its own country, most particularly when that foreign company has been guided by and is subject to the rules, regulations, and law of its own country."

Justice Phelan interrupted, "Mr. Veritelli, I understand your statement about the law, but your saying that there are no facts confuses me. Are you suggesting that the trial court can decide for itself what the facts are without regard to the actual facts contained in the record?"

"No, I am…"

Justice Canady interrupted. "What facts formed the basis for Judge Green's decision?"

Veritelli paused and then said, "The facts are akin to the popular saying right now that what happens in Las Vegas stays in Las Vegas…."

Justice Phelan smirked. "Are you suggesting to this court that the facts presented by your opposition should be disregarded? I would like an answer."

"Everything about this case occurred on foreign soil under foreign laws and regulations," Veritelli said. "For this court to second guess…."

Justice Canady interrupted again. "Second guess? Do you think it's second-guessing for this court to consider the complete record in this case? Is it second-guessing when the trial court failed to divulge the facts it relied on in dismissing the case? Do you think that the trial judge had the obligation to provide those facts to the record when counsel for plaintiffs specifically requested that he do so?"

Before Veritelli could respond, Chief Justice Haley leaned forward. "Has the government of India taken any action against Enpact's manufacturing and selling of generic Lorital?"

"Nothing whatsoever, Chief Justice."

Phelan countered testily, "Answer my question, please. And then answer the question of Justice Canady."

"Enpact has zero tolerance for unethical or illegal behavior." Veritelli gazed at Canady. "In fact, Enpact has been praised by the government in India for its meticulous and careful manufacturing practices."

Katie restrained an impulse to stand up and shout that the man was lying.

Justice Phelan said testily, "Perhaps you have forgotten my question, Mr. Veritelli. I will repeat it. Are you suggesting that the lower court can decide for itself what the facts are without regard to actual facts contained in the record?"

"No, Justice, I am not. What I am saying is that American courts are not the appropriate forums to question the legal relationship between Enpact and the Indian government and its regulation of drugs. Enpact, like all organizations that work at the cutting edge of science and medicine, is a work-in-progress. In doing so, it continues to improve its systems and processes, and remains fully committed to upholding the highest standards that patients, prescribers, and the regulators in India expect from the company. Enpact stays firmly committed to its philosophy of quality and patients first."

Justice Phelan shook his head. "You should be writing television commercials instead of practicing law. But, you are not answering my question." He looked around at the other members of the court. "Let the record reflect that Justice Canady's questions have also gone unanswered."

The Chief Justice looked angrily at Phelan. "I disagree with your observation. Mr. Veritelli has answered the questions." He looked at Veritelli. "Continue with your argument, counsel."

Before Veritelli resumed his presentation, Justice Anne Leibowitz, the newest associate justice, asked, "It seems that your position is that it does not matter what the facts of the case are because there is no legal basis for proceeding in this country against a foreign drug maker whose actions are regulated by a foreign government. Have I stated that correctly?"

"Yes, Justice Leibowitz, you have stated my position correctly. As a matter of law, this case does not belong in the courts of the United States."

Justice Phelan shrugged his shoulder. "Which way do you want to go here? You can't have it both ways. Either there are facts to be considered, or there are no facts to be considered. In this brief period of time you have said two different things. You are confusing me."

Veritelli's face reddened. "Justice, I…"

Haley interrupted. "Your time is up, counsel. Let's hear from the other side." As Chief Justice, Haley had absolute power and total control over all matters related to courtroom procedure.

Veritelli looked relieved. He picked up his papers and returned to his seat.

Katie took a deep breath and moved to the podium. She felt lightheaded. She placed her hands on the sides of podium and gripped tightly. She hoped no one noticed how badly her hands shook.

"Good morning, Chief Justice. Good morning, Justices," she began. "I'm Katie Hornsby appearing on behalf of the plaintiffs . . ."

Justice Phelan interrupted. "Hornsby? Like the ball player?"

"Yes, Justice Phelan. Like Roger Hornsby."

Phelan leaned forward and smiled. "I'm a long-time Chicago Cubs fan. Are you related to him? If so, I'll need your autograph before you leave the courtroom." There was a smattering of laughs from the small audience.

Haley scowled at Phelan.

Katie shook her head. "No, Justice Phelan, I'm no relation, but I respectfully suggest to this court that the game of baseball offers a remarkable analogy as an alternative to opposing counsel's Las Vegas comparison. If I may explain briefly, the object of the game of baseball is to score runs by crossing home plate safely. Looking at the big picture of this case, Enpact markets the dangerous and defective generic Lorital throughout the world, not only in India and not only in the United States. What the defendant is asking this court to do is to give it a free pass because it makes the drug in India even though a big part of the 'game' is being played here in this country. The defendant is suggesting that this court, the umpires in this game, declare the drug safe in this country while, in actual fact, the drug is safe nowhere. Not in India, the rest of the world, or in the United States."

Justice Phelan interrupted. "Safe nowhere. I like that analogy. All the more so when I recall that the Chief Justice of the United States Supreme Court said that we are umpires in robes." He flashed a grin at Justice Haley who glared back.

Katie continued. "Just as in baseball, there are rules and

regulations in effect in the United States that determine how the game should be played and the defendant should be required to play here by those rule."

Justice Anthony Scalici jumped into the discussion. "Are you telling us that the fact that Enpact has complied with all the rules and regulations of India should play no role in how we decide?"

Chief Justice Haley quickly added, "I was just going to ask the same question. What do you have to say about that, counsel?"

The smug look on Haley's face caused Katie's mind to go blank. She stood for a long moment and tried to gather her thoughts. She took a deep breath. "Every prescription drug marketed in the United States, including those coming in from abroad, is subject to the rules in the Federal Food, Drug and Cosmetic Act, which, in part, prohibits the marketing of an adulterated drug. There are no exceptions. As my written brief points out, Enpact makes more than thirty percent of the prescription drugs sold in this country. To rely on India's approval of the drug would be akin to using a different set of rules in our hypothetical game of baseball. It is a fair analogy because it would allow Enpact to play the game of baseball using the rules of softball with its shorter baselines and closer fences.

"In this context, the issue of the regulation of Enpact by the Indian government is a red herring. The footprint of Enpact's drug business is large in this country and in the state of Michigan and the sale and marketing of Enpact's drugs in this country and in the state of Michigan is subject to the laws and regulations of the U.S. Food and Drug Administration. As to opposing counsel's analogy about what happens in Las Vegas stays in Las Vegas, what happens in Vegas just doesn't stay there. It affects every city and state in the country and every person in the country."

Justice Phelan nodded his head and grinned. "I like the baseball analogy" He smirked at Phelan. "It's a big hit with me." The younger justices tittered at the comment.

Katie continued, "Adding to this analogy, the game also requires a level playing field. During my preparation for our position before this court, I came across a quote that summarizes our position very well. Quote, 'At a time when the complexities of American life seem to increase and acts of private and public misconduct are constantly coming to light, the focus of our system of justice should be on how to provide a level litigation field that is receptive to promoting our public policies and compensate those who have been damaged. Citizen access to the courts and resolution of disputes on their merits, not by tricks or traps or obfuscation…' End of quote."

"Counsel," Haley snapped, "That's a pretty big word. What is your definition of 'obfuscation?'"?

"Mr. Chief Justice, my understanding of the word 'obfuscation' is that it means 'evasive, unclear, or confusing.'"

"Are you accusing Judge Green of deliberately obfuscating your case?"

"I am not privy as to the reasons why Judge Green…"

Justice Scalici interrupted. "The Chief Justice wants to know if Judge Green deliberately obfuscated, as you put it, your cases."

"Justice, as I just explained, I am not privy to the reasons for Judge Green…"

Justice Robert Thomason joined in. "I think it is disrespectful both to Judge Green and this court that you accuse him of something deliberate. Accusing a trial judge of using tricks or traps

243

is a serious charge and I see no basis in this record of any such action by Judge Green."

Katie was upset by the responses to her use of the quote. She attempted to gather her thoughts. This was not going the way she'd intended.

Justice Scalici sneered at her. "Please don't tell us now, counsel, that you have used the word by mistake. Your hesitation tells me that you are thinking of doing exactly that."

Justice Phelan leaned forward. "Counsel, Justice Scalici is a mind-reader. He can also read fortunes. I don't see any harm in your use of the word 'obfuscation' and I recognize the statement you are quoting as being from Teddy Roosevelt. Is that right?"

A scattering of subdued laughs came from the small audience.

"Yes, Justice Phelan. That is correct."

Justice Phelan continued. "The quote containing the word 'obfuscation' also appears on page thirty-two of your brief, isn't that right? Tell us why you used that quote."

"Yes, Justice Phelan. I apologize. Before I made the statement I should have given the citation. The quote also includes, quote, 'Citizens' access to court…for the resolution of disputes on their merits exactly describes the essence of the Seventh Amendment to the U.S. Constitution.' End of quote. When I first read that quote, my thought was that I couldn't express the Seventh Amendment's essence any better than that. And the essence of merit resolution is exactly what was taken away by the court below in its order."

Justice Phelan smiled at the other justices. "And those words were used by Teddy Roosevelt, a former president of these United States?"

"Yes, Justice Phelan, that is correct." Katie stopped for a

moment. She'd lost her train of thought with all the interruptions. She looked over her notes. Her mind was a blank.

"Are you through with your argument, counsel? Because if you have anything else to say, you better get going because your time is limited." The Chief Justice glared at her and then shared a smirk with Justice Thomason.

"Thank you, Mr. Chief Justice." What she wanted to say was that speaking of obfuscation, this was exactly what you assholes were doing to her, but she kept her mouth shut while she attempted to organize her thoughts. Even though it was obvious that Phelan was on her side, this experience was frustrating as hell. It occurred to her that so far she had not given Justice Canady, the usual swing vote on the court, much fodder for his consideration.

She looked at Justice Canady. "This court has taken the high road in prior cases when the built-in conflict between corporate interests and the constitutionally protected rights of individual citizens has arisen."

Justice Canady nodded. He knew, as she expected, that she'd just referred to a "high road" statement in an opinion he'd written five years earlier. "The high road in this case is the need for this court to consider the underlying array of facts disregarded by the lower court in dismissing these cases. The trial judge initially dismissed the lawsuit before the facts that are presently before this court were discovered. After conducting discovery for ninety days, a detailed list of facts was submitted to the court that, nevertheless, dismissed the cases again without any attempt to consider these facts or indicate why they were not considered. Instead, the trial judge made a couple of sweeping proclamations in its opinion that included statements of purported facts that are untrue. To view this issue most simply, the court below decided a version of facts improperly in two regards. First, it is within the province of a jury to decide facts, not a judge. Second, even if the judge were to decide facts, a court should use all available evidence provided to it, irrespective of which party submitted the factual data."

Justice Alberto Alioto reacted. "You are confusing me, counsel. Are you saying that the court can decide facts or not? You seem to be suggesting that it can, so long as these are your facts and not those of your opponent." Several of the justices snickered and nodded in agreement.

Katie realized her mistake immediately. She'd gone too far and conceded something she should not have. "No, Justice Alioto, I am not suggesting that the lower court has the right to decide facts. I am just pointing out in this case when it did so, it not only took away the right of my clients to have a jury decide what facts were true, but made finding of facts which were false. In fact, the example before this court is perfect for understanding just why the founding fathers decided that citizens should be entitled to a jury trial in civil matters. The absence of a system of citizen involvement in the jury function was one of the core issues considered in the establishment of our constitution. The colonists were fed up with the petty tyrannies being imposed on them by British autocrats precisely because these tyrants did exactly what they wanted to do without any regard for truth and justice."

Justice Phelan smiled. "I wondered when you were going to get to the heart of your case."

Katie noted that Justice Canady moved forward and sat up. She took a deep breath. "This is my complete position. It is simple and basic…"

Justice Alioto interrupted, "Not so fast, counsel. What is your position on the fact that the defendant is based in India, makes its products in India, and is subject to the laws and regulations of that country?"

"Justice Alioto, as I stated earlier, this corporation from India is, in fact, providing more prescription drugs to citizens of the U.S. than any drug company in America. Eighty-three percent of all prescription drugs used in America are generic and Enpact provides..."

Justice Alioto held up his hand to stop her. "You've already said that. You don't need to repeat yourself."

Katie hesitated. The constant interruptions were wearing her down. "If this court rules in its favor, what Enpact really gets is total immunity, not only for itself, but for an industry whose products kill hundreds of thousands of our citizens every year. That concept, of course, is completely antithetical to the Seventh Amendment right to jury guaranteed by the Michigan and U.S. constitutions. Further, such a ruling would suggest that the FDA has no business regulating foreign-made generics, which is untrue. The FDA does regulate these foreign drugs when they come into the U.S. If this court decides that the U.S. is an inconvenient forum for dead or injured Americans to bring suit against a company marketing and selling billions of dollars of its products here, the entire domestic drug industry will simply relocate to foreign shores to take advantage of this nonsensical result. The net effect of this, of course, would put the entire U.S. population at risk from exposure to shoddy, sub-standard drugs."

She paused and took another deep breath. Several of the judges nodded in agreement. She should stop, she thought, but another point occurred to her. "Also, we have submitted documents as part of the record below that clearly indicate an unspecified relationship between Enpact and the American company Orex. When Enpact's generic Lorital and Orex's brand-name Lorital are combined, these two entities have ninety-three percent of the overall Lorital market which last year exceeded six billion dollars in sales in the United States…"

Justice Phelan interrupted, a deadpanned face. He'd clearly enjoyed this argument. "Excuse me, counsel, but does Orex's brand-name Lorital have the same content of mice and rat feces that its subsidiary Enpact has in its generic drug?"

The Chief Justice looked irritated by the question. "Your time is up, counsel."

Justice Mary Sodenberg interposed, "Chief Justice, it is requested that counsel answer the question before her microphone is cut off."

Haley glared at Katie. "Answer the question, counsel."

"We claim that generic Lorital is adulterated because of its content of various contaminants, including mice and rat feces as well as the more dangerous and deadly inconsistent and high doses of testosterone that is the cause of all the strokes and heart attacks in users, including my clients. These problems have not been reported or seen in the brand-name product and none of our clients were injured or killed by the brand-name product."

She hesitated and took another deep breath. "Thank you, Your Honors. That concludes my argument."

There was a smattering of applause from the few spectators and the Chief Justice transferred his glare from Katie to the gallery. "I will clear this courtroom if there is another interruption."

The room became instantly silent.

TOM BLEAKLEY

Chapter 29
July 2012

Judge Steven Green was served with the papers that announced Nancy was suing him for divorce. He was stunned. He rushed back to his office and called her immediately. "I can't believe you'd break up our marriage just because Abigail is upset about this Lorital situation."

"The fact that you pick just one small thing and focus on that is a perfect example of how out of touch you are with this family," Nancy responded. "It's not just that. It's the way you've been treating us since getting your damn appointment. We no longer exist in your little world. I don't know the person you've become. I've tried to talk to you about how you've changed, but you've refused to listen. You refused my suggestion of marriage counseling. You've left me no choice." She hung up the phone.

The order required him to move out of the marital home. But what hurt most was the restraining order preventing him from any contact other than supervised visits with his three daughters. If he'd want to spend time with them, he'd have to obtain permission from another judge, another circuit court judge with the same status as him. Fat chance he'd do that, he thought. Nancy's divorce lawyer had a well-deserved reputation for a take-no-prisoners approach and she'd lived up to that expectation.

He moved out of the house the next day after tracking down a place to live. He'd settled on a small rental unit on the ground floor of a fifty-year-old brick apartment building located just inside the county limits on the far east side of Detroit. His unit was located at the corner of the building some hundred feet from Eight Mile Road and the incessant hum of traffic on the six-lane road kept him awake the first night. Added to that, the air-conditioning unit constantly cycled on and off emitting a grinding noise at the beginning of each cycle. Although the night was muggy and warm, he opted for the noise of the highway, shut the unit down and opened the two small windows

# # #

"Katie, lover boy on line three." Leslie laughed.

Katie punched the right button. "Hi, Richard. I was just sitting here thinking about you."

"Good things, I hope."

"Always good." Katie smiled. "It's nice to hear your voice."

"Same here," Richard said. "I'm coming to Detroit this weekend just to see you."

"Me? Just me? No business?"

"Just you. No business. I hope you're not busy."

"I was going to go to Washington to consult with President Obama, but I'll call him and tell him I need to cancel."

Silence on the other end of the line. "President Obama?"

"It's a joke, Richard. I'm just teasing."

"A joke?"

"Forget it. I can't wait to see you. Do you want me to pick you up at the airport?"

The weekend was delicious in every way, Katie thought, after dropping Richard off at the airport Sunday afternoon. He hadn't said anything further about their relationship, but she felt that something was different, better than ever. She called Leslie when she got home.

"Have you ever been in love?"

"Only about twice a day since I turned fifteen. Why do you ask?"

Katie giggled. "I'm trying to be serious."

Leslie laughed. "Your weekend was obviously very good."

"Yes, it was. I think I'm in love. I can't stop thinking about him."

"He's a lucky man." Leslie hesitated. "Do you think he feels the same way?"

"I think he does. He's told me once that he loves me, but I was holding a gun to his head at the time. I know one thing, though— I've never felt this way before."

"Just be careful, honey. I've had a couple of long-distance romances, and they've never worked out. I don't want to see you hurt. I know I sound like a mother hen, but I just want you to be careful."

# # #

"There's a reporter on the line, says he want to talk to you about the Enpact case." Leslie said. "Should I put him through?"

Katie had been disappointed by the lack of media attention to her Supreme Court argument. There'd been nothing in any of the local papers. Four months had passed since then and, while she hadn't forgotten about the case, it was definitely on the back burner. For the past month, Gary had been in trial in Chicago and she covered his other cases for him while he was gone. In truth, there had been little time to think about the Lorital cases.

"Put it through, Leslie."

"Katie Hornsby? This is Matthew Dowd from the *Detroit Times*. I'm calling to find out your reaction to the Supreme Court's decision."

"I…I didn't know there was a decision."

"It came out this morning, a five-to-four decision in your favor. What's your reaction?"

Katie hesitated. "I can't comment until I read the decision. Can you send it to me? Who wrote the opinion? Tell me about it."

"Canady wrote it. You're going to like it. He usually sides with the conservatives. By the way, I was present at the arguments. Let me compliment you. You stood up to the Chief Justice and Scalici. Most lawyers wilt when they face these two guys. You didn't back down. You did a helluva job."

She blushed. "Thank you. I'd like to read the opinion before I comment."

"Give me your email address and I'll send it right now. Call me back after you've read it."

She waited for the email and then read the decision three times. Dowd was right. Canady's opinion was terrific. She scanned through the five pages of the opinion again and stopped at her favorite part: "During the Constitutional Convention in the late eighteenth century, our forefathers debated over the need for citizen juries to decide facts in civil trials. Initially, the concept was rejected, but when the original document was presented to the various states for ratification, the absence of a guaranteed right to civil trial by jury became a rallying cry for rejection. The founding fathers went back to the drawing board and James Madison drafted the language that was to become included in the Bill of Rights as the Seventh Amendment. No matter how many rules, regulations, or procedural roadblocks have been devised by Congress, various state legislatures, or by the court system to modify or eliminate this basic right, the essence of the Seventh Amendment still remains the law of the land. The plaintiff's contention that the drug is 'safe nowhere' is entitled to be considered by a jury."

She was thrilled. The statement was taken verbatim from her appellate brief. She spent a few moments thinking, wrote down what she wanted to say to the reporter and then returned his call. "Mr. Dowd, I have one thing to say and you can quote me." She began to read from her notes...

# # #

"That son of a bitch Canady's going to pay for this." Oliver Brewster took a large swallow of scotch and swirled the remaining liquid in the glass.

"What can we do?" Timothy Holt asked. "He's not up for re-election for three more years."

Brewster took another large sip, chewed on an ice cube. "You wait and see, my friend. Do you know how much these guys make for just giving a speech? He'll be happy to receive a hundred-dollar honorarium from a local bar association by the time we finish with him. He can kiss his sweetheart speaking fees good-bye."

He looked at Holt and grinned. "Our radio and TV guys will also rip him a new asshole. I've already got a call in to Rush."

He tossed back the rest of his scotch. "This battle is not over, my friend. Not by a long shot."

Holt smiled. "Anything on Hornsby or Patel yet?"

"Let's just say it's a work in progress."

# # #

Leslie walked into Katie's office and tossed a copy of the *Detroit Times* on the desk.

"You're a star." She smiled and pointed to the headline on the front page. "Hornsby Hits a Home Run" was emblazoned across the top of the page. "Just wait until you read the article. You're going to love it."

Katie sat and read Dowd's story while Leslie hovered over her, waited for her reaction.

A remarkable event occurred recently in the courtroom of the Michigan Supreme Court. Katie Hornsby, a Detroit-based first-year lawyer, whose credentials include receiving the highest score ever written on the Michigan bar examination, wove a detailed and formidable legal argument using a baseball theme in a hotly contested case that dazzled a majority of the members of the court as well as this writer. In its 5-4 decision announced yesterday, the court ruled that Hornsby's clients could continue in their suit against a drug company from India whose drug had caused heart attacks or strokes in the plaintiffs. An apt baseball phrase, "Safe Nowhere," was used in the opinion written by Justice Bryan Canady giving testament to the impact of Hornsby's argument on the court.

Hornsby commented on the court's opinion, "The majority

opinion simply and elegantly reaffirms the glory and beauty of the Constitution as it was intended by our founding fathers. The Seventh Amendment in the State of Michigan is alive and well today. It's about time that something other than the Second Amendment's right to bear arms got some attention in the press. Admittedly, the Seventh Amendment is not as sexy an issue as someone's right to walk into a Starbucks, a church, or a bar carrying a loaded weapon, but it's a heck of a lot more important for citizens of this country to have the right of holding someone who injures or harms others responsible for their acts."

The euphoria since Katie had first heard from the reporter hadn't worn off yet. She was on a high. It felt good. It was the headline of the article she liked best. She put the article aside and looked up at Leslie.

"You were right. I do love it."

Leslie said, "Your Seventh Amendment comment is going to get folks talking."

The office phone rang non-stop the rest of the day with calls from new potential Lorital clients. Surprisingly, Leslie also fielded a number of hate calls from those who didn't like Katie's comment about the Second Amendment. That afternoon she walked into Katie's office and smiled. "You're number one on a lot of peoples' shit list, girl. Calls are pouring in and people are complaining about your comparison between the Second and Seventh Amendments. Seems like a lot of people want you to insert your 'goddamn Seventh Amendment' someplace where the sun don't shine."

They shared a good laugh. Leslie added, "I also wanted to bring you attention to this." She pointed to an ad in the newspaper placed at the bottom of the first page. She read, "If you or a loved one has died or been injured by Lorital, you need to know your legal rights. Contact us. We are the Lorital product experts."

Katie was surprised. To her knowledge, their firm was the only one in the country with any Lorital cases. "I called the number," Leslie said. "It's a law firm in Philadelphia named Crumley and something, something. Ever hear of them?"

Katie shook her head. After Leslie left her office, she thought about her conversation with Gary the evening before when she'd finally reached him with the good news about the decision. "Katie, this is terrific," he had said. "But now you'll have to be prepared for the onslaught. Anybody taking Lorital who has so much as an in-grown toenail will call to see if they have a case. Other lawyers will come out of the woodwork scrambling for cases. This is going to be big. Keep in mind that we're a small firm with limited resources. We've got to stick with what we do best; taking a limited number of really good cases and work them to the best of our ability. We are not going to get caught up in a numbers game. We don't have the personnel and we don't have the money. The pig gets fat and the hog gets slaughtered."

"My dad used to say the same thing." Katie responded, making Gary laugh. "You say a lot of things that remind me of him."

"If he were alive today, I'm sure he'd be telling you how proud of you he is. That's another thought he and I have in common."

"You're going to make me cry. But thank you. That's nice to hear."

"In our business, Katie, the hog example is exactly how it is. I've seen it happen a dozen times. We've got to focus on the clients we have and get them ready for trial. Judge Green will give us a trial date soon and we'll have to be ready."

The phone calls from potential new Lorital clients poured into the office. By the end of the day, Leslie had scheduled twenty-two new client interviews. Katie thought about what Gary'd told her. The pig was indeed getting fatter. When does a pig become a hog?

TOM BLEAKLEY

Chapter 30
September 2012

"Gentlemen, I've called this meeting today to deal with an urgent situation that's come up in Michigan. I'd like to bring you up to date." Oliver Brewster stood before ALEC's board, which was comprised of upper-level executives from fifteen of the top Fortune 500 companies in the U.S. "I've monitored the situation closely. The Michigan Supreme Court surprised us by holding that Enpact is subject to suit in Michigan even though it's based in India. The decision was five-four against us. A judge we thought was on our side, William Canady, joined with the liberals."

"This ruling is likely to impact multinational companies in a lot of ways. Many of you keep considerable assets offshore to minimize tax liabilities. It is easy to consider how this current ruling could affect those situations. There are a number of other things you could also have trouble with..."

A voice from the other end of the table asked, "Do you have a plan in mind?"

Brewster nodded. "That's why I'm here. I need some broad-based assistance... including a lot of money."

"Tell us more. Tell us what you have in mind."

# # #

"This is Judge Green."

"Judge, this is Oliver Brewster. I'm in town and I wonder if you're free for a round of golf at our favorite course tomorrow? I've got a one-o'clock tee time tomorrow afternoon and we can have dinner later. I've got a couple of things I'd like to talk with you about."

Green was tired of eating his own cooking. He was tired of spending his evenings in a bar on Jefferson just outside the city limits of Detroit. It was a dive. So far no one in the joint had recognized him. He missed his wife and daughters. He missed them badly. He was lonely. Hell, yes, he'd play golf at Oakland Hills and have a nice dinner with Brewster. At least someone appreciated him.

He looked at his calendar. "There are a couple of things I can move to next week."

# # #

Green arrived at the golf course earlier than Brewster. A young man started unloaded his clubs from the trunk of his car.

"Good morning, Judge Green."

"Good morning." Green was surprised the young man knew his name.

"Mr. Brewster called and said he'd be about thirty minutes late. Would you like to go to the practice range and hit some balls in the meantime?"

"That would be nice. Thank you." He handed the young man a five-dollar bill.

"No tipping permitted, sir."

Green drove the golf cart to the practice range and hit balls. Brewster arrived a few minutes later. A short, heavy-set man was riding in the golf cart with him.

"Judge Green, I'd like you to meet Stanley Crumley. Stanley's a good friend of mine and he just happened to be in town, so I thought I'd bring him along."

The two men shook hands. Green looked at Crumley. "You're name sounds familiar. Have we met?"

Crumley shook his head. "Judge, I've never had the honor."

Brewster said, "Let's go play."

At the end of the round, Brewster and Crumley paid Green the hundred dollars they'd lost. Green was a terrible golfer. The other two men well understood the concept of customer golf.

"Ready for dinner, Judge?"

"I'm looking forward to it."

The three men sat in the men's grillroom and spent the next several hours drinking and eating.

Brewster took a sip of his bourbon. "How's your lovely wife, Judge?"

Green took a large swallow of his third martini. His speech was blurred. He didn't have to tell them he was going through a divorce. "Bad news, I'm afraid to say. My wife and kids have had difficulty accepting the demands being a judge puts on me. My oldest daughter is on a 'save the whale, love everyone in the world' kick. She hasn't liked some of the decisions I've made, and isn't shy about letting me know. My wife sides with her. They're critical of every damn thing I do. They simply don't appreciate the responsibilities a judge has…"

Crumley sipped his wine. "I solved a similar problem. My third wife is a judge…a federal judge."

"So then you know what I'm talking about."

Crumley smiled. "I understand exactly. My motto is, if you can't beat them, marry a judge."

The three laughed. Green didn't find it funny, but he laughed anyway.

Green looked at his empty glass. "It started even before I became a judge. They hated my NRA case. My wife screamed at me all the time. I stopped telling her about the case. We stopped talking about any of my cases."

Brewster leaned forward and put his hand on Green's arm. "I'm sorry to hear that. Anything I can do to help? A nice trip for the five of you someplace? Tell me what you need and I'll take care of it."

"That's really nice of you…but I think it's past that point."

Brewster said, "How is the campaign going?"

"Incumbent judges rarely lose in Michigan unless they screw up big-time. I don't think I'll have any problem."

Brewster hesitated. "Can we talk business for just a moment? Let me tell you a little about what Stanley does…"

# # #

The next week, Holt and Brewster met at the Fireside Lounge in Chicago for lunch. After ordering drinks, Brewster said, "You asked me to do something. I've got a suggestion. You can save

Enpact a hell of a lot of money and make things go away."

"I'm all ears," Holt responded.

"You've done the math and you've done your homework. Newton and that girl can hurt you bad. Real bad. If he gets a big verdict in his favor, cases will spring up all over the country and expectations will be high. All that stuff about Orex owning Enpact, what a terrible company Enpact is, can all go away. You can eliminate that risk."

"Whad'ya have in mind?

"Two things. Ever heard of bifurcation?

"Bifuhrcation? In what context?"

"Let's talk about a scenario. The way Enpact makes and sells its drugs is pitiful, agreed?"

"Y'all can go ahead and make your point."

"A typical trial of a civil case involves three related issues: negligence, causation, and damages."

"That's basic tort law. Go ahead. Continue."

"Some judges around the country separate out these issues for trial purposes. Let me ask you a question. How much easier would it be for your people to try a Lorital case if the only issue up first was whether or not the drug causes damage?"

"Leavin' out wrongdoing'?"

"Yes. That's the point."

"Hell of a lot easier for us if the first issue's jus' causation. That would stop Newton and that gal from runnin' off their mouths about rats and mice shit. How does that work?"

"Let me give an example. A judge in one of our cases involving a different drug where the issue of contamination was raised said it didn't matter unless it could be proved that the contamination caused the harm. If that couldn't be shown by competent expert testimony, then it would be prejudicial to allow any mention of the contamination when the jury was being asked to consider the issue of causation. We got the same situation here. The experts are going to say that it was the dosages of the drug that caused the harm, not rat or mice shit. There's no scientific proof that rat and mice shit causes strokes or heart attacks, and any mention of it would be prejudicial and inadmissible on the issue of causation. Understand? I'll get you the briefs from that case."

"It sounds good."

"Now let me tell you about another plan I think you're going to like. Stanley Crumley is drooling over an opportunity to jump into the Lorital litigation. I think that's the best thing that could happen for you."

Holt shook his head in disgust. "That scumbag? You kidding?"

"No, I'm serious. Let me lay it out. Crumley gets into the litigation and Green orders him to conduct settlement discussions while Newton does the trial work. You make a low but reasonable settlement offer that includes all the pending cases in the country and Crumley agrees to settle at that figure. Green approves the settlement after a hearing. It puts an end to the litigation. Crumley does this all the time. He takes a few million dollars in fees and the clients get peanuts, but that would be well worth it for you. Having Crumley in the ball game will keep that number down, way down. Everyone will walk away happy…except Newton."

Holt thought for a moment. "What if that backfires? What if this bidness goes sour? What if somehow the settlement gets botched up?"

"Got it covered there as well." Brewster said simply. "As a

backup, if the settlement doesn't go through, Judge Green orders that the trial of the case be bifurcated with the issue of causation being tried first by itself."

Their drinks arrived. The two waited until the waiter walked away.

Holt shrugged. "Y'all dreamin'. I don't see Newton going along with any of this."

"Don't worry about Newton."

"Pretty confident about Crumley? Who's to say he'll go along?"

Brewster grinned. "He loves the settlement idea. I've already talked to him. The same with the judge. If the settlement doesn't fly, Green's also comfortable with ordering the case to be bifurcated. He thinks he's going to be on the front cover of *Newsweek*."

Holt laughed. "He and Crumley'd fight over that. Doesn't Crumley call hisself the master of disaster?"

Brewster leaned forward and whispered. "Green and Crumley got along pretty damned well when we met at Oakland Hills last week. We had a good time . . . and a good talk. I didn't think it was appropriate to invite you."

The two men laughed. "Oliver," Holt said, "y'all a sneaky son of a bitch. You don't fuck around, do you?"

"Yes, but don't forget that I'm your son of a bitch. I get paid for results for the results I get. Any problem with that?"

Both men raised their drinks. Holt said, "Hell no. But let me ask. How do we keep Newton from screwin' this up?"

"Let's just say that there are ways."

"Trade secrets, eh?"

"Just leave it at that."

"Don't get caught."

"That's the least of my concerns."

Chapter 31
September 2012

Gary started the discussion. "What can I do for you?"

"It's not what you can do for us, but what I can do for you. Are you familiar with my reputation?" The speaker was Stanley Crumley, a fat, vertically challenged man with brooding eyes and pure white hair. He gave Katie the creeps.

Gary flashed a quick grin at Katie. "I remember the *Newsweek* article where you modestly referred to yourself as the 'master of disaster'."

"Good. We're on the same page then."

Crumley missed the "modestly" nuance, Katie observed.

"Same page?"

Leslie had given Katie everything she could find in the newspaper about Crumley in advance of the meeting. "The guy's an idiot," Leslie had told her.

Katie had the same reaction. The guy was an idiot and he also thought he was hot stuff.

"I deal in mass litigation. Do you remember Agent Blue or Gocal or the cigarette cases?"

"Of course. Who doesn't?"

"I settled those cases for billions of dollars. My reputation speaks for itself. That's what I'm here to talk to you about."

Gary gestured. "Go ahead. We're listening."

"I have more than eight thousand Lorital clients. Your numbers don't come close to mine."

Gary gave Katie a look and then turned back to Crumley. "I've seen your ads in the newspapers and on TV. How do you screen your cases?"

Crumley hesitated. "I don't handle our intake procedures but I hire only the best people."

"So you have no idea how many of these eight thousand cases are valid?"

"We have doctors on our payroll who make those kinds of decisions."

"You let doctors make decisions about what constitutes a valid case? I'm a licensed doctor, and I've found that I need my legal training to make that kind of assessment."

Katie was seeing a side of Gary Newton she'd never seen before. She was impressed.

"I told you I'm not involved in the selection process. But I'm not here to talk about my cases, but about how our firms can work together."

"And?"

"I'd like to work with you on the Lorital cases. There is strength in numbers. So far your track record is not so good, what with the judge throwing your cases out."

Katie saw that Gary was getting angry. "Are you aware that we've already reversed the judge in our Supreme Court?"

"I know what a great lawyer you are and what a wonderful background you have in complex medical and scientific issues. As I said, I want to work with you."

Gary rolled his eyes at Katie. "You want to work with us? Even though you think our track record is 'not so good,' as you put it."

"These cases cost money…a great deal of money."

Gary looked at his watch, then at Katie, and shrugged. "Why don't you just tell us what's on your mind?"

"There's strength in numbers. I want to add my clients to your litigation. We would be co-counsel on the combined cases."

"And?"

"I'll add my name on the pleadings as co-counsel, but you'll continue to be in charge of the litigation. The only difference is that…I'll handle all future costs and you'll have sufficient financial backing to continue the litigation."

"You're well known for screwing other lawyers in cases like this. Why would this be any different?"

Crumley ignored the question. "We'll set up a $500,000 account for costs. Both firms will receive ten percent of the total recovery of all clients, and you'll be the lead trial lawyer in all cases. We will provide whatever staff assistance you need, including lawyers and paralegals both for trial preparation and at trials. Given my extensive experience in mass tort litigation, I'll take responsibility for settlement negotiations."

Katie knew that the funding proposal might be of interest. Gary had called a short meeting with the firm's lawyers the week before and told them that how finances were being strained by the costs of the Lorital litigation. Obtaining a bank loan was inevitable. Since the Supreme Court decision, the firm had added sixty additional Lorital clients and turned down hundreds more. Gary had already rented vacant office space on the floor below to serve as a designated Lorital repository because the increasing number of files had threatened to overwhelm the existing storage space. The firm needed more space and definitely needed more money.

Gary thought for a couple of moments. "I need to think about this for a couple of days. I also have some questions. What happens if we burn through the $500,000? I don't understand the fee proposal. We have contracts with our clients for contingency one-third fees. I have other questions."

"Make a list of any questions you have. Call me in a couple of days and we'll talk. I hope we can do business."

After Crumley was gone, Gary called Katie back into his office. "I'll tell you what I think. I'd bet that everyone who responded to his ad is included among his eight thousand cases. There are probably, at best, only a hundred decent cases in that mix." He smiled. "But the cost issue is tempting. I'll give him a call tomorrow and talk with him some more."

# # #

Goddamn, Green was lonely. The incessant thumps of car wheels and blaring horns from Eight Mile Road made it worse, serving as a reminder that others had homes where loved ones waited. For the first week at this God-forsaken place, he'd blotted out his terrible loneliness with alcohol but discovered quickly that it'd done no good. For the past few nights, he'd sat in his dingy living room, air-conditioner off, windows open, and listened to the arguments and shouts of his neighbors. At least these were people in his life, he thought. He might not know who the hell they were, but they'd become a part of his after-work existence. It had started to affect him at work, though. He'd been pissed the day before when Stella reminded him that he needed a haircut. He'd wanted to tell her to mind her own damn business, but he hadn't. The worst part was nighttime, the sleeplessness; the endless hours he'd lay wide awake on the lumpy bed, looking up at the dark ceiling punctuated by the intermittent flashing of car headlights through the venetian blinds covering the window. He didn't know which was worse, the constant street noise, the flashing lights, or the fact that the other side of the bed was empty. He was a judge, goddammit. A judge. How could he be reduced to this hollow, barren existence? It was like being in prison. But if he had been in prison, at least he'd have someone to talk to.

He thought about the meeting with Brewster and Crumley, the agreement that'd been reached. He knew it was wrong, but he'd agreed anyway. What a whore he was. What bothered him most was that Abigail, one of the shining lights in his life, had been right. He was an asshole. He closed his eyes and turned over to the other side of the bed. This was no existence. Animals live better than this. How much longer could he tolerate this miserable situation?

# # #

Gary called the "master of disaster" and put the call on speakerphone while Katie listened. "Stanley, this is Gary Newton. I've got some questions."

"Go ahead. I've got a few minutes."

"Your proposed deal includes my firm's obligation to try your firm's cases if the need arises. Is that right?"

"Right. I have confidence that you can do the job for us."

Gary continued. "Each firm would receive ten percent of the recovery, according to your proposal. That's a twenty percent total fee on all cases. Our written contracts with our clients call for a one-third fee. Why would I want to agree to a reduced fee on all Lorital cases and then do all the trial work? It doesn't make sense. Maybe I'm not understanding what your proposal really is."

Crumley hesitated. "It's not just twenty per cent. I charge a standard rate of forty percent on any case I handle on a contingency fee basis."

"So, doing the simple math, you propose receiving thirty percent of a recovery while I get ten percent even if I spend the time and effort trying cases for you. Does that sound fair to you? It sure as hell doesn't to me."

Crumley paused. "Gary, you're right. We settle most of our cases. When I put the proposal together it never occurred to him that a case would go to trial. This is a minor detail. We can work it out."

Gary looked at Katie and raised his eyebrows. "Stanley, when was the last time you tried a lawsuit?"

Crumley laughed. "Most big corporations, if they know what they're doing, won't go to trial against me. The stakes are too high."

Gary gave Katie another look, wrote on the legal pad in front of him and slid it across the desk: "Doesn't answer the question."

"In theory," Gary spoke into the phone, "I think we can work something out, but the current fee proposal is unacceptable. Give me something more reasonable and I'll think about it. We can talk next week."

Crumley was peeved. "I wouldn't take too long. There are other lawyers that I can link up with. I came to you first because you were the first to file and you've already done considerable work."

"Not to mention the favorable Supreme Court decision and all the work we've done on the litigation already."

Crumley paused. "That, too."

By the sound of his voice, Katie surmised that Crumley was looking at his watch, anxious for the conversation to end.

Newton said, "I expect a reasonable time to respond and that we can agree on a reasonable fee arrangement."

"Of course, of course."

After the call, Gary smiled. "The sanctimonious son-of-a-bitch. He certainly is full of himself. Katie, do some research. See what his track record really is, rather than what he says it is. This 'master of disaster' bit troubles me. He sounds more like a salesman than a lawyer. A good salesman but still a salesman."

That evening Katie cobbled together a trove of information on Crumley. What she didn't find was interesting. There was no indication that Crumley—or anyone else in his office—had tried a case in the past ten years. What she did find was even more interesting. Crumley had been involved in the massive Agent Blue litigation. Tens of thousands of veterans from the Vietnam War had been exposed to the deadly effects of Agent Blue; a chemical intended to exfoliate the jungles of Vietnam to eliminate enemy hiding places. Injuries caused by the defoliant ranged from debilitating respiratory effects to profound brain damage. The post-war litigation to fund these damaged soldiers had gone on for more than a decade and all the cases in the country had been consolidated in front of one judge. Having one judge hear all the cases saved duplication of effort and it was believed that this was the most expeditious way to handle cases that involved huge numbers of plaintiffs.

Lawyers from three small firms in Tennessee, Alabama, and Florida had spent countless thousands of hours putting a solid case together against the manufacturer of Agent Blue. The three firms had spent more than $3 million of their own money putting the case together and had announced to the judge that they were ready for a trial against the defendant on the merits of the case. Three weeks before the scheduled trial was to begin, Crumley filed his appearance in the case on behalf of several hundred clients. The trial judge ordered the small group of plaintiffs' attorneys, now four in number, to meet in New York and instructed them to come up with a recommendation as to how to deal with the addition of Crumley and his clients. Crumley arrived at the meeting with the same proposal that he'd made to Newton—that the other three law firms handle trials while he conducted settlement discussions with the defendant. The trial judge liked the idea. He'd apparently welcomed the possibility that he wouldn't have to sit through a series of lengthy trials if all of the cases were settled. He ordered the three law firms to continue trial preparation, and Crumley was ordered to conduct settlement negotiations. Two weeks later, Crumley announced that a massive settlement had been reached, which put an end to the lengthy litigation and encompassed the claims of all Vietnam veterans as well as attorney fees.

Katie had read enough. She waited until she got in the office the next morning and placed a call to the lawyer from Tennessee who'd dealt with Crumley in that litigation. She explained the reason for her call.

"Good luck with that sonofabitch. I think you'd be making a huge mistake to let him anywhere near your case. In our case, each injured veteran received only about ten percent of the potential value of their cases while Crumley walked away with sixty percent of the attorney fees. Our three firms that had done all the work shared the remaining forty percent, which included our costs. We made some money but we'd earned it. Crumley walked in and stole the lion's share. All the trial judge was interested in was wrapping up the case, so he'd welcomed Crumley with open arms. So my advice to you is to steer clear of him. Excuse my language, young lady, but he'll screw you any way he can."

Katie sat in Gary's office and filled him in her findings. "I couldn't stop reading last night. It was fascinating. Time and time again, he's done the same thing and he gets away with it. The lawyer on the Agent Blue cases told us to stay as far away from him as possible."

"It's the nerve of the guy that I find irritating," Gary said. "Personally, I can't stand him."

Katie responded, "Did you know he tried to hit on Leslie? An old guy like that."

Gary looked pensive. "What will prevent him from filing his cases with Green even if we don't reach an agreement with him? Judge Green could put Crumley in charge of all the cases just to screw us over."

Katie shrugged her shoulders. "They didn't teach anything like this in law school."

# # #

Katie mulled Crumley over. She had a thought and placed a phone call to Richard. She wondered if Crumley was as well known and hated by powerful corporations as he was by his fellow lawyers. Maybe Richard knew something about him that would be helpful.

He was pleased to hear from her. "I've been so busy. I've been meaning to call."

"It's all right. We've both been busy. I've been taking in new clients. The phone has been ringing off the hook."

"How many clients do you have now?"

"Probably about sixty. I'm really not sure of the number. I've done about thirty interviews the past couple of days. We don't take everyone who calls. We try to be really selective. That brings me to why I'm calling. I need some advice on a business question."

"Tell me what's on your mind."

"Have you heard of Stanley Crumley?"

"The whole world has heard of Stanley Crumley."

"Have any experience with him?"

"Let me guess. He's moving in on your Lorital cases?"

"He's trying to do exactly that. I need any thoughts you might have about him."

Richard paused. "I can't help you. It's outside my area of expertise."

"I thought you might have some idea, but at least it gave me a good excuse to call and hear your voice. Will I see you soon?"

"I've got some business in Detroit coming up. I'm not sure of the date, but I'll let you know."

After the call, Katie went to bed and tried to sleep. She tossed and turned. At one point, she fell asleep only to awake because of a nightmarish thought. She stumbled out of bed and went back to her desk and made a note to speak to Gary the very first thing in the morning. Whatever we do, we've got to do it quick. Time was running out.

She went back to bed and, as she drifted toward sleep she thought about men. She was thrilled about her relationship, such as it was, with Richard. He was urbane, sweet, kind, gentle, good-looking, sexy— and old. The thought surprised her. Why had "old" entered her thoughts? What did "old" have to do with it? She tossed the notion around in her mind for a few long moments. She had to face the truth at some point in time that the relationship had no future and her hopeless infatuation with him was going to end. The inevitably of the end of this affair raised the question in her mind about why she'd never acknowledged the likelihood before now. She'd had other boyfriends and those relationships had all ended for a myriad of reasons. She thought about the first of her past breakups. Her eighth-grade heartthrob had nearly broken her heart when he'd told her he didn't like her anymore because the new braces on her teeth made her look funny. She'd cried for days when she broke up with her first real boyfriend when she was a high school senior. There was a pattern to her relationships, she thought. The fleeting nature of her past encounters with men all bore a striking resemblance; an eventual awareness of unmet expectations. Sometimes, a lot of times, she'd become bored when it'd dawned on her.

Her feelings about Richard, however, were different, on a higher plateau than any of her prior relationships. Richard was a full-grown man and around him she felt like a full-grown woman. She'd told him she loved him several times and she didn't miss that there was no reciprocation forthcoming. Her heart had ached ever since the last non-reciprocation. She sat up in bed and asked herself why she was having these thoughts at this moment. Was she missing something? Was there something that's occurred between the two of them that triggered her subconscious mind to bring these thoughts forward now? Was his failure to commit himself taking her down a road she didn't want to go? She grimaced and clenched her teeth until they hurt.

Her thoughts drifted to Lance Rebus, Jr. Why on earth was she thinking about him right now? He was the enemy, her adversary. Maybe Dr. Patel had been right. Maybe Junior was smitten. Lately, he'd been acting silly around her and he blushed constantly in her presence. Initially, she'd enjoyed his obvious discomfort and had done whatever she could to provoke him. But, if she was going to be really honest, she had to admit she liked him. She liked being around him. He was boyishly handsome and smart as hell. And he did seem to understand most of her jokes. Heck, a lot of people didn't seem to realize that her jokes were jokes. Her dad had always told her that if she had to tell someone that what she'd just said was a joke, it wasn't a joke. She'd resisted that concept. If she said something she thought was funny, it was a joke. Simple as that. Junior grasped the concept and sometimes he was the only one who'd laugh when she'd said something she'd thought was uproariously funny.

Her thoughts drifted to yet another man. A realization came to her. She knew exactly who Ev was. She sat up again. She was surprised it hadn't occurred to her before now. She jumped out of bed and went directly to her laptop. In less than a minute she'd confirmed what had so suddenly occurred to her.

Her alarm clock went off in her bedroom. It was time to get going.

# # #

In less than an hour, she was seated at her desk, waiting for Gary to arrive so they could talk about Crumley and the other realization that had gurgled to her consciousness the night before.

"You look exhausted. Did you sleep last night?" Gary looked at Katie with concern.

"Remember I told you about an 'Ev' who was at the depositions in India?"

Gary nodded. "You told me he wouldn't give his name to the court reporter."

"That's the one. I woke up last night and I remembered where I'd seen the name before. I checked it out on my laptop at home and I was right. His name is Everett Plimpf, the Fourth, and he's the CEO of Orex. What I don't know is why the CEO of Enpact's major Lorital competitor was present at my depositions and at Singh's home that night. It confirms what I've been thinking all along about a connection between the two companies."

Gary looked at her for a long moment. "I think it's obvious. The two companies have some kind of arrangement they don't want anybody to know about. That's what kept you awake all night?"

"No, not just that. I kept having a terrible thought that it might be too late to stop Crumley. He's walked in late on big cases before and taken over."

Gary nodded. "We'll ask the judge for an early trial date and then deal with Crumley after we get the date. That way he can't interfere with our early cases. Draft a motion for an early trial date. Get right on it. Also, have a subpoena served on Plimpf. Maybe we can prove that connection between Enpact and Orex."

"I'll do it today. Right now."

# # #

Katie finished the motion by noon and took the papers into Gary's office. "We're all set. I'll file it right away."

Gary read the motion and looked up. "Katie, I always enjoy reading your writing. You've done a great job. Get it filed."

Katie walked over to the courthouse and filed the original copy of the motion with the court clerk. Then she took the elevator to Judge Green's floor and walked into the courtroom. Stella was seated behind her desk and the courtroom was otherwise empty. She looked up and smiled at Katie.

"Good afternoon, Ms. Hornsby. What can I do for you?"

"I've got an emergency motion that I just filed with the court clerk. I thought I'd drop by with the judge's copy as well as get a date for the hearing from you."

"These Lorital cases are really heating up. This is the second emergency motion we've received today."

"Second?"

"A lawyer from Philadelphia has just filed eight thousand new cases and scheduled an emergency motion to ask the judge to consolidate the cases with yours. I'm surprised you don't know about it. You're supposed to be served before the papers are filed with the court. Judge Green has already set a date to hear the motion, next Friday at ten o'clock. I'll put your motion down for the same time."

Katie was dumbfounded. "Any chance of you putting our motion first? It's really important that the judge hears our motion first."

Stella smiled and nodded. "I know what's going on. I'll see to it."

# # #

Holt placed a call to Brewster as soon as he'd heard the news from Hempstead.

"Newton has filed a motion for a trial date. He's requested a date within the next four months. I thought you had things under control with Crumley."

"Settle down. Crumley has filed his cases and a motion for consolidation. The judge has scheduled a hearing for this coming Friday. Crumley will be flying in on his private jet from his vacation in Aruba to handle it himself. I've got everything under control. Everything's going according to plan."

TOM BLEAKLEY

Chapter 32
September 2012

Gary and Katie arrived at Green's courtroom fifteen minutes early. Hempstead and Rebus were already present and seated next to Timothy Holt. Stella looked up from her desk. "The judge is not here yet and Mr. Crumley's office just called to let us know he'll be a few minutes late."

Hempstead stood and walked over to Gary. "Good morning. What's the deal with these motions? Why the hell would a Philadelphia lawyer file eight thousand lawsuits in Detroit? Are you partnering with him?"

"Lester," Gary said, "you know as well as I do what's going on. Crumley's going to try to take over the litigation. That's his modus operandi." Gary nodded toward Holt. "Is your client here to make a settlement offer? Whenever Crumley comes into litigation, there's always money on the table."

"Holt is prepared to go to the mat. Enpact won't offer a penny."

The courtroom door opened and Crumley entered, followed by a small entourage of young lawyers. Katie counted seven. Crumley gestured for the group to sit in the first row behind counsel table. He wore an expensive suit with an appropriately matched tie and shirt. Katie's dad would say he looked like a million bucks. From what she'd read about Crumley, a million bucks was chump change. Crumley walked over. He extended his hand to Gary. As the two shook, Gary nodded toward her. "You remember Katie Hornsby."

"Yes, I do." He held out his hand to her. She hesitated and they shook. Crumley gave her the once-over. Katie blushed. His piercing look gave her the creeps. He looked at Gary. "Let's go in the hallway and talk. Just me and you."

Gary nodded towards Katie. "She's coming with me."

Crumley shrugged. "Have it your way."

They walked out of the courtroom and down the hallway.

Crumley looked at Newton. "I understand you've filed a motion for a trial date. Does this mean we're not going to work together?"

Gary hesitated, "I told you I'd needed some time to think about your proposal."

Crumley gave him a cold stare. "You do know that if you lose a trial, it makes it difficult to settle these cases, don't you?"

Gary didn't back down. "Quite frankly, I think these cases are winners. If there is going to be a settlement, it should come after I kick their ass at trial a couple of times. From what I hear about you, Stanley, we approach litigation much differently. My firm accepts cases that we think have merit. We don't advertise and we don't file a lawsuit for just anyone who thinks they might have a case just because they think they might have taken the drug. We set the criteria for accepting a case in the first place pretty damn high and the same goes for settling each case." Crumley paused. "Any good trial lawyer knows there is a risk in trying cases. I've heard a lot about you. I didn't know you were a cowboy."

Gary's face turned scarlet. "I'm not a cowboy."

Crumley stepped closer, whispered, "You know full well that

there's no such thing as a guaranteed win. You lose a case and you hurt all the rest of the cases. That makes you a cowboy."

"Quite frankly, Stanley, I know a hell of a lot more about this litigation than you do. I expect to use my knowledge to get the best for my clients. If I do that well, your clients will benefit too. That's my view and it doesn't make me a cowboy."

The two men glared at each other for several moments before Crumley frowned. "You've answered my question. We're not going to work together. Let's go back and talk to the judge."

Fifteen minutes later, Judge Green came into the courtroom and sat on the bench. Katie thought he looked terrible. He looked ten years older than the last time she'd seen him.

Stella called Katie's motion first.

Green looked around the room. "Is there anyone from the media in the courtroom?"

A young man dressed in blue jeans and a polo shirt raised his hand. "I'm here for the *Detroit News*."

Green looked perturbed. "Let's meet in chambers, counsel."

The entire group, minus the news reporter, crowded into Green's office.

Green said, "I've read the motions. I've thought a great deal about both of your positions." He looked first at Newton, then at Crumley. "These cases are unique in terms of numbers and trials involving more than eight thousand plaintiffs will bog this court down for years. I have no intention of letting that happen. I'm looking for a solution to the problem. I am going to grant both of your motions. First, Mr. Newton's motion for an immediate trial date is granted. Second, Mr. Crumley's motion to consolidate all of the cases is granted. With the staggering number of new cases, I think it's best if plaintiffs' counsel divides responsibility in two directions. I am ordering that Mr. Newton's responsibility will be trial preparation and discovery. Mr. Crumley will be responsible for exploring settlement."

Katie's thought about the ALEC letter Green's daughter had given her. This scenario had been planned well in advance of Crumley's entrance into the litigation.

Green turned and looked at Hempstead. "Mr. Hempstead, I would like the settlement committee to have a representative from the defendant. Do you have someone in your firm who can do this without taking away from your trial preparation time?"

Hempstead nodded. "I request that Mr. Holt be designated a member of that committee."

Green smiled and said, "Of course."

Gary and Katie exchanged looks. They were thinking the same thing. This had been well rehearsed. Gary interjected, "Judge. I would like to also be placed on the settlement committee."

Green looked at Crumley. "Any objections, Mr. Crumley?"

Crumley smirked. "No, Your Honor. We're happy to work with Mr. Newton on any aspect of this litigation, including settlement." He gestured toward his contingent of lawyers who'd lined the back wall of Green's office. "My law firm will also assist Mr. Newton in any way we can to facilitate trial preparation. I'll personally make myself available to try any of the cases with Mr. Newton."

Green nodded his approval. "That's very generous, Mr. Crumley. I am sure that Mr. Newton will appreciate all the help he can get. Now that we've established a working format, I am not going to delay this case any longer. Mr. Newton has sixty cases, and he will select one case out of the sixty to be tried. Mr. Hempstead, you will also select one of Mr. Newton's sixty cases, and those two cases will be tried together. We'll meet back here next Friday and I'll set a trial date then when you identify which two cases are chosen. I'll decide then the format we'll use at trial. My present inclination is to try the single issue of causation first, but I want both sides to submit recommendations as to how each of you think it should happen. Submit something to me by this coming Tuesday. Should these cases be tried at the same time or back to back? Should we try cause only or liability only? I need your suggestions. We'll have a final settlement conference on October 15th. If these cases aren't settled by then, we'll start trial the next day."

# # #

Gary and Katie sat in the conference room and discussed the upcoming events. Gary said, "I like Sharon Albright as our selection. What do you think?"

"She's a nice lady and the facts in her case are solid and straightforward," Katie replied. "The jury will be sympathetic. Who do you think the defense will pick?"

"I have no idea. Your guess is as good as mine."

Katie hesitated. "There's another item we should talk about. I started looking for information about Plimpf, the Orex CEO who goes by 'Ev.'"

"I remember. Anything new?"

"Not on him but while I was looking I discovered that Timothy Holt had been general counsel for Orex. Last year he left Orex and, at the same time, became outside counsel for both Enpact and Orex. I can't imagine Enpact would hire outside litigation counsel who also represented Orex if there wasn't some connection between the two of them."

"It does appear that it's not your imagination working overtime."

# # #

After the hearing, Holt, Hempstead, and Rebus met back in Hempstead's office.

Holt spoke first. "We're gonna choose Mark Stenson for trial."

"Mark Stenson?" Hempstead raised his eyebrows in surprise. "Why him?"

"That's right." Holt nodded. "I've read all your summaries about each of Newton's clients. His claim is the shakiest."

# # #

Oliver Brewster laughed like hell when Holt told him about the meeting with Green. "I'm going to wet my pants if you don't stop." The two men shared another hearty laugh. "So Green is doing what we want?"

"So fah," Holt said.

"I thought he would. What's next?"

"Several things. We all goin' raise the stakes a bit."

"In what ways?"

"Bes' you don't know."

Chapter 33
September 2012

Emily Stenson stood at the bathroom sink slowly shaking her head. She couldn't believe it. She must be imagining this or she might be mistaken. She held the vial away from her body as if to avoid the toxic effects of its contents. Mark hadn't worked a day in over three years, while she'd worked two backbreaking menial jobs to support their family. And now this. It was all so unreal. But it was more than just a bad dream. Mark was still taking the damn drug that had nearly killed him three years ago. She lifted the toilet lid and emptied the vial into the toilet.

"What are you doing?" She turned and looked up. Mark stood at the bathroom door, red-faced. "Just what the hell do you think you're doing?" He stepped in and reached over to grab the now-empty vial away from her. "You had no right to do that," he yelled.

She cowered away from him. "How could you do this? That drug almost killed you and you're taking it again?"

"It's none of your goddamned business."

Emily squared her shoulders. "You're suing the drug company that makes the drug. Just what do you think is going to happen when they find out?"

"They're not going to find out. I told you. It's none of your business."

"It is my business. I've worked my ass off the past three years to keep us from going under. I can't afford to buy the kids new shoes and you drive around in that fancy car of yours."

He stepped forward and slapped her. She fell to the floor. "I said it's none of your business."

# # #

Katie stood in front of Judge Green. If anything, he looked even worse than the week before.

"Your Honor, we've selected Sharon Albright's case for trial."

Green looked at Hempstead. "Mr. Hempstead. What is your selection?"

"Your Honor, we have selected…" Hempstead looked down at the legal pad in his hand. "…Mark Stenson."

Katie grimaced when she heard Stenson's name. Of all our clients, he was the worst, the absolute worst. Why would Enpact pick him? Getting Stenson prepared and ready for trial was going to be a nightmare and she couldn't stand being in his presence.

# # #

Katie reported the outcome of the hearing before Green. Gary sat at his desk, chin in his hands. "Their selection of Stenson surprises me."

"Me too. It's like they know what a problem he's been to us."

Gary rubbed his eyes. "For now, we'll just concentrate on Albright and Stenson. We'll meet with both of them right away to tell them what's happening. Call them and get them in here as soon as possible. Do we have their reports back from Alex and Jan yet?"

Katie made a note. "I know we have Albright's, but I'm not certain about Stenson. I'll check."

Chapter 34
September 2012

"Alex? This is Katie Hornsby." She described the judge's ruling on the selection of two clients for trial. "We need your evaluation of Stenson's records right away."

"Jan is working on Stenson right now. We'll get a report to you within the week."

"Do you think Jan would be willing to testify?"

"She's been following the medical literature and the news on generic Lorital, and she's mad as hell. My guess is that she'll say yes."

# # #

"Look at this." Jan Emrich pushed the small stack of Stenson's medical records across to Hartley. They were seated at the dining room table in their apartment that evening.

"What do you have?"

Emrich removed her glasses. "I think these records are phony."

"Tell me."

She gestured toward the records. "First, the chart on top is all handwritten by the same person. I'm not a handwriting analyst, but the writing in this record"—she tapped the chart with her index finger—"Some one person sat down and copied the entire medical chart by hand. There's more, that's not all…" She paused.

"Go on. You're going to make me beg, aren't you?"

"I'm going to make you do more than that." She reached out and touched his hand. "You're going to give me a nice back rub when we're through here. I've been sitting at this damn table all day and my back is sore as hell."

They smiled at each other. "Sounds good to me. So what else?"

"In Katie's notes from her interview of Stenson, he'd told her that he was in Alaska on a fishing trip when he suffered his heart attack. The next chart is a complete hospital chart from Dallas General Hospital of another patient, not Stenson. Someone has changed the name on each page throughout the chart to Stenson. His weight in this chart is listed as one hundred and sixty-five pounds. In the rest of his records his weight is always listed at two hundred pounds. There's no mention in any of the records of any dramatic change in his weight. Losing thirty-five pounds and gaining it back in two or three months is impossible. I can't imagine it not being mentioned in the records if it actually happened."

She handed Alex the discharge summary of the Dallas hospitalization and pointed to the weight discrepancies. The signature on the summary was a "Paul Henderson, M.D."

Alex looked up. "I know Paul Henderson. We were fellows together at Cleveland Clinic. We can solve this mystery quickly. I'll call him in the morning."

Emrich spent several minutes highlighting other discrepancies in the records. "Now you know why I think these records are phony."

Alex smiled at her. "Good work. Now about that back rub…"

# # #

Next morning, Katie was late getting to work. She'd been caught in traffic from an accident on the expressway. There was a message from Jan Emrich to call her back, but she couldn't take the time. She picked up the phone and told Leslie to hold her calls. Stenson and Albright sat next to each other while they waited for her in the conference room. She walked in and was struck by the odd dissonance between the two. Albright sat primly with her hands in her lap. She wore a dark blue pantsuit that complimented her trim figure. Her highlighted blonde hair hung to her shoulders and framed a face that conveyed innocence and lack of guile. She'd make a terrific impression on the jury at trial. Stenson, on the other hand, looked like a slob. He had a scowl on his face and wore a dirty, sweat-stained tee shirt that permeated the room with a rancid odor. Katie briefly considered asking Leslie to come in and spray the room with a deodorizer, but knew that would really set him off.

"Good morning. Let's get started." She checked her notes. She told them how the two of them had been selected for trial. Albright had a number of questions that Katie answered while Stenson sat and sneered. Katie turned to him. "Do you have any specific questions, Mr. Stenson?"

"Yeah. Why was I picked?"

Katie bit her lip. Gary and she had asked themselves the same question. The conclusion they'd reached was that his angry demeanor and slothful appearance would have a negative impact on a jury. "We don't know why they picked you. Is there anything in your background or medical history that you haven't mentioned to us that could be a problem at trial?"

He scowled. "Why would you ask me that in front of her?" He gestured angrily at Albright.

Katie tried to remain calm. "Mr. Stenson. From now on there are no secrets between any of us. We will be in a public setting and your entire life will be an open book. If there is something in your past you haven't told us about, you can be sure that the drug company will know about it and bring it out at trial."

Albright smiled and stood. "I have no problem leaving the room while you two talk. Why don't I wait in your office, Katie? I'll be more comfortable there." She smiled gently at Katie, sniffed twice, and tilted her head toward Stenson.

"Go ahead. You know where it is." Smart lady, Katie thought. She wished she could get away from the smell too.

She waited until Albright left the room and closed the door. She looked at Stenson. "A famous trial lawyer once said, 'If you have any skeletons in your closet, at least make them dance'. This is the time right now to talk about any skeletons you may have, Mr. Stenson."

He glared at her. "If I'd known this was going to be an inquisition, I'd never have come down here...and I really don't give a good shit about what your father said."

Katie took a deep breath. Here we go again, she thought. "This is not an inquisition. Mr. Stenson, in a case like this the drug company will know more about you than you know about yourself. The defendant spends a lot of time and money investigating the backgrounds of people who sue them. Obviously, you're troubled about something. Let's talk about it."

Stenson stood, moved around the table, and hovered over Katie. "I don't have to put up with your crap. Just get my case ready for trial and tell me when to be there." He stomped out of the room and slammed the door shut behind him.

Katie sat for a few moments with her head in her hands. She didn't have the slightest idea about what she should do about Stenson. His pungent body odor was bad enough, but his attitude was terrible. She went back to her office after giving Gary a quick rundown on Stenson's reaction. She spent the rest of the morning preparing Sharon Albright for her trial testimony. After Albright left, Katie thought about Stenson. If it took an entire morning to prepare a cooperative client like Albright, how much time would she need to get Stenson ready for trial? She picked up the phone messages. Jan Emrich had called three times.

Katie called her back.

"We should meet right away and talk about Stenson and his medical records. Alex's here with me. Come over and let us fill you in."

"This morning he just walked out of the office when I asked him about his background. He was really ticked off. I'll be right over."

Katie walked the five blocks to Hartley's small office at Receiving Hospital, Katie thought about Jan Emrich. Over the past few months, she and Emrich had become good friends. They shared a love for baseball and had gone to a few games together. She had toyed a couple of times with asking her for some advice about Richard, but the right opportunity hadn't presented itself yet.

Jan and Alex were waiting. Katie hugged them and sat down. Hartley summarized. "Jan looked over Stenson's records. They're either forged or faked. A hospital chart from a Dallas hospital mentioned the name of a doc I trained with at the Cleveland Clinic who's a friend of mine. I called him and he told me that he'd never heard of Stenson, never treated him. All these records are phony." He gestured toward the stack of records on the table.

Katie winced. Hartley continued, "He's scammed you guys. The question is why."

Katie asked, "Did he think we wouldn't find out? This explains why he was so angry this morning."

Emrich looked at Hartley and they both shook their heads. "We've never seen anything like this. We don't have a clue."

"He's a remarkably strange man," Katie offered. "He's been nothing but trouble since day one."

Hartley cleared his throat. "I bet he thought that he could make a quick buck from an early settlement. That seems the most likely explanation."

Katie pursed her lips. "If so, why would he be such a pain in the ass? During his first appointment, he gave me such a hard time I had to bring Gary in to pacify him. I've met with him three times and all he's done is argue and complain. This morning was the worst. I'd think if he wanted an early settlement, he'd at least try to be nice."

Emrich shrugged. "Gary's told us about you and Stenson." She hesitated. "What if…he's being paid by Enpact to spy?"

Hartley rolled his eyes. "Jan loves spy novels."

Emrich reached over and patted his hand. She looked at Katie and grinned. "Better than the trashy novels he reads. I don't mind it, though. I call it book-worm Viagra." She winked at Katie who placed her hands over her ears.

"Too much information."

The three of them laughed.

"I agree with Alex," Katie said. "He must be looking for easy money. I can't see why he'd be spying on us. What kind of information could he give them? I have to do something about him and his phony records. I'll talk to Gary. It's a good thing you discovered this now. Can you imagine what would happen if this came out during trial? You two are fantastic."

# # #

Katie mulled over the meeting with Hartley and Emrich as she walked back to the office. Gary was with a client and couldn't be disturbed so she had to wait. On impulse, she picked up the phone and dialed Stenson's number. What could it hurt?

"Mr. Stenson, this is Katie Hornsby. I'm calling to apologize for my rudeness this morning. I'm also letting you know that we're going to file a motion to postpone the trial date. We've had a problem come up with one of our witnesses and we need time to find a replacement."

There was a long pause at the other end of the line. "Which witness? Why?"

"Dr. Patel. As you know, he's one of our experts. He said he's changed his mind about testifying. He says if we force him to testify, he'll speak in favor of the company."

"Why are you telling me?"

She resisted making a sarcastic comment. "You've asked to be kept better informed. That's what I'm doing."

"How long will this take?"

"I don't know. I can't answer that right now."

"Let me know." He hung up the phone abruptly.

# # #

Later, Katie told Gary about her meeting with Jan and Alex. She told him about her phone call and what she'd told Stenson about Patel. "Alex and I both think he's just trying to get an easy settlement. I think that's why he walked out of the meeting with me. He didn't want me to find out he was a phony. Jan thinks he might be a spy for Enpact. Alex and I made fun of Jan for suggesting that Stenson was a spy, but after thinking about it I thought the phone call might be a way to test it. Particularly after he acted so screwy while he was here. Personally, I think the guy is just crazy. I made the call just to test Jan's theory."

"That was smart, Katie. It's possible that he's in bed with Enpact, but I agree with you and Alex. He's looking for a quick buck. I'm going to have to think about what to do next. In all my years of practice, I've never had a situation like this before. Just thinking off the top of my head, maybe the best thing to do is to call Hempstead and tell him. But that has some possible ramifications that could complicate things even further."

"I don't understand."

"The drug industry would like nothing better than to accuse us of filing a fake lawsuit. They'd jump at the chance here to make us look bad. We'll need to prove that we had nothing to do with the fake medical records." He thought for a moment and pursed his lips.

"Stenson is a little crazy. I want you to steer clear of him from now on. I'll take him over and you stay as far away from him as possible. I'll get him back in here and try to get him ready for trial. You take Albright and I'll take him. I'll string along with him for right now."

TOM BLEAKLEY

Chapter 35
October 2012

With all her time spent on the Lorital trial preparation, Katie felt like she'd abandoned her personal life. She'd been ignoring Richard. She hadn't seen him or spoken to him for what seemed like forever.

She checked her calendar and called him. "The big news is that we're either going to settle the cases or go to trial this month. I really need to see and be with you a couple of days. It's been too long and I miss you."

"I miss you too, Katie. The timing is perfect. I'm coming to Detroit next week and staying at the Ritz Carleton in Dearborn. I'll be there for three nights and you can come and stay with me. I've got business on Wednesday and Friday. We can take Thursday and do whatever you want. If the Tigers are in town, we can go to the ballgame. I'd like to see these Tigers you are always raving about. If they're not in town, we can do something else, still have some fun."

Katie smiled from ear to ear. It felt good. With Stenson and trial preparation such big concerns, she hadn't had much to smile about lately. "The Tigers are not only in town—they're in the post-season playoffs. I've already got two tickets for next Thursday. That sounds perfect, Richard."

"Plan on dinner with me at the hotel next Wednesday. I'll meet you in the lobby at six o'clock."

Katie bounced out her of her office and went directly to the front desk to share the news with Leslie. Leslie looked at her as she approached. "Well, well. Look who's got a big smile plastered all over her face."

Katie laughed and filled Leslie in on the details of the coming week. She was so excited she could hardly wait. She slept well that night.

# # #

Gary sat in his office and looked at the unkempt man sitting across from his desk. "As we promised you when you first came in, I'm going to be in charge of your testimony from here on through the end of the trial. So let's get started. I've got a list of questions here for you."

Stenson avoided eye contact with Gary. "What do I have to know?"

"What you know is not important. It's who you are that the jury will want to hear about. You and I are going to work together on what you need to tell them. I don't want to hurt your feelings here but the first thing you've got to do is clean yourself up. If you go into court looking and acting like a bum, the jury is not going to be impressed, if you dress and act like you are right now."

Stenson's eyes flared in anger. "You don't like me because I am not all dressed up fancy like you? Is that it?"

"No. That's not it at all. You look like a bum. You smell like a bum and you act like a bum. Let me ask you this…"

Stenson stood. "I don't have to take your insults. You're as bad as the girl."

"Sit down and shut up for a minute. If you walk out of here

right now, I am going to file a dismissal of your claim today. Either you help me get you ready for trial or you're out of the litigation. You've been nothing but a pain in the ass, and you know it. You're my client and I'll try to do my best for you, but I need your cooperation. If you're not willing to cooperate, we're through. Got it?"

Stenson stood still for a moment and then sat down. "Ask your questions. If the trial date is adjourned, why are we preparing now? Why did they choose me?"

Gary thought for a moment and thought about what Katie had said to Stenson. "We decided not to seek a postponement. The issue with the witness is resolved. We are going to use someone else to cover the same topics. I think they chose you…because of what I just said to you. You're a mess. You need to clean yourself up. If necessary, I'll buy a suit for you to wear in trial. You need to shave and get a haircut…and take a shower. I know it's hard to sit there and listen to me talk about you this way, but you have to be realistic. If I were defense counsel, I'd have chosen you for the same reason. Do you understand why it is important to clean yourself up?"

Stenson gripped the arms of the chair tightly. The two men stared hard at each other.

Finally, Stenson's shoulders slumped. "I'll do what you ask."

"Good. Now let's get on with some of my questions." He looked down at his notes. "How did you wind up in a hospital in Dallas?"

Stenson fumbled for a response. "I guess I was on a business trip or something."

"You don't know why you were in Dallas? Why you were

hospitalized there?"

Stenson looked down at his feet. "My memory is not as good as it used to be. I can't answer that."

"Do you remember the name of the doctor who treated you in Dallas?

"I was pretty out of it. I had a heart attack, you know."

"Who is your current doctor? We've asked you for that information several times, and you haven't given us a name yet."

"I'm not sure of his name."

"Where is his office?"

"I'll get the address for you."

"You don't know where his office is?"

"My wife drives me. I don't pay attention."

"I'll call her and ask her. By the way, why didn't you want her to be a party in the suit?"

"I have my reasons. Believe me, I have my reasons. You don't have to call her. I'll get the name of the guy for you."

"But why don't you want her in the suit? What are your reasons?"

"I don't think you need to know."

Here we go again, Gary thought. He moved on to the next question. For the remainder of the session, Stenson claimed a memory loss and was unable, or unwilling, to answer any more questions.

After Stenson left the office, Gary sat back and thought about the man. What had happened today didn't really matter. Stenson wasn't fooling anybody. In fact, it played directly into Gary's plans for trial. It was all a matter of timing.

# # #

The next Wednesday, Katie met Richard in the Ritz Carlton lobby. They walked into the elegant restaurant next to the lobby. She'd picked a dress she knew he'd like. As they walked to their table, the admiring glances of others in the room confirmed her choice.

When they were seated, Richard stared approvingly at her. "You look smashing." He leaned forward and took her hand. "It's so nice to see you again, particularly in that dress."

"Thank you." She blushed. "I thought you'd like it."

"I do…and so does everyone else in this room. I hope you don't wear it to court."

She shook her head and laughed. "I wouldn't dare. You know me better than that."

She blushed again. "Just thinking about being here with you has helped me to forget what I've been going through. We've got a lot of stuff going on right now at the office and it's nice to have this break."

"Anything new on your Lorital cases?"

"Our trial preparation is going great. I've met with Dr. Patel twice. You remember I mentioned him to you before? He's going to be such a great witness. He's such a smart man."

"You're making me jealous."

"No worries. He's old enough to be my grandfather."

"What's this Patel going to say?"

"He's so helpful. He's going to testify about all the awful things Enpact did. He says that in his twenty-five years in the drug industry, he's never seen such terrible things done by a drug company. He told me yesterday that the FDA has told him they are considering banning the company from selling its products in the United States."

"That's…really something. It sounds like he is going to be a big help." He picked up the menus on the table and handed one to Katie. "Let's think about food."

Richard obviously didn't share her enthusiasm about the Lorital case, she thought. "I can tell you're upset. I know you don't care much about lawsuits in America."

Richard glanced at her briefly. "We agreed that that topic is off-limit but, in fairness, I did ask you about the case."

Katie diverted her attention to the menu. She didn't want to do anything to annoy him. She placed the menu on the table. "I'm too hungry to eat."

Richard's smile returned. "Me too. We can address our hunger when we get upstairs."

They touched wine glasses. "It's a deal. Let's go."

# # #

Lance Rebus, Jr.'s time at the law firm had been the most exciting six months of his life. Most of the new associates who'd started with him had been rotated by firm management through two of the three sections of the firm already: probate, intellectual property, or litigation. Lance had been fortunate. His first rotation was the litigation section and he'd been assigned to Hempstead's team. After the first six weeks, Hempstead'd told him, "You're going to stay in litigation. The senior partner always skims the cream of the crop, buddy-boy, and you're it. You're staying with me." It was a dream come true, Rebus thought, and the best thing that had ever happened to him.

Lester Hempstead was a kind man and a giant in the law. He'd been generous beyond belief, in giving assignments to Rebus usually reserved for five-year associates. Rebus'd done everything except try a case and, given the high stakes in the cases Hempstead managed, he knew it would be a long time before that happened. Lance was excited about the upcoming Enpact trial. Hempstead had tapped him for second-chair status. Timothy Holt, Enpact's company representative, would sit between him and Hempstead at the defense table. Rebus would be expected to take detailed notes of everything he thought important that happened in the courtroom. He was thrilled about the opportunity, particularly to work so closely with Hempstead.

It was late in the evening and Lance sat at his desk. Mr. Holt had taken over his office during the daytime a week ago and would use it until the trial was over. Lance was expected to work in the conference room or the library. Given the bustle of trial preparation, there were usually two or three paralegals sorting through documents, or law clerks chatting away such as to make it difficult for Lance to concentrate. So when Holt left at the end of each day, Rebus would reclaim his office for the quiet and solitude. He just needed to make sure he didn't disturb any of Holt's materials that were scattered on top of his desk.

When he first sat down, Lance thought about his increasing fascination with Katie Hornsby. He blushed as he thought about her. The first time in that dingy and dusty document room at FDA headquarters in Washington, she'd walked in cracking jokes. He'd been both instantly mesmerized and terrified. She was the prettiest girl he'd ever seen. Forget movie stars and playboy models. She had it all over them, and being in the same room with her caused some kind of shut-down of his nervous system; blood rushed to his head, he'd get dizzy, and a tell-tale blush would announce the effect her presence had on him. His usual self-confidence simply dissolved in her presence. But he'd adjusted to her presence, and he no longer was tied-up in knots, although he did stumble on a few words at times when she was around. He smiled when he thought about when she'd called him Junior. He'd never tell Hempstead that the biggest reason he was looking forward to the upcoming trial was that he'd get to see her every day.

He thought about Mr. Holt, the client. He genuinely disliked the man and his syrupy Southern accent. He knew it was not the best way to feel about the representative of the largest client of the firm. It'd made him feel better when he'd learned Hempstead felt the same way.

Usually, Lance would just work around Holt's materials, taking care not to mess up anything. Tonight was different, though. He was angry with Holt. Twice this afternoon he had made disparaging comments about Katie and her boss. Preparing and trying to win lawsuits was one thing, but getting nasty and personal about the opposition was something else. Holt had called Katie a whore. As he looked about the desk, Rebus noticed a memo with Katie's name on it. He began to read. A wave of nausea had swept over him by the time he'd finished. He fought to maintain control. Try as he could, he couldn't focus on the rest of the work he had to do. He couldn't get his mind off the memo. He couldn't stop thinking about what he'd read. If Hempstead knew about this,

Lance would be terribly disappointed. He left the office and went home. He fought to sleep but the ugliness of the memo made it impossible. It was well after midnight, after he'd stared at the ceiling for several hours, when he decided what he needed to do.

# # #

Katie and Richard sat in box seats behind the Tigers' dugout. They watched while the Tigers beat the Oakland Athletics to move on to the American League championship series against the Yankees. Miguel Cabrera, the star of the Tigers, homered with two men on with two outs in the ninth inning in an exciting finish.

In the cab on the way back to the hotel, Richard said, "That was such a great game. Now I understand now why you rave about the Tigers so much."

"Detroit baseball fans are the best. The team has fans all over the country. Wherever they play, there are always Tiger fans wearing Tiger paraphernalia and cheering them on. The only other team who comes as close to having loyal fans around the country is the Chicago Cubs."

"Yankee fans are pretty loyal, too."

"Is this our first argument? If so, you lose hands down. I went to a Yankee game in New York once and the home crowd booed a Yankee pitcher who had his no-hitter ruined when a hitter singled in the eighth inning. They started singing 'Take Him Out of the Ball Game.'"

He looked at her and raised his eyebrows.

She laughed. "Actually, I made that up, but it is true that they booed the guy. That'd never happen in Detroit. Tiger fans are fans forever."

"You're such a jokester. I'll admit the home crowd can be pretty nasty in New York."

She placed her hand on his thigh and giggled. "I'm not just a Tiger fan but a fan of a Yankee fan." She moved closer. "So, now that we have our first argument out of the way, we can kiss and make up..."

He smiled and pulled her close. "I'm looking forward to that"

She snuggled closer. "Me, too."

Chapter 36
October 2012

The beginning of the workday is the busiest time of the day at the Starbucks in the lobby of the Buhl Building. Customers form a long line to get their morning fix before they head to offices throughout the building. By eight o'clock each weekday morning, the line snakes outside the shop and into the lobby of the building.

Leslie's morning ritual included the long wait as it gave her the opportunity to chat with friends and get her favorite coffee drink to take to the office. Her duties at the Newton office included making coffee, but she didn't like the bland brand that Gary preferred. As she listened to a cute story about a former co-worker's four-year old child, she felts a tug on her elbow. She looked up. Lance Rebus stood there. He leaned toward her and whispered in her ear, "Richard Lion is not who he says he is. He's one of the owners of Enpact." He turned and walked quickly away. Leslie left the line and rushed after him. He was out of the building and gone before she could catch up.

# # #

When Katie awoke, Richard was already gone. She replayed the night's events in her mind. Everything, absolutely everything, had been so perfect. She checked the room service menu and placed an order. Her cell phone rang and she was tempted to ignore it. She checked the caller ID and it was Leslie. She would not call unless it was important.

Leslie whispered. "Are you alone? Can you talk?"

"Yes. Go ahead. Is there something wrong?"

"I've told you before how I've run across Lance Rebus a couple of times at Starbucks in the morning?"

"Yes."

"Well, this morning he approached me when I got in line."

Katie giggled. "You're pretty damn cute. If I was a guy I'd try to talk to you, too."

"No. Wait. Listen." She told Katie what Rebus had said. "Then he turned and walked away. I ran to catch up to him but he ignored me and kept walking faster. I thought you needed to know right away."

"That is strange."

"Katie, you have to protect yourself. Why would Rebus do this?"

"He might be jealous but that's silly. How would he even know about Richard in the first place?

"Katie. You need to find out."

Katie thought for a moment. "You're right."

She hung up and looked around the sumptuous suite. Richard had left a briefcase in the closet. She carried it to the table, opened it, and removed a large stack of papers. There were also several new children's toys in the brief case, probably intended for his nieces and nephews, making her think of how thoughtful Richard was and how she shouldn't be snooping on him. This is crazy, she said to herself. But how in the hell would Lance Rebus know about Richard? She needed to answer that question.

Her breakfast arrived. She sat at the table and started reading while she ate. Whatever guilt she'd felt about snooping was quickly replaced by a sense of alarm. Her jaw dropped when she saw that the first few documents were memos about the Lorital litigation from Timothy Holt to Videda and Anugrah Singh. Videda Singh was the current CEO of Enpact, the guy she'd deposed in India, but who was this Anugrah Singh? He was probably the other brother who owned Enpact, but why were these documents in Richard's briefcase? She felt her heart rate accelerate and the palms of her hands became sweaty. She nearly gagged on a piece of toast. She continued to read. Each of the documents described in great detail Enpact's tactics in dealing with her and Gary. One of the memos described a carefully planned campaign to destroy Dr. Patel's credibility by accusing him of scientific fraud. She felt sick to her stomach but she couldn't stop reading. The next item was a letter from Timothy Holt that stopped her cold. It read, "Dear Anugrah, I'm so sorry to hear about your wife's illness and I wish her a speedy recovery. The burden of raising four small children is no picnic when one has good health, and it must be that much more difficult for her with her illness. You are doing important work for us and I am happy to hear that you will continue to do so. Your report on the FDA's plans for our generic Lorital is most helpful. Keep up the good work on the Newton law firm. From what you have said your dealings with Hornsby have been most enjoyable. Kindest regards, Tim."

Katie squeezed her eyes shut. Her sense of alarm had increased to terror. The room was spinning. She thought she was going to pass out. She forced several deep breaths and fought the panic that was building inside her. She squeezed her eyes shut. Oh my God, she thought. Richard is one of the Singh brothers. She slowly opened her eyes. This was real and it was happening to her. She had to keep going. The next memo described in detail her seduction by Richard. How in the hell would he have known where she was staying in Washington when they first met? Had she been followed? Were the phone lines tapped at the office? A cold chill swept through her body. What didn't Enpact know about her or the case?

It was no wonder that fat little asshole Singh was so persistent at his home in India. He thought she was an easy lay. She could only imagine what Richard had told his brother about her. The thought sent Katie into a crying jag. This was no broken love affair. She'd been used, toyed with, and the other brother had expected to get in on the action. She felt dirty. She'd fallen in love with Richard. What he'd done to her was the equivalent of rape, her mind as well as her body. Telling others, bragging about what he'd done with her and to her in detail. She broke down and cried until she had no tears left.

She froze and just sat staring at the wall in front of her. Her hands shook. She was cold. She was hot. She didn't know what she felt. She couldn't think. She couldn't cry. All her tears were used up. Death couldn't be as bad as this, she thought .She was mortified that the lawyers involved in the litigation knew about her relationship with Richard. This was terrible. Could she ever face these people again? Could she ever look Rebus in the eye? She was devastated that Richard had used her. She was such a fool. She started to hyperventilate again and willed herself to take deep breaths until her breathing returned to normal. She walked into the bathroom and looked in the mirror. She didn't recognize the haggard face that looked back at her. This was not simply a bad dream. What was happening was real.

She couldn't just stand there and stare at that anguished face in the mirror all day.

She dropped her nightgown to the floor and stepped into the shower. She let icy cold water flow over her body for a long time. It didn't stop her distress, but did allow her to start thinking about what to do. Her first clear thought was that Rebus had known about this and had the integrity to tell Leslie. Obviously, he'd taken a big risk. She just couldn't stand here and feel sorry for herself. Something needed to be done. A saying of her dad's came to mind. "Don't get mad, get even."

She decided what to do first. She dressed quickly and took the stack of documents down to the hotel's business center and had them copied. She used her credit card to pay, resisted the temptation to charge them to Richard's room. She returned to the suite, put the originals back in the briefcase, and placed it back in the closet where she'd found it. She'd thought briefly about leaving something that would let him know that she'd discovered his despicable act, but instead wrote a short note. "Something came up. I had to leave." She set her jaw so hard her teeth hurt. She grimaced as she added, "I love you" to the bottom of the note. She took a long look back at the suite while she stood at the door. "Richard Lion, you're a fucking asshole." She slammed the door shut.

Tossing out the f-bomb made her feel better, but not much.

The tears began again after the valet brought her car. Her eyes started to moisten before she started to drive away. She turned out of the hotel parking lot, pulled to the curb on a nearby residential street, and cried. He'd broken her heart. He'd betrayed her. She didn't know which was worse, the betrayal, the phony declarations of affection, or the telling of others. She'd cried once more until the tears stopped flowing. She blew her nose, wiped the remaining tears from her face, reminded herself of her dad's saying, and drove back to the office.

She had to deal with her angst immediately. She researched online for the name Anugrah Singh. More than a thousand entries popped up. In the very first one, there was a photograph of Singh—Richard Lion, as she knew him—in all his glory, the multi-millionaire former co-owner of Enpact who now lobbied for his former company. In a further article, she discovered that he, his beautiful Indian wife, and four small children lived in a large mansion on the New Jersey shoreline. The home had been featured in several prominent architectural magazines. She thought about all the lies she'd been told by him. There was no roommate in a New York apartment. His apartment story was a sham. She'd given herself so completely. The whole thing had been rigged. She nearly gagged again.

Included among the documents was a magazine interview in which Singh described the Indian surname as being the American equivalent of Lion. She felt so stupid. Stupid and angry. Ashamed of herself for being so dumb, so gullible, so trusting.

She raised her hands and covered her eyes, squeezed her eyelids tightly shut. She tried to protect herself from the emotions she was feeling; a mixture of betrayal, rejected love, anger, and hate. She thought about her dad. She missed him so much. She forced herself to concentrate on his face, his eyes, and his familiar smile. She needed him now. She needed to be held. She needed him to tell her that everything was going to be all right, that she'd done nothing wrong. When she opened her eyes, her retreat to this safe place vanished. She couldn't help it, but her tears started again. He was going to be one sorry son of a bitch. "Don't get mad, get even," she repeated to herself.

She walked out to the reception area. Leslie looked up from her computer. "I can't imagine how terrible this is for you." She stood up, placed her arms round Katie and held her tight.

"Come back to my office. I need to talk."

Katie briefly filled Leslie in on the events of the morning. "Thanks to you, Leslie, I won't be making a bigger fool of myself. I'm so embarrassed. I need to talk this through with you before I tell Gary."

"Sure thing. Let's do it downstairs right after work and we'll talk our way through it all."

"I really need that." Katie started to cry again.

Leslie stood and hugged her again. "Katie, go to the bathroom and wash up. We'll work this out after work. We'll take care of that fucking asshole."

Later, the pair left the office and went downstairs to the Buhl Bar in the lobby of the building. They sat and talked and drank the rest of the evening. Katie told Leslie all the details about Richard Lion.

"What a son of a bitch. I'll kill him for you if you want." Leslie learned forward and took Katie's hand. "What are you going to do?"

"My thinking right now is fuzzy. I've got to come up with something."

"I have an idea." Leslie smiled and patted the back of Katie's hand. "I think you may like it."

Leslie spent the better part of an hour explaining to Katie what she had in mind. When she finished, she looked at Katie. "What do you think?"

"Leslie, I think it's brilliant."

Leslie smiled. "You do understand that you'll have to do some things you might find distasteful? Pretending that you still like him?"

"Distasteful? Such a funny word. How about ball-crushing instead?"

"Ball-crushing? I love it."

Katie held her glass up. "Here's to ball-crushing. I love you, Leslie. You are such a good friend...and you are so damn smart."

Leslie clicked her glass against Katie's. "Let's drink to good friends and ball-crushing...and to Plan A."

They didn't count the number of drinks they'd had the rest of the night, but it was more than a few. Neither of them noticed the brooding guy at the other end of the bar who'd sat by himself and watched them all night.

The bartender stopped by their table. "We'll be closing in a half hour. Your tab is twenty-two bucks."

As he walked away, Leslie looked around her. "Oh crap. I left my purse upstairs."

Katie patted her hand. "Drinks are on me. Don't worry about it."

Katie opened her purse, pulled out some bills, put them on the table and smiled at Leslie. "I can't drive like this."

Leslie returned the smile. "I can't either. I'll call you a cab."

Katie nodded numbly. "Please."

Leslie laughed. "You're a cab."

"I think you just told a joke but I'll be damned if I can figure it out." Katie thought for a moment. "While you're at it, call yourself a cab, too."

Leslie laughed loudly. "I'm a cab."

"I still don't get it."

They stood arm-in-arm and worked their way outside to the street corner and waited for the cabs. Katie took the first one. As Leslie waited, she realized she needed her purse in the office. She went back into the building, rode the elevator up to the twelfth floor, and unlocked the door to the office. There was no need to turn on the lights, as she knew exactly where she'd left her purse in the reception desk. She could see her way from the dimly lit outside corridor. She retrieved the purse and turned to leave. Mark Stenson waited in the shadow of the opened front door.

He stepped out of the shadow as Leslie approached. He swung and his fist connected solidly with her jaw. She fell to the floor. He stood over her for a moment and waited for a reaction. There was none. He bent over, picked up her purse, opened it, and dumped its contents around her body. He stood up straight, thought for a moment, and kicked her hard in the rib cage.

"Let this be a lesson. This is payback."

He stood over her and placed a call from his cell phone. He spoke quietly into the phone. "I'm standing in the lobby of their office. I'm going to get the records right now. Anything else while I'm here?" He listened for a moment. "Got it." He disconnected the call and put the phone back in his pocket. He turned on his flashlight and walked back to Katie's office. He looked around and was tempted to scatter the files that sat on her desk. He found the box of trial exhibits and removed several documents, folded and put them in his pocket. He fished in his pocket, found the note and placed it in the center of the blotter on her desk and worked his way back to the lobby

Stenson looked down at the unconscious figure on the floor, kicked her again in the ribs, turned and closed the office door behind him. He took the stairs down. This worked out much better than he had thought. He would have had to find a way to get the exhibits during his preparation for trial, but this was better. He got back at Leslie for blowing him off.

Chapter 37
October 2012

Dealing with Richard was on Katie's mind as she approached the office early the next morning. Her eyes were blood-shot, her face puffy, and she still felt a little drunk, like hell warmed over. She placed her key in the office door and was surprised the door was unlocked. She walked into the still-dark space and nearly tripped over the prone figure.

She turned on the lights and saw Leslie sprawled on the floor. Leslie must have returned to the office rather than go home and just fallen asleep on the floor.

She bent over and nudged Leslie on the shoulder. "You look how I feel."

There was no response, and Katie looked at her friend more carefully. There was a large bruise on her face and blood on the floor next to her head. Somebody had done this to her. She nudged her friend again. No response. Katie noticed the scattered contents of the purse for the first time.

"Leslie. Can you hear me? Wake up." Katie fought a sense of panic. She stood, strode quickly to the reception desk, and called 911. She returned to Leslie's side after the call and thought about what to do until help arrived. She rubbed Leslie's shoulders gently, willed a response. Leslie emitted a slight groan and her eyes fluttered open.

Katie leaned close, said softly, "Leslie, honey. Help is on the way."

Leslie mumbled, "I hurt." She closed her eyes and groaned as she attempted to move.

"Hush. Just lie still." Katie continued rubbing her shoulders. She felt so helpless.

Two police officers arrived together with two emergency technicians. Katie was ordered to move away from her friend.

While the technicians looked Leslie over and placed her on a cart, one policeman approached Katie. "What happened here?"

"She's Leslie Gibbons. She works here as a paralegal and receptionist." She gestured toward Leslie. "I'm Katie Hornsby. I'm a lawyer here. We hung around the bar downstairs late last night. We were both going to take cabs home and I went first. I don't know why she came back up here. When I got here this morning, I found her."

"Do you know anybody who would do this?"

Katie shook her head. "Someone must have followed her and robbed her." She gestured at the scattered contents of the purse.

One of the emergency technicians nodded toward the policeman. "We're ready to go."

"I'd like to go with my friend. Can I put the stuff back in her purse so she can have it? Her ID is in there. She may need that for treatment."

"This is a crime scene. You can't touch anything. It will all stay here until we're through with it. Go ahead with her. We'll talk with you at the hospital if we need more information."

Katie held Leslie's hand during the trip to the hospital and stayed with her the entire time she was in the emergency room. She had Alex paged and he'd come down and took over her treatment. Leslie couldn't remember anything about last night. Xrays were taken of her chest and several ribs were fractured. Her jaw was not fractured, but several teeth had been loosened. She didn't remember why she'd gone back to the office rather than going home in a cab. Her mind was a blank. She was admitted to the hospital for observation and Katie went back to the office and knew her friend was going to be in good hands.

She sat in Gary's office and told him about the evening, then went to her own office. She sat down and noticed that the box containing the Enpact trial exhibits had been moved from where she'd left them the day before. She quickly scanned through the materials and discovered that the medical records for both Albright and Stenson were missing. A chill swept through her entire body. She started shaking and couldn't stop. All of this was happening because of the Lorital litigation, she realized. It couldn't be for any other reason. First Richard, and now this. She rushed to Gary's office and spent the next two hours telling him, through her tears, about everything that had happened. She'd been too embarrassed to tell him about Richard before.

"Katie, I can't believe that Hempstead's office would have anything to do with this. I'm so sorry you've had this happen. I don't know what else to say."

"It's Leslie and the case I'm worried about." She forced a smile. "The only real damage is to my ego. I thought he really liked me. But Leslie was hurt bad. She has fractured ribs." She couldn't help herself. The tears started. Gary walked around the desk and held her in his arms until she regained her composure.

"Take the day off. Go home and rest. A good sleep may help. I won't let the police know about the exhibits. Let's keep it to ourselves for now. There may be a way to turn this to our advantage. Let's both think this through and talk about it after you've taken care of yourself."

"I'll be all right." She attempted a smile through her tears. "There's so much to do. That's what they want. They want to interfere with our work. I can't let them. Fortunately, we have extra copies of exhibits in the conference room. Leslie made a duplicate set so I didn't have to lug the box back and forth between my office and the conference room." She thought for a moment. "And Alex and Jan have another set of the medical records, too."

She went back to her desk. With Leslie in the hospital, Katie was on her own insofar as dealing with Richard. The key to their plan was to continue the relationship with Richard as if nothing had happened. He had to stay clueless. She spent several hours and combed through the various documents she'd copied from his briefcase. It was fortunate that whoever stole the medical records hadn't looked inside her brief case. The more she'd read, the angrier she got. Don't get mad. Get even. She reminded herself again and again.

She ran the plan by Gary. He listened quietly. "There's some new information. Crumley just called and said he's reached a settlement. He's going to present it to the judge at the settlement conference. When he told me the numbers involved, it took everything I had to keep from laughing. I'll take care of it. But this is how I suggest you use it while you do your Richard thing…"

# # #

Katie gritted her teeth and placed the call to Richard. "Hi. I just had to call you to share my excitement."

"What's going on?"

"Stanley Crumley just called. Enpact is offering us a really huge settlement amount, much larger than we'd ever dreamed. Crumley put it together and we're hoping we can get the judge's approval."

Richard was quiet on other end of the line. Katie asked, "You still there?"

"You sound upset, like you've been crying."

Katie shuddered. "I…I have been crying. Tears of joy." You asshole, she thought, gritted her teeth.

"You must be excited. You've worked so hard on this and you must feel great."

"I do, and I miss you. When can we get together?" Doing this was difficult. She fought to restrain herself from lashing out at the man.

Another long pause. "I'm going out of the country for a while, but I'll be back."

"How long will you be gone? I can't wait to see you." Katie clenched her jaw.

"It'll be a month or so."

"A month? I can't wait that long. Can't we get together before you go? Let me see if this changes your mind. I've got two of the best seats in the house for next Tuesday's game between my Tigers and your Yankees. Please, please, please try to make it. I'll definitely make it worth your while." She clenched her teeth so hard her jaw hurt.

"Let me see what I can do."

Once the call ended, Katie sat and took several deep breaths. This was the most difficult thing she'd ever done. The plan would fall apart if he didn't change his plans about going abroad.

He called back an hour later. "Katie. Good news. I've cleared my schedule and will come in Tuesday afternoon. I've arranged for a suite at the Westin, close to your office."

"Richard, I can't tell you how excited I am." Katie grimaced. "I've got a big smile plastered on my face." Asshole, she thought again. She clenched her teeth and grimaced.

"Hopefully I can keep that smile on your face the whole time I'm there."

"How sweet you are." She gritted her teeth again. Her jaw ached. If it turned out that Lion had something to do with hurting Leslie, she was going to kill him.

Chapter 38
October 2012

Three days later, Leslie was back to work, taped up and banged up. She could barely move but insisted on coming back because there was so much work to be done on Lorital.

"May I help you?" She smiled at the pleasant-looking guy who approached her desk. "Do you have an appointment?"

"What happened to your face? Are you all right?"

Leslie forced a grin. It still hurt to smile. "The other guy won," she joked.

The man hesitated a moment. "I have no appointment but I'd like to speak with Mr. Newton."

"Mr. Newton is out of town. Can you talk with someone else? Is there anything I can help you with?"

"I'd rather speak with Mr. Newton...unless there is someone else here working on the Lorital cases."

"There is someone else. Ms. Hornsby is handling the litigation together with Mr. Newton. She's in the office. Would you like to speak with her?"

"Sure. Why not?" He shrugged his shoulders.

Katie came out of her office to the front desk in response to Leslie's call.

"I'm Katie Hornsby. What can I do for you?"

"I'm Dimitri Pavel. Is there someplace we can talk? I've got some information that may be important for you on Lorital."

"Come on back to my office." She led the way. When the two

were seated, she asked, "Are you a potential Lorital client?"

Pavel smiled and shook his head. "No, I was a client here on a different matter about fifteen years ago. Both Mr. Riley and Mr. Newton did a very good thing for my family and I am here to return the favor. I have something interesting for him." He spoke with a clipped foreign accent she found charming.

"Tell me what you have. I know Mr. Newton will be sorry he missed seeing you."

Pavel smiled gently, cast his eyes down. "I mean no disrespect, but I would like to speak with Mr. Newton. Perhaps you could reach him by phone?"

Katie picked up the phone. "Leslie, will you track Gary down and get him on the line? It's important."

Katie hung up and said, "While we're waiting, can you give me an idea as to what this is about? I understand why you want to speak to Mr. Newton and I'm not offended in the least."

"I'll tell you the background. I am a waiter at Oakland Hills Golf Club. I have been there for more than twenty years. I work in the men's lounge. Many famous people pass though and I have waited on them all. I could write a book. I remember people and names very well. That is part of my job, to remember and call people by their names. Judge Green is the judge on your Lorital cases, is that right?"

Katie nodded. "Yes, that's right."

"A couple of months ago, Judge Green was a guest at the club and I waited on him."

Katie wondered where this was going.

"Do you know the name Oliver Brewster? Have you heard of ALEC?"

Katie thought about the letter Green's daughter had given her. "I know about ALEC but I've never heard of Oliver Brewster."

"Let me try another name. Stanley Crumley?"

"Yes. Mr. Crumley is another lawyer who has Lorital cases in front of Judge Green."

The phone rang. Katie answered and put the call on speakerphone.

"Gary? I have a Mr. Pavel in my office, a former client of yours. He has information that he'd like to share with you. We're on speakerphone." She nodded to Pavel.

"Hello, Mr. Newton."

"Hi, Dimitri. It's good to hear from you. How's Sarah?"

"Sarah's very well. Thanks to you and Mr. Riley."

"I'm happy to hear that. She's a bright and beautiful little girl."

"She's not so little anymore." Pavel smiled. "She's in her third year at the University of Michigan, an all-A student. You and Mr. Riley made that possible."

"Third year? That's wonderful. You and your wife raised her well. You get the credit. We were just doing our job but we were pleased how well it came out for her."

"Let me tell you why I'm here."

"Go ahead."

"A month ago I was at work in the men's lounge at Oakland Hills Golf Course. I am a waiter there. I have followed what is happening in your Lorital cases in the newspapers. I waited on a table of three men. Judge Green, Stanley Crumley, and Oliver Brewster. I recognized the name of Judge Green and I knew he was the judge on your case. I knew Brewster and I'd heard him brag about ALEC while I served him drinks at an earlier meeting."

Gary interrupted. "ALEC? I know about ALEC. Green met with Crumley and someone with ALEC here in Detroit?"

"Let me finish and I think you'll understand. I also knew about Stanley Crumley because I see his ads every time I open a newspaper. Your Lorital case has received a lot of publicity. I put two and two together and figured that the three of them were up to no good. They'd had a few drinks and were oblivious to anything going on around them. I videotaped a part of their conversation while I cleared a table close to theirs."

There was silence on the other end of the line. Gary said, "Has anyone seen it?"

"No. It's a video recording on my phone. I think it's really important for you to know about."

"I'm out of town until tomorrow. Do you mind showing it to Ms. Hornsby?

"No, I don't. I meant no disrespect to her but I wanted you to know about it before I let her see it."

"Let me put it this way, Dimitri. I'd trust her with my life."

Katie blushed and Pavel smiled at her. "That's good enough for me. It was nice speaking with you, Mr. Newton."

"Thank you. And don't forget to say hello to Sarah and your wife for me."

"I won't. Good-bye."

The line disconnected and Pavel said, "May I show you?" Katie nodded and the man removed his smart phone from his pocket. He fiddled with it for a moment and then handed it to Katie. "Watch the screen. I think you will find it very interesting. Before you start, let me tell you about Oliver Brewster, the third man at the table. He is a big shot with ALEC, which is shorthand for the American Legislative Exchange Council. I looked it up. It's a conservative organization that tells politicians around the country what laws to pass." He gestured toward the phone. "Go ahead and watch."

Katie held the phone up and pushed the button. On the screen, she instantly recognized Green and Crumley. The third man apparently was Brewster. The recording was clear and distinct. Green was speaking, "She and the kids have had difficulty accepting the demands the judgeship puts on me. My oldest daughter is on a 'save the whale, love everyone in the world' kick. She hasn't liked some of the decisions I've made and isn't shy about letting me know. My wife has joined in. They're critical of every damn thing I do. They simply don't appreciate the responsibilities of a judge."

Crumley said. "I solved a similar problem. My third wife is a judge...a federal judge."

Green responded. "So then you know what I'm talking about..."

Crumley said, "I understand exactly."

Green continued. "It started even before I became a judge. They hated my NRA case. My wife screamed at me all the time. I stopped telling her about the case. I stopped telling her about any of my cases."

Brewster leaned forward and put a hand on Green's arm. "I'm sorry to hear that. Anything I can do to help? A nice trip for the five of you someplace? Tell me what you need and I'll take care of it."

Green responded. "That's really nice of you...but I think it's past that point."

Brewster spoke. "Can we talk business for just a moment? Let me tell you what Stanley does. He handles big cases like Lorital and he serves an important role for all of corporate America in that regard. Litigation has gotten out of hand in the United States and if it wasn't for Stanley, many large corporations would have been forced out of business and ruined financially a long time ago. Stanley is a man of reason. He is always willing to cooperate with us by pushing for settlements that are within reason and within the means of corporations so they are not ruined financially. In your Lorital cases, for example, you can use Stanley to wrap this litigation up quickly, relieve the congestion on your case docket, and become the hero for resolving a huge piece of litigation in a way that can serve as a model for judges in the future."

The video ended. Katie sat for a moment, stunned by what she'd just seen.

"Can I keep this?" Katie held up the phone.

Pavel shook his head. "I need my phone. But I can send the video to you on your cell phone right away. Give me your number."

Two minutes later, Katie confirmed that the material was stored on her phone.

"Will you lose your job if this is used? If the club finds out it was you?"

Pavel nodded. "Probably. I would hope it would not be necessary to make it public to be of benefit to you and your clients. I trust Mr. Newton and I know that he will do the right thing and not do anything to jeopardize my job." He paused and smiled. "The good your firm has done for me and my family can never be returned. This is my small gesture of thanks. My daughter, Sarah, was born with a very serious birth defect as a result of her mother taking a drug during her pregnancy with Sarah. Mr. Newton and Mr. Riley handled her case and she received a generous settlement that has allowed her to lead a normal life. My gratitude to Mr. Newton can never be fully repaid."

Katie felt tears in her eyes. "This is a very brave thing you've done. I'm grateful you came here and I can assure you that we will do nothing to harm you."

After Pavel left the office, Katie called Newton back and told him about the conversation in the videotape. Gary whistled. "You know what this means?"

"I'm not sure. What can we do with it?"

"It puts us back in control. Just sit on this for now. Meanwhile, make sure nothing happens to that videotape."

When the call ended, Katie sat at her desk and thought, what kind of force was at work against them? First Richard, then Leslie and the medical records, and now this. Did this happen routinely in America? Was there any part of the founding fathers' declaration of "justice for all" in play here? She thought about the obstacles they faced in the Lorital cases. It was daunting.

TOM BLEAKLEY

Chapter 39
October 2012

The lawyers on all sides were present in court for the scheduled settlement conference. After the bailiff called the proceedings to order, Judge Green started. "Mr. Crumley, do you have anything to report?"

Crumley, gnome-like but dapper in a black suit, green shirt, and blue tie, stood. "Yes, Judge. We have reached a settlement."

At the announcement, a murmur passed through the courtroom. More than fifty of the Newton clients were present. It was the first they'd heard about any settlement.

Green gaveled them quiet. "Let's listen to what Mr. Crumley has to say."

"Judge, the plaintiffs acknowledge there are many difficulties in the various cases and, as a result, I have negotiated a reasonable settlement to reflect these difficulties and to end this litigation to the benefit of all parties. After numerous conferences, the defendant has agreed to pay our demand and we propose that the court approve a final settlement of all cases in the amount of $120 million. Mr. Newton has agreed with the terms of the settlement. In recognition of the work done by plaintiffs' counsel, one third of that amount will be awarded to counsel for plaintiffs divided according to the percentages of cases each of the two firms have in litigation. Of the total of 8,060 cases, my firm has 8,000 and Mr. Newton's firm sixty cases, which amounts to a rough gross value for each case of $15,000. $5,000 of this amount on each case will go to lawyers' fees."

The firm's clients booed when Crumley finished his presentation. Judge Green again gaveled the room to order. "If these interruptions continue, I will empty this courtroom. I would like to hear now from the defendant."

Hempstead stood. "Your Honor, I believe that Mr. Crumley has correctly stated the settlement terms. As a factor in considering the reasonableness of the proposed settlement, as Mr. Crumley has stated, there are major problems in the plaintiffs' cases. It is my understanding, as an example, that the plaintiffs' principal expert witness, Dr. Deepak Patel, has changed his opinion and requested that his name be withdrawn from the witness list. He has apparently threatened to testify favorably for the defendant."

Bingo, Katie thought. Two birds with one stone. Both Richard and Stenson were spies. Katie looked over at Gary and fought back a grin. He'd had been right. It was smart to have waited on Stenson. She turned around and looked at the group of their clients who'd come to court. She wasn't surprised to find out that Stenson wasn't among them.

Green paused and took a deep breath. "Mr. Newton, do you have anything to say?"

"Your Honor." Newton stood and surveyed the room. He smiled at his clients. "There is something missing in the amount of settlement mentioned by Mr. Crumley. He did call me and tell me the figure he's mentioned in court this morning, bit it was my understanding he was speaking only about his eight thousand cases. He does not speak for the clients of our firm. The only agreement I could possibly recommend on behalf of my clients is the amount of $2 billion. What Mr. Crumley wants to settle his so-called 8,000 cases for is not my concern. My only concern is for the clients I represent who have been legitimately injured or killed through the carelessness and neglect of the defendant. One additional demand, however, is equally important to my clients. In addition to the $2 billion payment, Enpact must agree to take generic Lorital off the market. I might add that these two demands are non-negotiable. Take it or leave it."

Timothy Holt turned and looked back at Oliver Brewster, seated in the back of the courtroom. He shrugged his shoulders. What was this all about?

Judge Green was angry. He pointed at Newton and Katie. "I'll see the two of you in my chambers right now." He stormed off the bench.

Gary and Katie walked into Green's chambers. He'd taken off his robe and it was slung over the back of the couch. He was madder than hell. Katie saw it in his eyes.

"What did you think you're doing out there?"

Gary responded. "All I was doing, Judge, was responding to Crumley's ridiculous settlement statement."

Green stared hard at Newton. "As you may recall, I gave Crumley the authority to negotiate a settlement in this litigation and that is what he's done. It was my understanding that you agreed to it. I'm going to approve the settlement and you're going to be stuck with it. With you losing your expert witness, I don't see you having much choice. Your grandstanding out there was totally out of order."

Gary turned and nodded at Katie. She pulled out a cell phone pre-set to the videotape. "Just take a minute and look at this videotape, Your Honor. It is one minute, thirty-seven seconds long." She stood, reached across Green's desk and placed the phone in front of him.

Green picked up the phone. "I don't know how to operate these damn things."

"Let me get it started." Katie stretched across the desk and started the video. She stood while the judge watched. By the end of the tape, beads of sweat had formed on his forehead. The best part of this, Katie thought, is that Green's daughter and the ALEC letter didn't have to be revealed. She could keep her promise to the young girl.

He looked up angrily. "Where did you get this?"

"With all respect, Judge, that question does need to be answered. However, there are two questions that should be asked. What do we intend to do with this tape? And what are you going to do to keep us from doing it?"

Green's face reddened. "Are you trying to blackmail me?"

"Call it what you will, Judge. That's you in the video, not us. Your life will change in a heartbeat if this comes out. Particularly if your family finds out what you've done. Strike one. Particularly if the media receives this tape and plays it non-stop on every news cycle for two to three days. Strike two. And, most of all, if the Judicial Tenure Commission sees this tape, your public life will be over...and I expect you will be disbarred as well." Katie paused. "Strike three...you're out."

She looked at Gary and he nodded. They waited for Green's response.

"When I expose your threats, you'll both be disbarred."

"I suggest you think very carefully about that." Katie said. "I also suggest that you think very carefully about what I'm about to suggest." She was surprised at herself, at her sense of calm. With all she'd gone through with Richard and Leslie, this was child's play.

Green grabbed the phone and threw it in a wastebasket. He looked up at the two of them. "Get out of my office."

Katie stayed calm, but this was not the reaction from Green they'd expected. She felt her heart beat hard in her chest. She glanced at Gary for support. He nodded again. Her hands shook and sweat covered her body. Neither she nor Gary made a move to leave the office.

Green stared hard at Gary. "I wouldn't have expected something like this from you."

Gary returned the judge's glare. "The feeling is mutual, Judge. I have a hard time understanding why you'd do something like this. What are you getting out of it?"

Green broke eye contact. "I don't have to answer your questions."

Gary looked at Katie, then back at Green. "Your refusal to answer says a lot. You are getting something. They've promised you something and you've been caught red-handed."

Green looked away. Gary nodded at Katie, who gritted her teeth and said quietly, "There are four other phones with this video downloaded and ready to go. One is locked away in our office safe. The others are sitting on my desk in envelopes addressed to your family, to the Michigan Judicial Tenure commission, and to the *Detroit Free Press*. All I have to do is make a phone call and they're in the mail. You can keep the phone you just threw away, but your dilemma is not going to go away by threatening us or throwing us out of your office." She paused. "I think your most important consideration here is what exposure of this will do to your kids. I know you have three daughters. My dad, bless his soul, died recently and I know what an important role he played in my life. If I'd ever found out he done something like this…"—she gestured toward the phone—"it would have killed me. So, think about how your girls will feel if this becomes public information." She took a deep breath and folded her arms.

Green's hands visibly shook. He sat silently, tried to keep the movement of his hands from betraying his discomfort.

Katie pressed further. "I met one of your daughters at an earlier motion in your courtroom. She's a beautiful and bright young woman. You're not only going to screw up your own life but hers, too."

Green's face was purple. He rubbed both eyes, ran his hands threw his hair.

Katie spoke softly. "Now, are we going to talk about this like adults?"

"Goddamn it. Sit down."

Katie sat down next to Gary, took another deep breath, and slowly exhaled. She wasn't through with what she had to say. "This is what we, the three of us, are going to do." She opened the file in her hand and handed a sheet of paper to the judge. "Read this."

Green scanned the document. He couldn't focus. He looked up at Gary. He avoided eye contact with Katie. "Just tell me what this is about."

Katie responded. "All we're interested in is fair play." Gary nodded. Katie continued. "We're not asking for the moon. We just want a fair playing field. We want you to act like a judge. We don't know what kind of deals you have struck with these people, but that's all out the window now. Is that too much to ask? Let me also say that we won't hesitate to use this video against you if you try to weasel your way out of this. That's not going to happen. Don't test us."

Green was stunned. He couldn't find a place to put his hands that would stop them from shaking. He looked at Katie. "What do you want?"

"It's right there in the paper I handed you." Katie summarized the contents of the document. "You'll read everything but the last paragraph in the courtroom right now. That last paragraph tells you how the trial will be conducted. That part of the message can be saved until later."

When she finished, Green was still. "You don't leave me much choice."

"You're absolutely right. You have no choice." Katie glared at Green. "Keep in mind that we're not asking you to do anything other than what you should have done in the first place." She paused. "Also, don't forget that if you don't do what we've said, I'll walk right out of your courtroom and make a call to our office and have the packages with the phones sent out. That's a promise, not a threat."

Katie and Gary stood.

"We'll wait in the courtroom while you get yourself together," Gary said. To Katie's surprise, Gary extended his hand to Green. "Judge, sometimes the worst thing that happens turns out to be the very best. I sincerely hope that this is the case for you. The words that have been spoken inside this office right now will stay among just the three of us. You have our word on that."

Green stood and slowly extended his hand to Gary. "I appreciate that." The two men shook hands. Green then looked at Katie and extended his hand. As they shook, she saw tears in his eyes. Katie's dad always told her, before he knew she was headed to law school, that if you shake hands with a lawyer, you should count your fingers. She wondered if the admonition also applied to judges. She bit her tongue to keep from smiling. Why did she almost always try to make everything a joke?

"I need about ten minutes. Go wait in the courtroom."

As she and Gary walked out of the chamber, she couldn't help it. She stopped and looked at Gary, held up both hands. "Ten fingers." She grinned. "My father said to always check..."

Gary held up his hands too. "I know what you're going to say. My dad said the same thing..."

They both laughed until tears streamed down their faces. Gary hugged her. "Katie, you were terrific. That took a lot of guts."

Fifteen minutes later, Green returned to the bench and read from Katie's slip of paper. "The court is satisfied that the position of Mr. Newton on behalf of his clients is reasonable and proper. The court specifically directs the defendant to consider Mr. Newton's demands in private conference today and to continue to do so until an appropriate resolution of this matter is reached. Mr. Crumley's offer of settlement as to the Newton plaintiffs is specifically rejected on this court's express determination that it fails to adequately compensate these plaintiffs and appears to be nothing more than a thinly veiled attempt to provide Mr. Crumley an excessively large legal fee. Mr. Hempstead, you and your client may use my conference room to conduct negotiations. If a satisfactory settlement cannot be reached today, this case will proceed to trial immediately."

Green placed the paper on his desk and looked up. "Have I made myself clear?"

Hempstead stood. "Yes, Your Honor. Crystal clear."

Holt's face reddened. He glared angrily at Green and turned to look at Crumley with a look of puzzlement.

Crumley stood and waved his arms. "Judge, there must be some misunderstanding. You specifically gave me with the authority to conduct settlement negotiations on behalf of all the plaintiffs in this litigation..."

Katie figured the master of disaster was engaged in yet another theatrical stunt, except this time she knew that Green wasn't going to pay it any attention.

Green leaned forward. "Let me stop you right there, counsel. I have ruled. It's as simple as that. What you and the defendant can work out with your clients is not at issue here. You can negotiate a separate settlement, but the Newton clients are removed from your arrangement. Do you understand?"

"Yes, Your Honor." Crumley turned and looked at Holt, shrugged his shoulders.

# # #

An hour later, a red-faced Holt sat alongside Hempstead and Rebus in Green's conference room. He looked at Newton. His angry stare was frozen. He sputtered. "Listen to me. What y'all are demandin' is outrageous, you unnerstand? Y'all aren't interested in discussing settlement. You want a trial."

Gary glanced at Katie and returned Holt's stare. "I'd put it differently. We're not afraid of going to trial. And, your drug has to be taken off the market."

Holt narrowed his eyes. "*That's* not gonna happen. *That's a* deal breaker. *Sorry's gonna* be *your* middle name."

This man was a piece of work, Katie thought, using his exaggerated Southern accent as a tool of intimidation.

Gary stood. "No need for threats. Let's talk to the judge." He stood and the rest of the small group followed him back into the courtroom.

Stella nodded and waved them through. "Go right in. The judge is waiting on you." They filed into Green's chambers.

Gary took the lead. "Judge, we're at a stalemate on settling these cases."

"Will it do any good if I talk to both sides separately?"

"No, Your Honor," Gary said. "I don't think that's necessary. We're so far apart, it would be a waste of your time."

Green looked at Hempstead. "Do you agree?" Green avoided eye contact with Holt, who glared at him.

Hempstead nodded. "Yes, I do."

Green shrugged. "We'll start trial tomorrow morning."

Katie flinched and Green said, "Is there something wrong with tomorrow?"

"I've got tickets for the Tigers and Yankees game tomorrow."

Hempstead responded. "I've got tickets, too, Judge."

"We'll start the day after tomorrow."

Katie blushed. "Thank you, Your Honor."

Green looked at the four of them. "This date is firm. If there are any issues, bring them up right now. Each side will have five trial days to present your case and I'll allow each of you forty-five minutes for opening statements and one hour for closing arguments." He stopped. "If there's nothing further, I'll see you all Wednesday morning."

Holt interjected. "How are we going to proceed? I'd like some clarification on the scope of the trial, Judge. A simple issue, causation, could be tried first and would give the court the best use of its time. If the jury finds that the product doesn't cause any problems, then the case is over and it wouldn't be necessary to waste a lot of your time trying sixty individual cases."

Green paused, reached for Katie's piece of paper and read the last paragraph. "The case will be bifurcated. Proofs on the two individual plaintiffs and the liability of the defendant will be presented first. If the jury finds liability and causation, then we'll go to separate damage proofs for the two individuals." He looked at Newton and nodded slightly.

# # #

"It's a perfect setup."

Hempstead sat back in his office chair and looked across his desk at Timothy Holt.

"How so?"

Holt checked his notes. "Stenson's a big problem for Newton."

Hempstead raised his eyebrows. "I'm not sure what you're getting at."

"I've got some stuff in my briefcase that I'll bring in the morning. It'll make your job a hell of a lot easier."

Hempstead nodded. "Get it for me now and I'll get my staff right on it. By the way, Newton hasn't withdrawn Patel from his

347

witness list."

Holt lifted his big chin. "My sources tell me it's just a matter of time, a matter of time…"

# # #

"It's Chief Justice Haley on the line."

"Thanks, Stella." Haley was the last person on earth Green wanted to hear from. He knew what was coming.

"Good afternoon, Jerry."

A pause. "This is Chief Justice Haley. Have you got time to chat for a bit?"

"Yes…Chief Justice. I do."

"You've upset a lot of people. What the hell happened? Why did you back away from Crumley's deal? "

Green closed his eyes and thought about what to say. "I don't know how familiar you are with…"

"You were supposed to approve the settlement. Didn't you understand that?"

"Yes, I…"

"So what the hell happened?"

"I…thought it was the right thing to do."

"Do you have any idea of the damage you've caused?"

Green didn't respond.

Haley continued. "You don't, do you? What are you going to do to correct this problem?"

"I don't view it as a problem…"

"Goddammit, it is a problem, a big problem." Haley exploded.

Green held the phone away from his ear.

Haley continued. "This is what you're going to do. Write it down." He spoke for another ten minutes while Green took notes. When the conversation ended, Green sat with his head in his hands. He felt like a lap dog being passed back and forth. He stood and tossed the notes in the wastebasket.

# # #

Abigail Green was in a quandary. She'd had plenty of time to think about her reactions to her dad. If she was going to be honest with herself, she'd treated him badly. The problem was she didn't know how to make it better, to extricate herself from the dilemma she'd created and the alienation she'd caused for him. She'd been present in her father's courtroom at the settlement conference. She'd found out the date from Stella and skipped school to attend. When her dad had walked back into the courtroom and thrown out that Crumley's settlement and sided with Ms. Hornsby's firm, she'd known that he'd done the right thing. It made her so proud that tears streamed down her face. She went home and tried that evening to work through her misgivings by raising the issue with her mother.

"Mom, I've been thinking a lot about dad. I feel terrible about the mess I've made."

Nancy set her book aside. "Honey, why do you think you feel that way? Come and sit down and let's talk about it."

Abigail sat and looked at her mother. "I feel so guilty. I love Dad and I said so many terrible things just to hurt him because I was so mad."

Nancy took Abigail's hand in hers, raised it to her cheek and held it there. "I've felt the same way. You and I are alike that way. Sometimes we say things we don't mean because we're angry. The problem is how to undo the hurt it causes."

Abigail looked at her mother, a tear rolled down her face. "That's exactly how I feel. I start thinking about wanting to tell him I'm sorry, but when I think too much about it I start getting mad all over again." She paused to rub her eyes. "I don't know what to do. I don't want him to hate me."

"Your father will never hate you. He loves you."

"Why are you divorcing him? It's my fault, isn't it?"

So that was what was really on her mind. Nancy resisted the impulse to tell her daughter that her husband had isolated her emotionally. Since his judicial appointment, he'd put a freeze on the relationship that had become unbearable well beyond how he'd handled the situation with Abigail. She chose her words carefully. "It's not your fault and don't ever think that because it's not true. What has happened between your father and me is totally unrelated to your situation with him."

"I started it all." Abigail's tears flowed freely down her face. "I went to court today and I was wrong about him."

"You had school today."

"I skipped school.

She spoke to Nancy in detail about the day's hearing. When she'd finished, Nancy had tears in her eyes.

"No. You didn't cause us to break up. The timing was purely coincidental. Your father and I were well on our way to breaking up before your problems with his handling of this Lorital case. But I'm so pleased that you saw him today. It sounds like he came to his senses about the case."

Abigail stood abruptly. "I don't believe you. You're saying this just to try and make me feel better." She stomped out of the room.

Nancy sat and thought for a long time.

# # #

An all-hands meeting took place that afternoon at the Newton law firm. The group was seated in the firm's conference room to discuss the plan for trial: Gary, Katie, Leslie, Deepak Patel, Alex, and Jan.

Gary started the meeting. "We start trial the day after tomorrow. The three of you will testify in the following order. Deepak, you'll go first and lay the groundwork for causation, then give an opinion on Enpact's conduct. Jan will follow with a brief course in pharmacology, so the jury understands the science involved, and then give her opinions on both causation and wrongdoing. Alex will wrap up the testimony by giving opinions on both cause and wrongdoing. You will not be repeating each other's testimony, but will emphasize the bases of your opinions from your respective areas of science. I will present Deepak and Alex. Katie will present Jan. Any questions so far?"

The small group shook their heads.

"Stenson is a setup, well beyond the spying issue," Gary continued. "The key is his selection as the representative plaintiff for Enpact. Why would they choose him? They think we don't know about the phony records. The question is how we handle it. A lot of pieces are falling into place, but what do we do with it is the question? Leslie has just come up with some interesting information about Stenson."

He nodded toward Leslie. She checked her notes. "A friend of mine obtained some financial information. Three days before he first came into our office, Stenson deposited a check in the amount of $20,000 into a bank account that's separate from the joint account he has with his wife. I don't know who issued the check yet, but my friend is working on it. Stenson claims that he's been out of work for the past three years, but he's actually received $35,000 a year from a company that doesn't exist, and all that money has gone into the same bank account. He's paid no income tax on any of these amounts while his wife has worked two jobs to support the family since his heart attack."

Gary looked at Leslie and smiled. "I don't suppose you can tell us how your friend got all that information?"

"My friend is a little...shy, but he knows a lot about computers." She grimaced as she tried to grin; the fractured ribs and her bruised jaw were still painful.

Katie thought her friend really looked cute with her spiked hair surrounding two blackened eyes. She interjected, "I called Stenson's wife and asked her about the family's income. She clearly has no idea that Stenson has received any of the money that's in his separate account. He also drives a new Jaguar bought and paid for by the mystery company. He's changed in the past few weeks. Very aggressive, stays out late, and comes home drunk. She cried when she told me he hit her. Her biggest news was that Stenson is still taking Lorital."

Leslie shifted in her chair. She grimaced again. "There's more. My friend also followed Stenson the last time he came down here. Stenson went directly from here to a small law office in Southfield and spent more than three hours in conference there with two lawyers from that firm and a man named Timothy Holt."

Everyone in the room shared glances.

Gary looked around the room. "Yes. That's right. Our so-called client is working for the other side. It's exactly as you suspected, Jan." He nodded toward Emrich. "Leslie's information today confirms it—that and the fact that he's still taking the drug. I've tried to figure out how best to use this new stuff. The problem is in disclosing how we got it."

"Leslie," said Katie, "Tell them about the photographs."

Leslie grinned and grimaced once more. "I was getting to that. There are photographs of Stenson and Holt leaving the Southfield building together. Holt walked Stenson to his car where they stood talking for a while. This was a couple of days before I was attacked. I think it was Stenson who hurt me. I can't prove it, but I have this feeling." She described Stenson's attempt to get her to meet him for drinks.

Katie piped up. "The day after Leslie was hurt, there were trial exhibits regarding Stenson missing from the exhibit box, his fake medical record. Leslie's thinking that it was Stenson who beat her up makes it likely that he was the one who took them." She thought for a moment. "Fortunately, we have other copies."

Gary looked at Leslie and then Katie. "I don't want either one of you to be alone with him for a minute. I can arrange for a bodyguard."

Leslie interrupted. "That won't be necessary, Gary. Katie and I've got some mace now. That son-of-a-bitch will get a full dose if he as much tries to come near us." Katie nodded in agreement.

Hartley asked, "Who is this Holt?"

"He's national counsel for Enpact," Gary responded.

"Interestingly, he's also national counsel for Orex."

Patel exclaimed, "Holt was the one who hired me for Enpact."

Gary thought for a moment. "Leslie, do you think your friend would agree to appear at trial and testify about the photographs? That would be good enough to tie Stenson to Enpact without going into the question of how your friend got all the financial data."

Leslie smirked. "I can certainly try."

Katie looked around. "Leslie's very good at getting what she wants." The group laughed while Katie's cell phone buzzed. She checked caller ID. Right on time. She looked at the others. "You guys have to excuse me. I've got an appointment." She stepped outside the conference room and answered the phone.

"Hey, Richard. I've been waiting for your call."

"I'm here. Governor's suite. The twenty-ninth floor."

"I can't wait. I've got another hour of work and then I'll be there."

"Any thoughts on where you'd like to go for dinner?"

"Who said anything about eating?'

They both laughed.

"Katie, you're such a tease."

"We can eat in your room later. I told you I've got something special planned. We don't have to go to the ball game."

"I can't wait."

Katie hung up and went back into the conference room. "Can I borrow Leslie for a few minutes?" The two went into Katie's office and went over the plan again. The timing had to be perfect

Chapter 40
October 2012

Katie stood in the hallway outside the door of the Governor's suite for a minute, took several deep breaths, and tried to control her shaking hands. Here we go, she said to herself, and knocked on the door.

Richard opened the door. He was dressed casually in khakis and a button-down blue shirt. "Katie, come in and give me a big hug."

He enveloped her in his arms; she fought to avoid cringing from his touch. She focused on the reason she was here. Don't forget, she reminded herself; don't get mad, get even.

"I'm happy you came all this way just to see me."

He kissed her deeply and, although repulsed, she forced herself to surrender to the moment. Leslie had told her to think like an actress. She was acting in a play and this was a role she was playing. She did the best she could to respond. She stiffened as his hands started to wander.

He stopped, held her shoulders at arm's length, and looked at her. "Is there something wrong? You seem so distant."

"I'm just tired. It's so nice to see you. I haven't eaten since morning. Can we order something now?" She found it difficult to look at him.

"I thought you said you weren't hungry."

She hesitated. "I was so excited to hear from you, I forgot I was hungry. A little food won't interfere with what I've planned."

355

She forced herself to smile coyly.

They looked over the room service menu and Richard called in their order.

This was the tough part, Katie thought. What was going to happen until the knock on the door? She resisted asking him about the health of his wife or about his four children. What else could they talk about? The weather?

"So…" She forced a smile. "Have you come up with any more thoughts on how to get on first base without making a hit? As I recall, you still have a couple more to go."

Richard looked perplexed. "You bring me all the way here to talk about baseball? This is your special plan?"

"When was the last time you went to a game?"

Richard laughed. "You did bring me here to talk about baseball. I don't believe it. The last time, however, was that Tigers game."

"You call yourself a Yankee fan and they're still in the playoffs and you haven't been to another game? Doesn't seem to me that you're much of a fan." She tried hard to keep an edge out of her voice.

Richard's smile disappeared. "Okay. Something's wrong. Something's bothering you. Tell me."

Katie couldn't look at him. "I…I told you I'm tired and I haven't eaten. I feel lightheaded. That's all." And she hated him with all the passion her heart and soul could muster. He had ruined her life. Could she ever trust another man again? Could she ever commit to a relationship with the intensity that she'd given to him?

The knock on the door echoed throughout the room. "Room service."

Richard stood and answered the door. A uniformed police officer from the Wayne County Sheriff's Department stood at the door.

The officer stepped forward and placed his foot in position to hold the door open. "Richard Lion? Anugrah Singh? I am serving you with a subpoena to appear at trial this week in the matter of Albright versus Enpact. Together with this subpoena is an order entered by Judge Steven Green enjoining you from leaving the city of Detroit until such time as you may be permitted by Judge Green."

The officer handed Richard two documents. "Sir, please sign here acknowledging that you have been served these papers." He handed Richard a third slip of paper and held out a pen.

Richard appeared confused. "What's going on?" He looked over at Katie who stood back, away from the door. "Have you done this? I don't understand." He looked back at the officer. "You cannot do this to me. I am a citizen of India."

Katie walked forward, moved past Richard, and stepped behind the deputy. "I'll see you in court next week, Mr. Singh." She walked away, never looking back. She loved the look of sheer panic on his face and was amazed by her own sense of composure. She'd worried that she'd just stand there and break down, but instead she felt so calm. It was unreal. The sadness and tears were over. Just last week she'd thought she was going to die when she'd discovered Richard's deceit. Now, anger had become her default emotion.

The deputy accompanied her to the elevator. "Say hello to Leslie for me," he said shyly.

"You were great, Brad. Thanks so much." Katie paused. "You

really should give Leslie a call sometime, take her out for a drink." She winked at him. "I know she'd like that very much."

# # #

Judge Steven Green had done much soul-searching since he'd been confronted with the videotaped evidence of his perfidy. Initially, he'd been in shock and incapable of appreciating the full ramifications of his conduct. After a sleepless night, he got out of bed the next morning with a clear understanding of the jeopardy he'd created for himself. Shame permeated him such that he could barely look at his reflection in the bathroom mirror. Nancy had battered him relentlessly ever since he'd been appointed to the bench and Abigail had joined the battle since her discovery of the ALEC letter. He saw clearly now why they'd done so. The meeting with Gary Newton and Katie Hornsby had been a stark wake-up call. He'd placed his professional career at stake. It was difficult for him to face the truth, but he knew he needed to do something about it. He'd been an idiot. Could he ever undo the damage he'd done to his family? He needed to talk to someone. He needed to work through his current situation with someone who could be trusted. He grimaced when he realized he didn't have a single friend he could call. How pathetic was that?

When he arrived at his chambers, he sat down and closed his eyes. He didn't have any choice. He picked up the phone and called home.

"Nancy, I'd like to ask a favor."

There was a pause at the other end of the line. "What is it?" Her tone told him she wasn't happy to hear from him.

"Can you give me the name and phone number of the marriage counselor you wanted us to see?"

"Don't you think it's a little too late to take that route? Or are you and the Chief Justice going to go for counseling?"

Green stifled an angry response. He closed his eyes. He needed to remember why he was doing this. "Nancy, I'm so sorry for the way I've acted toward you—and the girls. I want to do something about it but I don't know what to do or how to do it. Maybe the marriage counselor would provide some answers..."

"You've not only broken my heart, but your daughters' as well."

"I've hurt you terribly. I know that. I know that saying I'm sorry now probably doesn't mean a thing. But I do want to do whatever it takes to set things right." He paused. "Whatever it takes."

"I'm not stopping divorce proceedings if that's what you're thinking. I'm willing to sit down with you and a marriage counselor. That's as far as I'll go. Talk is cheap. You'll have to show us you're serious. Your daughters need that much."

TOM BLEAKLEY

Chapter 41
October 2012

This was the big day, the first day of trial. Katie looked over at Gary as they left the office for the courthouse. "I'm nervous. I can't even think of any baseball trivia. My mind's a blank."

Gary laughed. "That's pretty nervous."

As they walked, Gary added, "Speaking of baseball, this is like opening day of the season. It's your first game as a big league pitcher. Once you make that first pitch, get that first inning out of the way, and you'll be fine."

Katie stopped him short. "This is your way of trying to make me feel better?"

They looked at each other and laughed. Gary said, "I guess it didn't work."

They walked into the building and waited at the elevators. When they reached the tenth floor, several teams of reporters with TV cameras stood outside the courtroom. They pushed their way past and declined comment when microphones were shoved into their faces. They went into the courtroom where the entire defense team was already in place. The courtroom was packed with spectators. No one from the defense team looked at them as they sat down at counsel table. Except Rebus. He and Katie exchanged brief glances and he looked quickly away.

Gary leaned over and whispered. "Here's another one. You're going to sing the national anthem; forty-three thousand people in the old ballpark are staring at you, another two million on television. This…"—he gestured around the courtroom—"couldn't be as bad as that."

She laughed. "You haven't heard me sing. My feet are the only part of me that's not shaking."

Their clients walked into the room and joined them at the table. Katie was surprised that Mark Stenson had cleaned up so well. He wore a clean, pressed dark suit and a white shirt and tie. His hair was trimmed neatly, but the biggest surprise was his demeanor. He seemed relaxed and the nasty smirk was gone. Sharon Albright also looked nervous. The two clients sat next to each other between Gary and Katie at the table closest to the jury box. Katie made sure that Sharon sat between her and Stenson. Katie checked her purse. Her can of mace was readily available.

The jury venire consisted of fifty-nine potential jurors seated as a group in the first three rows of the courtroom. Six of the fifty-nine people would be selected by lot initially, and the lawyers would be permitted to ask each a few brief questions. Judge Green warned that the lawyers would not be permitted to argue their cases during jury selection. Any attempt to do so and that lawyer's opportunity to question the juror would be halted. Challenges for cause would be followed by peremptory challenges. Each side had an unlimited number of challenges for cause but was limited to ten peremptory challenges.

At the office, Gary had given Katie a short tutorial on the process of jury selection and the type of juror they wanted. "The objective in jury selection is to eliminate people who have biases against our clients."

"Sounds impossible," Katie said. "How can you do that in such a short period of time?"

Gary smiled. "You'll be surprised by now much information a potential juror will divulge. What they do with their free time is important. Do they volunteer? What do they watch or read? Questions about what news or TV shows they watch. What magazines they subscribe to give clues as to what they may be thinking about lawsuits. The point is to ask open-ended questions: how, what, where, when, and why types. Get them talking. Don't give them a chance to just answer yes or no. The key to good jury selection is to listen to what they say. My favorite question is to ask them to tell me the name of one person who's dead who we all know and respect. Most jurors say 'my grandmother' and that tells me that they don't follow directions well. If they say 'Ronald Reagan' or Martin Luther King' that gives me huge insight as to where their allegiances may be. Sometimes I just get a feeling about a potential juror and have no good reason for it. I rely on this sense if I think the juror will hurt me and just get rid of them. We can excuse a potential juror for any reason other than race, although in actual practice that happens every day. African Americans are like a plague to corporate defendants. They're considered way too generous, too liberal in their leanings, too willing to give away someone's money to the victims whether they deserve it or not."

"What kind of jurors will the defendant want?"

"They'll look for people involved in the health care system and those who like authority figures. They'll also look for people who hate lawyers. The insurance industry has spent millions of dollars the last few years hammering the public with phony claims about the impact of lawsuits on big business and placing the blame on greedy lawyers."

Katie nodded. "I had a lot of negative reactions from people even before I started law school when they found out I wanted to be a lawyer. I didn't even tell my dad before he died because I knew what he'd say."

Gary continued. "My personal opinion is that African Americans are more skillful in assessing bullshit when they hear it. White folks tend to believe anything a defense lawyer says because they've heard nothing but insurance-company drivel about unnecessary lawsuits. If we looked into it, we'd probably find that ALEC has funded all the publicity about unnecessary lawsuits."

Two days before, Katie had reviewed the two-page questionnaires filled out by each of the fifty-nine potential jurors and taken careful notes. She and Gary spent that afternoon discussing the pros and cons of each potential juror. "It's really a crapshoot," Gary said. "The goal is to get rid of the obvious people who could really hurt the case. Jury selection—obtaining a good jury—is a matter of luck. As I said, the key is to get them talking."

Stella stood. "All rise. Court is now in session. The Honorable Steven Green is presiding."

Green strode to the bench and the trial was underway.

Jury selection took three hours.

Gary leaned over and whispered, "I'm satisfied with everyone in the box right now. Anybody you don't like?"

Katie shook her head. "I really like the fireman, juror number four." She nodded toward the jury.

Gary smiled. "And he really likes you. The other two good-looking guys in the back row like you, too."

Gary stood. "The plaintiffs are satisfied with the jury, your Honor."

Gary and Katie felt good about the final jury mix: four African Americans, two retirees, and the three male jurors in their mid-thirties who couldn't keep their eyes off Katie. At the end of the case, only six members of the jury would deliberate. Verdicts in criminal cases required unanimous agreement among the jurors whereas in civil cases in Michigan, only five out of six votes were necessary to render a verdict. Three of the nine jurors selected were alternates in the event that one or more of the six couldn't deliberate for any reason. After Green had sworn in the nine jurors, he briefly explained to them what the case was about.

"There are going to be two issues in this trial you will be asked to decide. Rather than go into detail with you about those two issues, I'll let the lawyers tell you. Let me just simply indicate that the only questions before you are whether Enpact, the defendant drug manufacturer, is liable to the two plaintiffs in this case, Sharon Albright and Mark Stenson, for making and selling generic Lorital and whether or not generic Lorital caused heart attacks in either Sharon Albright's husband and Mark Stenson, or both. That's it. Now, let's hear from Mr. Newton in his opening statement."

Hempstead stood. "Your Honor, before we begin opening statements, there's a matter that needs to be taken up by the court. Can we approach the bench?"

The judge nodded and the lawyers gathered at the sidebar. The following colloquy took place outside of the hearing of the jury.

Green looked toward Hempstead. "Go ahead, counsel."

"Judge, we had something rather unusual happen and I need to call it to your attention. A gentleman by the name of Richard Lion was served with a subpoena as well as an injunctive order in this case. It was unusual in that Ms. Hornsby, one of the plaintiff attorneys, lured the gentleman to a hotel room here in downtown Detroit where he was served by a Wayne County deputy sheriff. Ms. Hornsby was present when the papers were served and, immediately after, walked away with the deputy sheriff, which suggests that the two of them were friends. Your Honor, the order for injunctive relief was signed by you."

Green raised his voice. "Let me stop you right there, counsel. Are you suggesting that the subpoena or injunction was improper?"

"No, Your Honor. I am requesting that both be quashed. Mr. Lion is an extremely busy person and a citizen of India. Being subject to a subpoena and an order requiring him to stay in Detroit until his testimony is over is unreasonable on its face. Mr. Lion denies any knowledge of the facts in dispute in this litigation and I have an affidavit for you signed by him to that effect. It would serve no worthwhile purpose to encumber a person who has no personal knowledge of the facts of this case for a week or more. I ask that both the subpoena and the order of injunctive relief be quashed."

Gary looked at Katie. "You take the response."

Katie looked at the judge. "Your Honor, I will represent that Mr. Lion is none other than the former co-owner of Enpact, who owned the company with his brother who has already been deposed in India. It should be noted that there was no objection by counsel to the other brother's testimony. Mr. Lion goes by two names, apparently whenever it is convenient to hide his association with Enpact. His real name, in fact, is Anugrah Singh and he currently serves as a paid lobbyist for Enpact on matters pertaining to the marketing of Enpact's drugs, including generic Lorital, in the United States. In an abundance of caution, the man was served with two identical subpoenas, one listing his last name as Singh, the other as Lion. I requested earlier this week that you issue an ex parte injunction preventing Mr. Singh from leaving the city of Detroit until the completion of his testimony. In my motion I attached several documents of Mr. Singh's that clearly depict his involvement in and knowledge about generic Lorital. For this reason, we would request that the court deny Mr. Hempstead's motion to quash."

Green spoke without hesitation. "The court is satisfied that Ms. Hornsby's recitation of the position, identify, and facts surrounding the witness is accurate and, therefore, there is no need to quash the two orders involving his appearance at trial. Your motion to quash is denied, Mr. Hempstead, and Mr. Singh will remain in Detroit until he is called as a witness. Anything else before we begin?"

Hempstead shook his head. "No, Your Honor."

Katie couldn't resist smiling. Singh was going to get what was coming to him, she was certain.

# # #

Green addressed the jury. "I'm sorry about the delay. As you could see, there was a matter that needed to be addressed. Now, let's hear from Mr. Newton in his opening statement."

Newton stood, straightened his tie, and approached the podium. The courtroom was silent. He spoke without notes in a quiet conversational tone. "Every trial is a story. The story that will be told to you during this trial is how the negligence and wanton disregard for human life by a major drug company has caused the death of Sharon Albright's husband, Ralph, and a nearly fatal heart attack in Mark Stenson. I am Dr. Gary Newton and, along with my colleague, Katie Hornsby, seated over there at the table, are pleased to represent these clients, Sharon Albright and Mark Stenson, in the matter you are being called upon to decide. We will present evidence to you about the dangers of a drug sold throughout the United States by the defendant in this case, Enpact Pharmaceuticals. During these opening remarks, I will give you an outline of what we intend to prove to you through the testimony of three of the most knowledgeable doctors in America about the dangers of the generic form of the drug Lorital. In addition to these three expert witnesses, you will hear from our clients and excerpts of deposition testimony taken from Enpact employees in India that will be read to you. You will also receive an instruction from Judge Green that you should consider deposition testimony as though it is testimony given live here in open court. There will also be a witness who was an employee of Enpact who will provide information to you about the sales of generic Lorital in the U.S. as well as other information about the efforts Enpact has taken to let users and the federal agency, the FDA, know about the dangers of generic Lorital use."

Gary paused and looked at each of the jurors. They were paying close attention. "Let me tell you now what the proofs will show about the dangers of generic Lorital…"

Twenty minutes later, Newton concluded his opening statement, "At the end of this phase of the trial, I will be asking you to deliver a verdict in favor of the plaintiffs."

Hempstead stood. "Objection, Your Honor. Can we approach

the bench?"

Green nodded and the lawyers for both parties gathered at the sidebar out of the hearing of the jury.

Hempstead whispered, "Your Honor, I move for a mistrial on the basis that Mr. Newton has improperly interjected the issue of wrongdoing by his continuous use of the word 'danger' during his opening statement. The issue before this jury is not about whether a drug is a danger to the user but whether the drug causes strokes or hearts attacks. Also, he referred to himself as 'doctor,' and he also improperly planted the seed that this is only the first phase of a trial which suggests to the jury that there are other issues they may deal with later on."

Green looked at Hempstead through narrowed eyes. "Mr. Hempstead, you are reaching a bit. Your motion is denied. A drug that causes harm may reasonably be construed to be a dangerous drug. And, from what I know, Dr. Newton is a licensed medical doctor and he is also correct that this is the first phase of the trial."

Newton cast Katie a quick grin as they returned to their seats.

Judge Green nodded at Lester Hempstead. "Mr. Hempstead, your opening statement, please."

Hempstead stood and buttoned his coat jacket. He walked over to the jury box and put his hands on the rail. "Members of the jury, Enpact Pharmaceuticals, my client, is going to present evidence that when a person uses its drug, Lorital, according to the prescription issued by doctors, it is safe and effective in the treatment of a serious medical condition arising because of the aging process...."

Hempstead took fifteen minutes and laid out the defense he was going to present. He concluded, "The proofs will show that the generic version of Lorital is as safe as the brand-name version. It does not present the danger to users suggested by Mr. Newton. In addition, there may be a surprise or two presented about the individual plaintiffs in this case." Hempstead turned and looked at Stenson. "We are here today because of those two people." He pointed to Stenson. "You will hear testimony that just because someone has brought a lawsuit, that doesn't mean the case is valid. Bringing a lawsuit against a company like Enpact, standing alone, is meaningless. There must be some truth and substance as to what is claimed." He looked back at the jury, thanked them for their attention, and sat down.

Green spoke to the jury. "Let's break for lunch now and the plaintiffs will start their case this afternoon."

As Gary and Katie walked back to the office, she said, "Hempstead knows about Stenson."

Gary nodded. "That was obvious. We're just going to let this play out like we planned."

# # #

Conventional wisdom in presenting a complex drug product civil case calls for the systematic building of a set of facts and scientific information to allow a jury to feel comfortable about their understanding of the subject. Gary felt that if a jury poorly understood the background it was possible they would think that the injured party wanted to be awarded money on the basis of sympathy. He wanted the jury to be clear on the drug information before he presented the clients who were injured. The proof of injuries or death without the scientific background would be meaningless.

He stood and addressed Green and the jury. "Plaintiffs call Dr. Deepak Patel."

Timothy Holt sat upright, as if an electric shock had been applied to him. He glared at Hempstead. The two men whispered back and forth. Holt's face turned a deep scarlet. Hempstead shook his head at Holt and returned his attention to the courtroom.

When Patel was settled in the witness chair, Gary approached him. "Good afternoon. Would you state your name and tell the court and jury what you do for a living?"

"My name is Dr. Deepak Patel and I am a medical doctor with a second doctorate degree in pharmacology. Until very recently I was the Director of the Department of Research at Enpact."

"Tell us how you happened to go to Enpact."

"It is a simple story. Are you familiar with Orex?"

Patel looked at the jury and several of the jurors shook their heads. "It is the company that makes brand-name Lorital."

The jurors nodded.

"For the past twenty years, I have practiced community-based medicine at a clinic in Brunswick, New Jersey, about fifty percent of the time. The other fifty percent of my professional time has been spent conducting research on various drugs at the request of pharmaceutical companies. One of the studies I conducted was a comparison between trade-name Lorital and generic Lorital, as reported in various published research articles. About three years ago, Orex management asked me to present a talk on this paper to its entire sales staff. In this particular paper, I'd compared Orex's reported adverse reactions of the original trade Lorital with those from generic Lorital. I found that generic Lorital had problems that the trade-name product didn't have. Generic Lorital was causing cardiovascular problems in men at the usual dosage levels being prescribed. Apparently, someone from Enpact was present at the talk and that company started recruiting me to join their company as its research director. I was flattered and I believed what they were telling me, that they were interested in improving the safety of their products. I believe now that they hired me just to shut me up."

Hempstead was on his feet. "Objection, Your Honor. Request that the jury be instructed to disregard the last statement on the basis that it lacks relevancy to the issue in this case. Also, how can the witness know why he was hired?"

Green leaned forward. "Objection overruled. Dr. Patel said it was his belief that he was hired to be shut up, not that he thought it was the defendant's belief."

Gary turned and shared a quick grin with Katie. This was going better than expected. He turned back to Patel. "When did you start thinking there might be a problem at Enpact?"

"Almost as soon as I got there. I should have asked more questions before I agreed to take the job, but I didn't. The laboratory facility was much smaller than I thought it would be. They led me to believe I was going to be taking over a big research department and that I could make it bigger and better. I think there were only eight people in the department when I got there. Only three had any type of scientific training. The lab equipment was shoddy and most of it was outdated. It was not a very pleasant beginning. I feel guilty now because the money they were paying me blurred my objectivity, the money and the promises. I thought things were going to get a lot better but they didn't."

"Was there anything specifically that happened to make you suspect there was a problem?"

"Dr. Elizabeth Barrett, a respected colleague who, like me, had just recently started working at Enpact, came to me with the testing results that Enpact used to get FDA approval of generic Lorital. The tests they submitted were identical to the results for brand-name Lorital, something that simply doesn't happen. That's why she came to me. The results were too perfect and raised her suspicions that the tests were fake. That's when I started my investigation. I was in charge of a few Enpact employees around the world who were members of my department. I asked them to gather some specific information about our products and, when they reported back, they confirmed that our suspicions were right. When I asked to bring this to the attention of the board of directors, my requests were ignored. Shortly after, everything started spiraling out of control. A distinguished physician from India called me and told me his research showed that an Enpact antibiotic had caused seven hundred children's deaths because the packages actually contained no antibiotic."

Patel paused. Katie thought he was close to tears.

Gary asked him gently. "What did you do with this information?"

"Dr. Barrett and I did the same thing with generic Lorital that this doctor had done with Enpact's generic ampicillin. We arranged for a large sample of generic Lorital to be tested for purity and strength. The products were obtained from our own warehouses. Many of the sample tested, about one-third, contained three times the amount of active drug that the package labeling said. Some packages contained no drug at all." He looked sadly at the jury and shook his head. "I had worked all my life to build my scientific reputation, and now it seemed on the verge of collapse. I cannot explain to you what I was going through."

Katie picked up the well-marked copy of Dr. Barrett's deposition and handed it to Gary.

Gary approached Patel. "Listen to this for a moment." He read part of Dr. Barrett's testimony to him. "Other employees, as well as Dr. Patel, told me that it was customary practice at Enpact to perform bio-equivalency testing on trade-name products and submit those test results to the FDA rather than tests done on our products. As I understand it, that has been the customary practice here at Enpact for several years."

He looked at Patel, then the jury. "Was that the customary practice at Enpact?"

Patel's expression turned grim. He turned to the jury and nodded. "It's true but it was only the tip of the iceberg. As I mentioned, the information about the lack of quality—the dangerous dosages of Enpact products including generic Lorital— are more important than these fake equivalency tests. Someone needs to know this in order to understand how and why Enpact causes damage in users."

Gary asked, "What else?

"As I mentioned earlier, I received a call from the respected doctor in India who discovered the problem with Enpact's ampicillin, Dr. Geer. I then retrieved a copy of his research that was published in a respected peer-review journal, which confirmed what he told me."

"When you use the term 'peer-review,' what does that mean?"

"Peer review is the process of review that occurs when research is submitted to a reputable medical or scientific journal. Before the research can be published, the paper is sent out to three independent scientific reviewers who work in the same scientific area as involved in the paper in question. If those peer reviewers approve the publication of the research, then the journal publishes it. Peer review is the hallmark of acceptable scientific evidence. As a scientist and a physician, I do not rely on research that is not peer-reviewed."

"What did you do with this information?"

"Finding out about the tragedy of the seven hundred dead children was the final straw. When I found out about this, I went to Enpact's CEO, Mr. Singh. I tried to tell him what was happening. He didn't want to hear it. He threw me out of his office and fired me on the spot, but it didn't matter. I quit before he could."

Gary checked his notes. "Dr. Patel, in your earlier response you mentioned some research that you presented to the company that makes trade-name Lorital. Can you tell the jury about that research?"

"Yes. The brand-name Lorital had been on the market for a few years and was widely used without any apparent problems. When the generic Lorital began to be used, there were a great number of heart attacks and strokes reported in men, even younger men, who were using the generic drug. This had not been seen previously with the trade-name product. I prepared a paper that looked in detail at several studies that addressed the comparative rates of problems. To make a long story short, it was clear that the generic Lorital was causing problems about twenty-five times more frequently than the brand-name drug."

"Did your research at the time determine the reason why

generic Lorital was more dangerous than brand-name Lorital?

"No. It did not."

"Did you subsequently acquire information that led you to conclude why this was happening?"

"Yes."

"Do you have an opinion as to whether generic Lorital is more dangerous than brand-name Lorital?"

"Yes. It is my opinion that generic Lorital is much more dangerous than brand-name Lorital, because of the way it is made in the production facility. What happens there is that drug tablets that are supposed to have the same dose of testosterone as every other dose actually have a widely varied amount of drug. Some, as in the ampicillin situation, have no drug at all and some pills contain dosages more than three times greater than stated on the package labeling. In my opinion, it is those particular tablets or pills that contain excessively high doses of testosterone that cause heart attacks or strokes in persons exposed to these dangerous levels. I also should add that I have personally walked through some of Enpact's factories that make the drug. I have questioned workers who've made the drug. Rats and mice run around the factories like they are pets. The workers are all unskilled and very careless in handling the materials. Most workers do not have even a high-school education. The conditions are deplorable."

"Does generic Lorital, with reasonable medical and scientific certainty, carry a much higher risk of a user having a heart attack or stroke than with the trade-name product?

"Yes. It is my opinion with reasonable medical and scientific probability that generic Lorital carries a much great risk of harm than trade name Lorital. Much greater. To the point of being unreasonably dangerous. It should not be on the market."

"Before you knew that this case was in litigation, did you have that opinion and did you share your opinion with the CEO of Enpact?"

"Yes and yes. I submitted a written report to the CEO of Enpact prepared by Dr. Barrett and me with exactly those conclusions."

"Speaking of your report, do you have a copy of it with you?"

Patel shrugged and nodded. "I do, but I have not shown it yet to anybody outside of Enpact. When I left the company, I signed an agreement to not take anything with me. I've kept a copy. I know that Enpact considers the report to be a corporate document because it was written while I was working for them. So I wasn't certain I could share it with anyone else. I'm not sure that I can share it with you right now unless the judge orders me to."

Gary asked Patel, "Did they give you anything in return for signing this agreement?"

"They gave me six month's severance pay and told me they gave me that much because of the signed agreement. They told me that if I didn't sign the agreement, I would only get one month's severance pay. They paid me to keep the report quiet, to keep my mouth shut."

"Dr. Patel, I would ask that you surrender your written report to the court reporter and that it be marked as Plaintiff's exhibit Number 42."

Hempstead thundered. "Objection, Your Honor. The scope of the information in Dr. Patel's report extends well beyond the limitations on proof in this trial. I request that the court review the report in chambers before it determines its admissibility."

Green nodded. "I will look at the document overnight and rule on it in the morning. For now, let's have it marked for identification only."

Patel handed his report to the bailiff who turned it over to the court reporter.

Gary looked at the judge. "Your Honor, could I request that you tell the jury why the numbered exhibits will not be presented to them in sequence?"

Green nodded at Newton and looked at the jury. "As part of my pre-trial order all exhibits must be numbered and disclosed to the other party before the trial begins. Many times the exhibits are not presented in sequential order during trial because the timing of their use at trial cannot be predicted. Do you understand?"

The jurors all nodded.

"Thank you, Your Honor." Gary paused. "Dr. Patel, why did you put your professional life in jeopardy by attempting to bring the information about generic Lorital to the attention of upper-management at Enpact?"

Patel answered without hesitation. "My actions are consistent with my Indian heritage. While I am now a citizen of the United States, I am originally from India and I am proud of my Indian ancestry. We are an honest and hard-working people. We are rooted in an ancient civilization and culture that values truth and integrity. Despite this noble tradition, this is not the way Enpact runs its business. It is dishonest and wrong to sell poorly made and dangerous drugs that hurt people. This is not who we are—and we need to prove that to the world. That is why I have done what I've done." He smiled at the jury. Most of them smiled back.

Gary checked his notes and then looked at the jury. "That's all the questions I have, Your Honor."

Green looked over at Hempstead. "Counsel, you may proceed with your cross-examination."

Hempstead stood and walked to the podium with a legal pad in his hand.

"Good afternoon, Dr. Patel."

"Good afternoon, sir."

"Earlier, you mentioned your paper that compared the rate of adverse effects seen in brand-name Lorital users with those in generic Lorital users. Is that right?

"Yes. That's correct."

"You undertook to look into the potential differences between the two forms of the drug? Your research indicated there was a difference and you published your conclusions, did you not?"

"Yes. That's right."

"Would you agree that the phrases 'look into,' 'seek,' 'examine,' 'explore,' 'delve into,' 'study,' and 'investigate' are all terms that are synonymous with the term 'research'?"

"Yes. Of course."

"You just agreed that you 'looked into' the differences between the two forms of the drug in the study we are talking about. Right?"

"That is right."

"You not only agree that you 'looked into' the relationship, but you also contend that your study constitutes a research finding. Right?"

"That's correct."

"And we can also agree that you published the results of your research. Right?"

"Yes. That's right."

"Isn't it true that your so-called research on this supposed comparison between the two forms of the drug was not subjected to peer review before it was published?"

"That's true. If I may explain…"

"Does this statement sound familiar? 'As a scientist and a physician, I do not rely on research that is not peer-reviewed.'"

Patel cast a glance at Gary. He had a slight grin. "I can explain."

"There is no question pending that requires an explanation. Either the statement I just read sounds familiar or it doesn't. Just to make sure we're talking about the same thing, I'll repeat the statement. 'As a scientist and a physician, I do not rely on research that is not peer-reviewed.' Does that sound familiar or doesn't it?"

"Yes. I said that earlier."

"Let me see if I understand correctly what has happened here. Just a few minutes ago, you said that as 'a scientist and a physician you do not rely on research that is not peer-reviewed.' After you said that, you told us that generic Lorital was more dangerous than the brand-name product based, in part, on your own non-peer-reviewed so-called research. Have I got that right?"

"There is an explanation."

Hempstead turned and looked at the jury. No one had fallen asleep. He said to the judge, "Your Honor, I'd request that you instruct the witness to answer the question he so clearly wants to avoid answering."

Green leaned toward Patel. "Answer the question, doctor. Mr. Hempstead, you will also refrain from making sarcastic comments."

Hempstead smiled. "Your Honor, with all the hoopla going on, I request that the court reporter read the question back to Dr. Patel so that he's clear on what question needs to be answered." Hempstead looked at two of the jurors and winked. Both responded with broad smiles.

The judge nodded at the court reporter. She picked up her notes and read. "Let me see if I understand correctly what has happened here. Just a few minutes ago, you said that as 'a scientist and a physician you do not rely on research that is not peer-reviewed.' After you said that, you told us that generic Lorital was more dangerous than the brand-name product based, in part, on your own non-peer-reviewed so-called research. Have I got that right?"

Hempstead looked at Patel. "Do you have the question in mind?"

Patel's bearing never changed during Hempstead's cross-examination. He responded in a firm voice. "Yes. That's right. I'd like to explain..."

"Your lawyer can do that, if he wants." Hempstead turned to the jury and smiled. "Finally, Dr. Patel, is it true that generic Lorital made and sold by Enpact has been approved for marketing by the Indian equivalent of the FDA here in the United States?"

"Yes. That's true, but..."

"Thank you, doctor. That's all the questions I have."

Katie sat there with a thousand thoughts running through her mind. This kind, intelligent man had been treated with contempt by the wily Hempstead. She was concerned that the experienced lawyer may have cast a cloud of doubt around Patel's opinions that might fool the jury.

Green looked out at Newton. "Any redirect, Dr. Newton?"

Gary jumped to his feet. "Dr. Patel. Am I your lawyer, as Mr. Hempstead's last statement suggests?"

"No, Mr. Newton. You are a fine lawyer, and if I ever needed a lawyer I would come to you. But no, you are not my lawyer. I am an independent expert witness and the former Director of Research of Enpact Pharmaceuticals."

A grand slam home run, Katie thought.

Newton continued. "Dr. Patel, you indicated during your questioning by Mr. Hempstead that you had an explanation for his question on the peer-review issue. Can you give the court and jury your explanation now?"

"Yes, I will. Mr. Hempstead's question focused on my review of fourteen outstanding peer-reviewed published studies that compared various aspects of the two forms of Lorital. Mr. Hempstead is exactly right when he pointed out that my review was not peer-reviewed, but the research articles that I relied on in preparing my paper were all peer-reviewed. That is to say, the data I relied on in drawing my conclusions was all peer-reviewed. My article was an attempt to summarize this peer-reviewed literature and then make my review available as quickly as possible to physicians who have the responsibility to prescribe drugs in a safe manner to their patients. I discussed this time concern with the editor of the journal that published my article. He agreed that the time it would take for my study to undergo peer review, usually about six months, would keep this information from physicians for an unacceptable amount of time and it would be likely that more people would be hurt. Also, this type of review is generally not subject to peer review. I will freely acknowledge that I probably should have been more careful in calling my paper 'research,' when it was just an extensive review of many peer-reviewed papers. I apologize to the jury...and to Mr. Hempstead for his apparent confusion."

Gary looked at the judge. "That completes my questions, Your Honor."

Katie felt like standing up and applauding. What an awesome rebuttal. She hoped the jury understood the importance of Patel's testimony.

Green looked at the jury. "That's enough for today. We'll start at 9 a.m. tomorrow. Please be here in the jury room fifteen minutes early. Do not talk with anyone about this trial. Do not read any articles that may appear in the news or watch any news shows that discuss this case. Have a good evening."

Hempstead approached Gary after the jury filed out. "Could you consider calling Lion tomorrow so he doesn't have to sit around all week?"

Gary nodded. "That'll be Katie's call. I'll talk to her and let you know."

TOM BLEAKLEY

Chapter 42
October 2012

Katie had a lot of questions about how she was going to approach Richard's cross-examination. She needed time to think about how she was going to proceed and she needed time to talk with Gary about her intended approach. She was unwilling to give up her preparation time just to accommodate the asshole.

Gary called Hempstead and told him that they would not call Lion the next day. Katie was relieved because her time tonight was limited, and she and Gary both had a busy day ahead of them. Jan Emrich was coming into the office tonight for her trial preparation and Katie was going to present her testimony tomorrow. Gary was also going to present Alex Hartley. If there was sufficient time during trial tomorrow, Katie also planned on reading some of Dr. Barrett's testimony. At some point, she would also read the other Singh brother's deposition.

Then, there was Mark Stenson. Katie sat in Gary's office and they discussed Stenson. Gary said, "I'm ready for him. What do you think we should do about the timing? When should we call him to the stand?"

"I've been thinking. I think he needs to go on before Jan testifies."

Gary shook his head. "I disagree. The element of surprise is so important in how we do this. Let me explain…"

As Katie walked back to her office, she thought about Gary's idea. He was right. A trial was like putting pieces of a puzzle together. Not only did all the pieces need to fit together, they had to be introduced at the right time.

# # #

Katie had just finished her preparation of Emrich. Leslie popped into her office. "Katie, I'm going downstairs for a drink. Join me?"

"I need an hour. Can you wait?"

"I'm going now. I'll wait for you down there."

"While you're waiting, Leslie, can you think of any other ideas as to how you think I should handle Richard?"

"That's simple. You should hit the son of a bitch over the head with a sledgehammer." They both laughed. "But I'll think about it for real while I'm waiting. See you later, girlfriend."

Katie sat in her office and looked at the stack of papers on her desk. She had thirty-nine exhibits lined up for questioning Richard. She'd culled those thirty-nine from the two hundred or so she'd discovered and copied from his briefcase at the hotel. There was one particular letter than Lion had written to Timothy Holt that brought tears to her eyes every time she'd read it. She'd been too embarrassed to show the letter to Gary or even Leslie. She removed the letter from the pile and looked at it again. The part that bothered her most and invoked a terrible feeling of shame and angst said, "Katie likes to drink and she likes sex. And she likes to drink and have sex. The more she drinks the more sex she likes to have. She is particularly adept at…"

Throughout the trial, she'd noted that Holt stared at her with a look that made her uncomfortable. Now she knew why. She felt ashamed, sad, and angry. She wondered how many people other than Holt and Lion had seen this document. The other Singh brother? Hempstead? Rebus? Was her sex life a subject of discussion at defense trial planning sessions? At the water fountain in Hempstead's office? She was diminished, humiliated, and embarrassed. Leslie was right. Richard deserved to be hit over the head with a hammer. What kind of man would do something like this to another human being? She sat and cried for a few minutes. Would she ever be able to trust any man again?

She dried her eyes, composed herself, and finished writing her list of questions for Emrich and headed down to the bar.

Leslie smiled when Katie approached her at the bar. Katie ordered a beer, handed Leslie Richard's letter, and sat back. "I need to get this into evidence. I'm so embarrassed to show this to you but I really need your advice."

Leslie's eyes teared up as she read the letter. Then she looked up at Katie. "Big fucking deal. Okay, so you like to drink and have sex. Name me one person who doesn't? That's no big deal. But the problem for you, Katie, is that there's a double standard in how women are treated in situations like this. You've got a long career ahead of you. You have to protect yourself and your reputation, or else you'll never hear the end of it. You have no choice but to keep this out of evidence or you'll be known forever in this legal community as a slut. It's unfair as hell, and it wouldn't happen if you were a guy, but that's the reality. Do you really need it to be in evidence?"

"I need part of the letter in evidence. Not the sex part but another part."

"There must be a way." Leslie paused. "Have you heard about

redacting?'"

"I know what redacted means. How would that work here?"

Leslie explained. She nodded at Katie. "You haven't touched your beer."

"Leslie, you mesmerize me with your brilliance. You should be a lawyer. I'm going to talk to Gary and tell him that he should send you to law school. I've got to go back upstairs and put this all together. You understand and see things that most people miss." She stood and gathered her notes.

Leslie grinned. "Thanks honey. Go."

# # #

The next morning, the jury was seated. Judge Green took the bench, and looked at Katie. "Ready to call your next witness?"

"Yes, Your Honor. Plaintiffs call Dr. Janet Emrich."

Emrich stood and walked to the front. Stella administered the oath and she settled into the witness chair.

"Good morning, Dr. Emrich. Would you state your full name and occupation for the court and jury?"

"My name is Janet Emrich. I have a doctorate degree in pharmacology and I teach pharmacology at the Wayne State University School of Medicine. I am also an adjunct professor of pharmacology at both the Medical College of Ohio and the University of Michigan medical schools."

"What is pharmacology?"

"Pharmacology, most simply, is the science of drugs."

Gary sat and watched the interaction between the two women. At the same time, he cast glances over at the three male jurors who'd found Katie so interesting. All three were seated on the edge of their chairs. Their eyes moved back and forth between Katie and Jan as Katie asked questions about Emrich's education and training. Gary smiled to himself. The two women had the jury's attention. They hung on every word.

"Can you tell us your employment background?"

"Yes. Just after I completed my doctorate training in pharmacology, I was hired by the Food and Drug Administration."

"What did you do at the FDA?

"I was a drug monitor for seven different drugs."

"What does a drug monitor do?"

"I had the responsibility to continuously monitor information from a variety of sources regarding the safety of the drugs I was assigned."

Katie raised her voice. "What sources provide safety information?"

"First, and foremost, the drug manufacturer receives information about its drugs from patients, doctors, and medical researchers. Another major source of information is the peer-reviewed scientific or medical articles in the medical literature. A third source is patients or doctors who contact the FDA directly. I should also state that it is the responsibility of the drug manufacturer to collate and send any information about adverse reactions it receives to the FDA. I would prepare a monthly report from all these sources and indicate in any particular situation if I thought a problem was developing with a given drug. The monthly report was part of an ongoing assessment of every drug in determining whether some type of regulatory action was necessary to assure that the drug was as safe as possible for the public."

"You said that the drug manufacturer had the responsibility to report any negative information about its drug to the FDA. What happens if the drug manufacturer receives such information but doesn't send it along to the FDA?

"Before I answer that, can I give some background?"

Katie nodded.

Emrich looked at the jury. Part of her preparation last night had been to remind her of the need to establish eye contact with each of the jurors. "All drugs have problems that can occur in users. There are two things that must be considered when a doctor prescribes a drug. The first is whether or not the drug is effective for the condition it is going to be prescribed and the second is whether there are any risks associated with the taking of the drug. This is known as the benefit versus risk ratio. Both the patient and the doctor must be fully aware of the benefits and the risks that might result from the use of a drug."

Emrich smiled at each juror and nodded. They nodded back.

Emrich continued. "Now to answer your question, when a drug manufacturer fails to notify the FDA about adverse reactions, neither the FDA, the doctor, or the patient has sufficient information to assess the benefit-risk ratio of that drug. That means it is impossible for the drug to be used safely. This, by the way, is a major problem in the U.S. In most countries of the world, physicians are required to report adverse reactions to both the drug manufacturer and the regulatory agency of the country. In the U.S., reporting of adverse reactions by physicians is voluntary rather than mandatory so many incidents are not reported in the first place. This underreporting is one reason why it is all the more important to report what a manufacturer does receive."

Katie stepped toward the witness stand. "At my request, did you review documents at FDA headquarters on generic Lorital?"

"Yes."

"Did you review all of the documents in the possession of the FDA that pertained to generic Lorital?"

"Yes. I took a trip to Washington and my former colleagues put out everything they had from the manufacturer."

"Were adverse-reaction reports contained in the materials you reviewed at the FDA?"

"There was not a single adverse-reaction report sent by the manufacturer to the FDA on generic Lorital. If the FDA had received any, I would have seen them during my visit."

Katie raised her voice again. "Not a single one?" She looked at the jury to assess whether or not they were getting this. All of them appeared attentive.

"Not a single one."

"Are drug manufacturers required by federal law to provide all adverse reactions to the FDA?"

Emrich looked at the jury, smiled slightly. Gary noted that the three male jurors smiled back, as did several female jurors.

"Yes."

"Did you also review documents in the possession of Enpact, the manufacturer of generic Lorital, in your overall review?"

"Yes."

"Were there adverse-reaction reports in the Enpact documents?"

"Yes. There were a substantial number of adverse reports that described heart attacks or strokes occurring in users of the generic form of Lorital."

"Would knowledge about this significant number of adverse reports of heart attacks and strokes be an important piece of prescribing information for a physician to have in making an intelligent benefit versus risk evaluation in deciding to prescribe generic Lorital to a patient?

"Yes. I should also mention that I examined the labeling of generic Lorital. There was no mention whatsoever of any of the possible adverse reactions they'd received from users and doctors. There was no way a physician or a patient could make a benefit-risk assessment without knowing this information."

"Do you have an opinion based on your training and education in pharmacology, your work at the FDA, and your subsequent teaching of pharmacology at three medical schools, whether or not the generic Lorital manufactured and sold by Enpact was unreasonably dangerous and increased the risk of heart attacks and strokes in the users of the product?"

"Objection, Your Honor." Hempstead's voice startled everyone in the courtroom. "I object on the basis that this question is well beyond the guidelines set forth by the court in establishing the issues in this trial."

Green shook his head. "Objection overruled. Please answer the question, doctor."

"Yes, I do have an opinion. Generic Lorital is unreasonably dangerous to users of the drug because it definitely increases the risks of suffering either a heart attack or stroke. The key to it being more dangerous is two-fold. About one-third of generic Lorital produced by Enpact contains more than twice the amount of testosterone than is stated in the package insert. The second is that there is no statement about the adverse reactions known to Enpact that will allow for a benefit-risk assessment in deciding whether the drug should be used."

"At my request, have you reviewed the medical records of both Ralph Albright and Mark Stenson for the purpose of determining the role of generic Lorital in whatever damage has been caused to them?"

"Yes, I have."

"Have you formed opinions about the role of generic Lorital in causing whatever medical injuries were suffered by Ralph Albright and Mark Stenson?"

"Yes." Emrich hesitated. "Yes."

"Let's take your opinions one at a time. Dr. Emrich, what is your opinion about the role of generic Lorital in causing the death of Ralph Albright?

"It is my professional opinion that generic Lorital caused the death of Ralph Albright, within reasonable scientific certainty. Mr. Albright was fifty-seven years old when he died and had one well-documented heart attack five years prior to his death. Well-controlled peer-reviewed studies have shown that testosterone given to men under the age of sixty-five with a history of cardiovascular disease create a significantly greater risk of experiencing either a heart attack or stroke. I understand that the jury has already heard the testimony of Dr. Patel about his work comparing generic Lorital with the trade name Lorital. From that work it is known that more than one-third of all generic Lorital sold in the U.S. contains three times greater the dosage of testosterone than is actually intended to be used. A dangerous situation, indeed. It is well known that there is a direct correlation between the amount of testosterone taken and the incidence of adverse effects. The higher the dose, the greater the risk of harm."

Katie paused and looked over her notes carefully. "Let's talk about the plaintiff Mark Stenson. Did you review his medical records?"

"Yes. I reviewed several medical records that were stated to be those of Mr. Stenson."

"Before we get to those records, did you do anything else in preparing for your testimony regarding Mark Stenson?"

"Yes, I did."

"Can you tell the court and jury what else you did in relation to the claim of Mark Stenson and his claim that generic Lorital caused him to suffer a heart attack?"

"Yes. Shortly after my first thorough review of Mr. Stenson's records, I contacted several of the physicians who purportedly treated him and whose names appeared in his records. Additionally, I arranged for a former investigator from the FDA to make inquiries about two of the medical hospitalizations contained within the records of Mr. Stenson."

"Did you arrive at any conclusions from those activities?"

"Yes. The FDA investigator reported back to me that the records containing Mr. Stenson's name were not, in fact, about Mr. Stenson, but were instead that of another patient who had participated in a drug trial conducted by Orex Laboratories on both generic and trade-name Lorital."

Hempstead was on his feet. "Objection. Your Honor, can we approach the bench?"

Judge Green waved the lawyers to the side bar. When everyone was in place, Green said. "What is your objection, Mr. Hempstead?"

"Judge, I wanted to discuss this out of the presence of the jury. Mr. Newton's office provided us with Mr. Stenson's medical records and this is the first time I've heard from him or Ms. Hornsby that they are not actually his records. Before we proceed any further with direct examination, I'd like to conduct a voir dire of the witness as to whose records these are."

Green looked at Katie. "Your response?"

Gary stood and put his hand on Katie's shoulder. "Let me handle this." He looked at Green. "Judge. Rather than stand here and argue, I request that you allow us to present some additional evidence that will answer Mr. Hempstead's objection. There is a witness in the hallway we'd like to have testify right now who can provide a thorough explanation of why these records happen to be at issue now. Knowing Mr. Hempstead as I do, I'm certain that he doesn't know some facts about our client, Mr. Stenson. For tactical reasons, I don't want to say in advance what we intend to present to the jury. I can assure you, however, that what will be presented will deal squarely with the objection Mr. Hempstead has raised and will save court time in the process."

Hempstead thought for a moment. "This is highly irregular and improper. What I hear Mr. Newton admit is that Ms. Hornsby has failed to lay a proper foundation for Dr. Emrich's testimony. Without a proper foundation, her testimony is inadmissible and should be stricken from the record. The jury should be instructed to disregard the testimony."

Gary shook his head. "Judge, that's nonsense and Mr. Hempstead knows it. Experts testify all the time before a foundation for the rendering of opinions has been admitted into evidence. The control of the timing of admissible evidence is solely within your discretion. The information that the waiting witness will present is important evidence that if presented now will facilitate the jury's understanding of Dr. Emrich's opinions...and will provide the appropriate response to counsel's objection."

Green's face conveyed his obvious confusion. He sat silent for a long moment. "I'm going to permit the witness to testify now on the express assurance by Mr. Newton that the testimony will be limited to the scope of Mr. Hempstead's objection."

The lawyers returned to their respective tables. Green looked toward the jury. "We're going to interrupt Dr. Emrich's testimony and hear from another witness. Dr. Emrich, please step down." He nodded at Katie. "Go ahead. Call your witness."

Katie turned to the back of the room and nodded. A slight balding man with a neatly trimmed beard stood and walked forward. Stella administered the oath and the man took the witness stand.

Katie addressed the witness. "Sir, please state your name."

"My name is Earl Freidberg."

"Will you tell the court and jury what you do professionally?"

"Yes. For twenty-five years I worked as an investigator for the FDA. My work there called for me to investigate incidents that occurred from time to time that involved fraudulent claims made by those conducting research for pharmaceutical houses. The thrust of my efforts involved evaluating compliance with regulations pertaining to the Food Drug and Cosmetic Act, which is the law of the land insofar as the regulation of drugs in the U.S. is concerned. I performed detailed analyses of medical records of research subjects and in-house unpublished research conducted by pharmaceutical companies. Three years ago, I left the FDA voluntarily and started my own business doing the very same thing on a contract basis for drug companies."

Katie looked at the jury. They were playing close attention.

"Mr. Freidberg, did you work with Dr. Janet Emrich while you were at the FDA?"

"Yes. Dr. Emrich and I worked together several times on issues pertaining to the safety of several drugs on the market in the U.S."

"Did Dr. Emrich contact you with regard to certain medical records pertaining to a Mark Stenson?"

"Yes. She provided me with a large package of medical records purporting to be of a patient named Mark Stenson who claimed to have suffered a heart attack from the taking of generic Lorital."

Stenson leaned over and whispered to Gary. "I have to use the bathroom. I'll be right back." He stood and walked quickly out of the courtroom.

Katie continued. "What did Dr. Emrich ask that you do with these records?"

"She came to my office in Grand Rapids, Michigan, and told me that she'd been retained as an expert witness on behalf of the plaintiffs in this litigation. She told me that she had serious doubts about the validity of the records that were provided to her about Mark Stenson."

Katie turned and looked over at the plaintiffs' table. Stenson's chair was empty. Her mind went blank. Where is he? Where did he go? She fought to regain her composure. She turned back to Freidberg. "Did…did you review and conduct an investigation of the records on your own?"

"Yes. I did."

"Did...did you reach any conclusions about Dr. Emrich's concerns about the Stenson records?"

"Yes. I conducted a thorough investigation of the records in the same manner as I did when I was at the FDA. I concluded that Mr. Stenson's records were fake. During my investigation, I found that two physicians who prepared most of these records had done other work previously for another company that currently markets the brand name Lorital. I had several encounters with both of these men when I was at the FDA and these involved serious breaches of federal regulations. Quite frankly, I was surprised that they were still involved in research projects for drug companies. I assumed they'd been banned by the FDA from this kind of work. I confronted both of them with my findings on the Stenson records and both admitted they had constructed the records to make it appear that Mr. Stenson had suffered a major heart attack from taking generic Lorital. They both also admitted that the request to do so had come from a representative of the company that makes brand-name Lorital, a company by the name of Orex."

A collective murmur from the audience in the packed courtroom became increasingly louder. Judge Green pounded his gavel. The room became silent. "Another outbreak and I'll clear this courtroom."

Katie looked over the jury. They were on the edge of their seats. She looked back at the plaintiff's table. She stepped over to Gary and whispered. "Where's Stenson?"

Gary whispered back. "He's gone to the bathroom."

She turned to Freidberg. "Did you prepare a written report of your investigation and conclusions?"

"Yes. I did."

"Your Honor. At this time I offer Exhibit 38 into evidence." Katie distributed copies to Stella and Hempstead. Stella passed the copy to Judge Green.

Green examined the document and looked up. "Exhibit 38 is admitted."

Katie faced Freidberg. "That completes plaintiff's presentation of Mr. Freidberg. Thank you, sir."

Green leaned toward Hempstead and frowned. "Do you have any questions, counsel?"

Hempstead stood. He looked shaken. He was at a loss for words. "If I may have a moment, Your Honor. Perhaps the jury could take a break?" He looked over at Holt whose face was beet-red.

TOM BLEAKLEY

Chapter 43
October 2012

Stenson was nowhere to be found. Gary went into the men's room on the floors below and above the tenth floor. When the break was over, the jury returned to the jury box and Freidberg to the witness stand. Gary approached the bench with Hempstead and Holt. "Judge, Mr. Stenson is missing. He left the courtroom during the testimony of the last witness and said he was going to the bathroom. We've searched on several floors for him. He's gone."

Green was perplexed. "Your client has a right to be present during this trial. Are you willing to waive that right and continue?"

Gary responded. "Judge, with all due respect, I think it is clear that Mr. Stenson is no longer a viable plaintiff in this litigation, given what we've just heard from Mr. Freidberg."

"So what do you want me to do? Declare a mistrial?"

"No, Your Honor. That would be a tremendous injustice to Sharon Albright. Maybe…" Gary had a glint in his eye. "Maybe Stenson could be considered a defendant." Gary and Katie were the only ones who smiled.

Holt sputtered and Hempstead replied. "Mr. Newton's suggestion is preposterous. We do agree, however, that a mistrial is not necessary. I'll have no questions for the witness. Why don't we just proceed for the time being? This is an unusual situation and we need time to think about it. I'm certain that Mr. Newton and I can work out an appropriate explanation for you to make to the jury. I'm sure they're as confused as we are."

Green looked at Newton. "What's your response?"

"I have no problem with Mr. Hempstead's suggestion just to move this case forward. I do think at some point, however, that all of us are going to have to deal with the Stenson issue. We can't pretend that he never existed...or that the records weren't falsified." Gary turned and gave Holt a harsh look and added, "Or that someone in this courtroom isn't responsible for this charade."

Green sat back. "Let's get going. I'm not going to say anything to the jury right now. Half of the jury, maybe all the jury, may not have noticed that he's not here. Without knowing why he's gone or where he is, flagging his absence for the jury might be a mistake."

Back in the courtroom, Green spoke to the jury. "We're going to resume trial right now. Mr. Hempstead has elected not to cross examine Mr. Freidberg so he will be excused and Dr. Emrich will come back to the witness stand."

As Emrich passed Freidberg on her way to the witness stand they exchanged nods and slight grins.

Green learned toward Emrich after she was seated. "Doctor, you are still under oath. Ms. Hornsby will continue with your questions."

Emrich smiled at him. "Thank you, Your Honor."

Katie walked to the podium. "Dr. Emrich, we were discussing your evaluation of medical records prior to Mr. Friedberg's testimony. In connection with your review of the Albright records, what other data did you use in arriving at your conclusion that generic Lorital caused Ralph Albright's death?"

Emrich thought for a moment. "I relied on the current medical literature, Dr. Patel's research, my own training, education, and experience in the field of pharmacology, Dr. Barrett's deposition testimony, data you provided me from the FDA, and documents from Enpact."

"Let's switch topics for a moment. Do you have an opinion as to whether or not Enpact's selling and distributing generic Lorital to users in the U.S., including Ralph Albright, met with acceptable standards established by the regulations and law of the U.S.?"

Emrich looked at the jury. "Yes, I have an opinion. It is my opinion that Enpact did not meet acceptable standards for a pharmaceutical company in making and selling generic Lorital in the U.S. Generic Lorital is an adulterated product in violation of the federal criminal statute known as the Food Drug and Cosmetic Act. I should point out that Michigan has a law virtually identical to the federal act and my opinion would be the same if Michigan law were to be used as a basis of my analysis, rather than the federal law." Several jurors nodded their heads in understanding.

"Thank you, Dr. Emrich. That completes my direct examination, Your Honor."

Katie turned and walked to her seat. Stenson's chair remained vacant.

Hempstead stood and walked close to the witness stand. He stared at Emrich for a moment. "I couldn't help but notice, doctor, that Ms. Hornsby didn't ask you why you left the FDA. You were fired from that agency, weren't you?"

Emrich glared at Hempstead. "I lost my job because I was a whistleblower..."

Hempstead interrupted. "So your answer is 'yes.' You were fired."

"As I stated..."

"Your Honor, could you please direct the witness to answer the question? It is capable of being answered yes or no."

Green nodded toward Emrich. "Answer the question."

Emrich nodded back, looked at the jury, and smiled. "I was fired, but..."

Hempstead said forcefully, "No buts about it. You were fired."

"If that's a question, I disagree. I was fired simply because I told the truth about the dangers of a drug and I also disclosed that my immediate boss was taking money from the company who made the drug. He had a longstanding arrangement with the medical director of the company who provided call girls for my boss whenever he went to Washington. If my exposing this information reflects incompetency, then I'll admit to being incompetent, but I don't think it does..."

The jurors were surprised by Emrich's outburst. Several looked at each other with widened eyes. Others smiled. Only one juror obviously disapproved. He sat with his arms folded. Gary made a note of his reaction.

Hempstead appeared rattled by the response. He looked at Judge Green. "Move to strike the answer as non-responsive to the question."

Green thought for a moment. "Given that the witness will likely give the same answer on redirect examination, in the interest of saving time the objection is overruled. Please ask your next question, Mr. Hempstead."

Green's ruling surprised Hempstead and it took a moment for him to gather his thoughts. "You are not a medical doctor, are you?"

Emrich smiled at the jury. "No, and I don't claim to be."

Green leaned toward her. "Just answer the questions. Avoid the commentary."

Hempstead smiled. "Thank you, Your Honor. Dr. Emrich, you don't treat patients or prescribe drugs to human beings, do you?"

"No."

"Specifically, you don't treat people suffering from heart attacks?"

"No, I don't. Nor do I treat people suffering from strokes." Emrich smiled at the jury.

Most of the jurors, Katie noted, enjoyed Emrich's tart responses.

"You have never made a benefit versus risk assessment on a patient, have you?"

"I conduct rounds at the medical center with students, interns, and residents almost every day and I discuss benefit versus risk assessment on individual patients with the entire group. But I cannot make the decisions legally to prescribe drugs based on my benefit versus risk assessments."

"In forming your opinions, did you say you relied, in part, on the published writings of Dr. Patel as a basis for drawing your conclusions?"

"Yes."

"Would that include the non-peer-reviewed article that he's written?"

"I am under the assumption that everything Dr. Patel has written about the dangers of generic Lorital has been peer-reviewed."

Hempstead's smile said it all, Katie thought. He concluded, "That's what I thought. Thanks for your time, Dr. Emrich. That concludes the cross-examination."

Green looked up. "Any redirect counsel?"

"Yes, Your Honor." Katie stood and approached Emrich, unsure of how to phrase the question. As it stood right now, she and Gary faced the possibility of Judge Green's striking the testimony on causation of both Patel and Emrich if he accepted the already-conceded point that both witnesses had made about requiring peer-reviewed scientific evidence as a condition of giving an opinion on causation. From the looks of concern on the faces of several jurors, they understood exactly the dilemma Katie faced.

"Dr. Emrich, if you were to find out that one of Dr. Patel's publications in which he summarized the peer-reviewed available scientific evidence on the dangers of generic Lorital was, in fact, not peer-reviewed, would that change or modify the opinions you have expressed here today?"

Emrich appeared unfazed by the question. She answered without hesitation. "Not at all. Not at all. When a researcher reviews the works of other scientists and draws conclusions based on their peer-reviewed studies, it is perfectly acceptable to publish an article that is not peer-reviewed."

"And why is that?"

"The process of peer review is time-consuming. Peer review involves submitting a paper to at least two other scientists of standing in the appropriate scientific community. These independent scientists assess both the quality and validity of the paper being considered and it is a process that takes time, often up to a year. If there is reliable scientific data that has already been peer-reviewed that indicates a potential or real danger to takers of a drug, the quickest and most efficient way to spread that information is to summarize it and have the summary published as quickly as possible without the necessity for further peer review. Lives can be saved if information regarding harm is disclosed earlier. The earlier the better."

Whew, that was a close one. Katie checked her notes. "That's all I have. May Dr. Emrich be excused, Your Honor?"

Green looked at Hempstead. "Any follow-up, Mr. Hempstead?"

Hempstead shook his head. Green said, "The witness is excused. Let's take a short break."

As the jury filed out, Gary whispered to Katie. "You were fabulous. Katie. I have a problem, though. Hartley just texted me that he can't make it this afternoon. A sudden emergency came up. He's not available until tomorrow. Can we call Singh now? Are you ready?"

She nodded.

Gary walked over to Hempstead. "We'll call Singh next. Can't have him waiting around too long. His wife and four children might miss him too much."

Hempstead shrugged his shoulders and said nothing.

# # #

Mark Stenson was surprised no one had tried to stop him when he walked out of the courtroom. Listening to the man with the German name testify about his falsified records, he realized he had to get out of there fast or he'd wind up in jail. He walked directly to the bank of elevators and pushed the button. He didn't notice the man who followed him out of the courtroom. The good-looking man stood alongside him until the elevator door opened and they descended to the ground floor together. Stenson was preoccupied with his thoughts and tried to think what he should do next. The disclosure of the false records didn't happen the way it had been planned. It was supposed to have been the Enpact lawyer who exposed the records, not his lawyers. Holt had told him that Hornsby was going to take the fall for trying to get forged records into evidence. All he was going to have to say was that he'd known nothing about it. He'd practiced his story so many times that he'd almost started to believe it. Now, he had to get as far away as possible and wait until things cooled down. He'd stop by his house and retrieve some of the hidden cash and simply disappear for a couple of months. He'd tell his wife he was going to take a break from their marriage. She'd probably welcome the idea. All they'd done the past several weeks was argue and bicker. He didn't notice that the man trailed behind him to the third floor of the parking structure where Stenson had parked his car.

Stenson opened the door and got into the vehicle. He was startled by the looming presence of the man forcibly holding the door open. He opened his mouth to say something but the bullet that tore through his brain stilled his voice and life instantly. Plimpf looked around. The area was deserted except for the two of them. He removed the silencer from the weapon and placed it in his coat pocket. Stenson had to be dealt with, he thought. Other than Holt, he was the only one who could clearly tie Orex to the fake medical records. Holt could always claim lawyer-client privilege but Stenson could be forced to testify. This was a necessary precaution. He'd be forced out of Orex if his role came out. He spent several moments arranging the scene. He placed the weapon in Stenson's left hand, curled the dead man's fingers around the grip. He retrieved a slip of paper from his wallet and placed it in the glove box. He stood back and studied his handiwork. Everything was in place. It would be assumed that Stenson was distraught because of the revelation his medical records were phony. In a fit of anguish and despair, he'd fled the courtroom and killed himself. Plimpf had purchased the weapon in Stenson's name three days earlier, and the receipt was now in the glove box. He knew that Stenson was left-handed and he'd placed the weapon in that hand to correspond with the placement of the fatal wound in the left temporal area of his brain. He removed his latex gloves and walked away.

# # #

After the break, the jury was seated and Green took the bench. "Call your next witness, Mr. Newton."

Katie stood. "The plaintiffs call Richard Lion, also known as Anugrah Singh under the adverse-witness statute." Katie knew that under Michigan law, a party calling a witness from the opposing side was entitled to cross-examine the witness, rather than be limited to a direct-examination format. It was necessary to invoke the adverse- witness statute to do so. The advantage of cross-examination, Katie knew, was that she could ask leading questions that suggested answers and limit the witness to responses that either agreed or disagreed with her suggested answers. She had prepared her questions for Singh based upon her intention to do so.

Rebus left the courtroom and retrieved Singh. He came forward, was administered the oath, and took the seat in the witness box.

Katie's hands shook. She took a deep breath and began. "What name would you prefer to be called by in this courtroom?"

Singh smirked. "Richard Lion will do just fine."

"You executed and signed an affidavit after you were subpoenaed to testify in this case, did you not?"

"I don't remember."

"The purpose of this affidavit was to try to prevent you from being called as a witness, to avoid having to testify in front of this jury, wasn't it?"

Singh smirked again. "If I don't remember this affidavit, how could I possibly know what its purpose is?" He smiled at the jury.

Katie restrained a sudden impulse to call him a smug, lying son of a bitch. Slow down, girl, she warned herself. She took a deep breath.

"Let me refresh your memory. Exhibit 2 is a copy of an affidavit filed by your lawyers in which you claim to be a resident of India. Is that correct?"

"Whatever you say."

"Let me read from Exhibit 2. 'I am a resident of the city of New Delhi in India.'" Katie walked up to Singh and handed him the document. "Look at the lines that have been highlighted and tell the jury whether I have read that correctly."

Singh smirked. "Yes. You read very well."

"Now look at the bottom of Exhibit 2 and tell the jury whether or not that is your signature administered under oath on a document filed with this court."

"Yes, that's my signature. I don't remember taking an oath when I signed it. Nor do I know if it is a document filed with the court." He looked over at the jury and smirked again. Most of the jurors sat with their arms folded.

"Exhibit 2 is offered into evidence at this time, Your Honor. I request that the court take judicial notice that it is a document, in fact, filed in these proceedings and purports to be an affidavit signed under oath by Mr. Singh or Mr. Lion…whatever his real name is."

Green nodded. "The exhibit is admitted and the court takes judicial notice that it is part of the court record submitted by the defendant. It is admitted for use by the jury for any purpose."

Katie thought for a moment. "Your Honor, at this time I request an instruction from the court to the jury on what judicial notice means."

Green paused. "The jury is instructed that the document is exactly what Ms. Hornsby represented it to be in her examination of the witness."

Katie stepped close to the witness stand. "You and your brother founded Enpact?"

"Yes."

"And the two of you are the co-owners of Enpact?"

Lion hesitated and looked over at Holt. "That's privileged information. I cannot answer that."

"Privileged information? Let me show you Exhibit 3 and have you read to the jury the portion that is highlighted on the first page of the exhibit."

Katie handed the document to Lion. He looked at it briefly. "I don't see where you want me to read from."

Katie grabbed the document away from him. "I'll read it for you." For the record, Exhibit 3 is an Enpact advertising brochure that was distributed to every doctor and pharmacy in the U.S. She read from the first page. "Enpact is owned jointly by Anugrah and Videda Singh and the two brothers founded the company on February 10, 2001." She pointed out the language to Lion. "Have I read that correctly?"

"Yes, you read very well." He sneered.

Katie paused. "Is the New Jersey home where you live with your wife and four children in the country of India?"

Hempstead jumped to his feet. "Now she's getting ridiculous with her questions, Your Honor."

"I'll withdraw the question, Your Honor." Katie said quickly. She looked at the jurors, who appeared to be enjoying the show. The three male jurors exchanged amused glances.

"You have four children and a wife in your home in New Jersey, is that correct?"

"Yes."

"It's true that your immediate family uses the surname Singh in their everyday living? Your children use the last name 'Singh' in school and your wife uses the last name 'Singh' on her personal checking account? Is that correct?"

"Yes, that's correct."

"Under the name 'Singh' you and your brother created and own the drug company Enpact. Is that right?"

"That is correct. I thought I answered that already." Singh maintained his smirk.

"You are a current employee of Enpact, is that right?"

"I am retained by Enpact on a contract basis."

"What are your responsibilities on behalf of Enpact? What type of work have you contracted with Enpact for you to perform?"

"I lobby for Enpact in Washington D.C. with regard for the products that are sold in the U.S."

"Do you have any scientific training whatsoever in the field of medicine or pharmacology?"

"No. My education is in the area of economics and business management."

Katie looked at the jury and took a deep breath. Here we go, she thought. In the next few minutes, she was going to put her professional career on the line. It was a risk she had to take because it was the right thing to do.

"Is spying on lawyers who bring lawsuits against Enpact part of your contractual responsibilities with that company?"

Singh sat up, looked at Hempstead and Holt, and then at the judge. "I'm not sure what she is asking," he said.

"Let me break it down for you then. Do you understand what spying is?" Katie glanced at the jury. They were listening closely.

"Spying? Do you mean like wiretapping or intercepting email, things like that?"

"Let me clarify your confusion. I mean the word 'spying' exactly as you would use that word if you, for example, wrote a letter to someone telling them about your spying activity on behalf of Enpact?"

Hempstead jumped to his feet. "Objection, Your Honor. This line of questioning has gone far afield. It's been interesting listening to counsel prattle on and on about something totally unrelated to this lawsuit, about something that might appear in a spy novel."

Green rubbed his chin. "I assume, Ms. Hornsby, that you intend to relate this line of questioning to the current lawsuit?"

"Yes, Your Honor. I have just a few additional questions that will tie it to this case."

"Go ahead. Proceed."

Katie nodded to Gary who retrieved an easel with several large posters from a corner of the room and set it up in front of the jury.

Katie turned the first poster over and read it to the jury. They could also read directly from the poster. "I am particularly enjoying my spying on Ms. Hornsby as per my contractual obligation for Enpact." She looked at Singh who had a puzzled expression. "Let me ask you first, Mr. Lion also known as Mr. Singh, have I read that statement that appears on the poster in front of the jury correctly?"

He smirked again. "Yes. As I said earlier, you are a very good reader."

Several jurors shifted in their seats.

His smugness rankled Katie but she now knew for certain that he had no idea about what was going to happen. "Do you remember making that statement in a letter you wrote to Timothy Holt, the gentleman seated over there next to Mr. Hempstead?" Katie pointed at Holt.

"I don't remember any such statement or letter."

"Your Honor, we have pre-marked Exhibits 4 and 4A. Exhibit 4A is a redacted copy of Exhibit 4. At this time I request that Exhibit 4A be admitted into evidence." She walked over to Hempstead's table and handed a copy of the redacted exhibit to him. She took another copy, along with the unredacted version, to Stella who handed both documents to the judge. She took a third unredacted copy and walked to the witness stand. She hesitated for a moment and decided to withhold the exhibit from Singh until the predictable objection was resolved.

"Any objections, Mr. Hempstead?"

"If I may have a moment to speak with Mr. Holt, Your Honor?"

Green nodded. Hempstead handed the exhibit to Holt who shook his head after he read it. He leaned over to Hempstead and whispered something.

Hempstead stood. "We have a matter we would like to take up out of the presence of the jury."

Green waved the lawyers to the sidebar.

Hempstead whispered. "There must be some mistake, Your Honor. This letter is addressed to Mr. Holt who has just read it and he says he has never seen it before."

Katie spoke. "Your Honor, it may be appropriate at this time for the court to read the unredacted letter in its entirety. I've given you two separate documents, Exhibits 4 and 4A: the entire letter and a redacted version. For sake of the record, I will describe proposed exhibit 4. It is a letter from the witness to Timothy Holt, who sits at counsel table as the designated representative of Enpact, and addressed to him at his position as general counsel of Orex Pharmaceuticals in Brunswick, New Jersey. I direct the attention of the court to the specific language of exhibit 4 in this letter, which is the same language on the blown up poster, displayed in front of the jury. The statement reads, 'I am particularly enjoying my spying on Ms. Hornsby as per my contractual obligation for Enpact.' That is the only language, other than the mention of Mr. Holt's apparent other place of employment, that I intend to use during my cross examination of Mr. Singh, or whatever his name is. Exhibit 4A, the redacted copy of exhibit 4 for the jury contains only the name and address of Mr. Holt, the statement just read, and the signature of the witness. Everything else on the document has been covered up by writing over the words with black ink, rendering the remainder of the document totally illegible. My position is that any other portion of the document is irrelevant, prejudicial, and inadmissible."

Green read the unredacted document. His face reddened. When he finished, he looked up. "Do you have anything more to say, Ms. Hornsby?"

Katie looked directly into Green's eyes as she spoke. Tears began to stream down her face. Her hands shook uncontrollably and she didn't know what to do with them, where to put them. "Yes. I have a dilemma. I'm fighting a double standard. This is always awkward for a woman."

Gary placed his hand on her elbow to steady her. He handed her his handkerchief and she used it to dab her eyes. She took a deep breath. "Teenage girls and young women face this kind of thing all the time. As an example, when someone takes a risqué photo of a boy and a girl at a party and posts it on Facebook or Twitter, the girl is called a slut. There's no equivalent word that will destroy the boy's reputation for doing the same exact thing. Once the label is attached to the girl, her life is never the same. There are any numbers of instances throughout the country that have led girls in similar situations to commit suicide. This is the situation we have here. I'm risking my professional career here by trying to do the right thing, to bring truth into your courtroom." Katie glanced over at Holt who stood there smirking. That bastard was enjoying this. "Anyone who has teenage daughters would understand my dilemma. I'll have no choice but to withdraw the document if you allow the full document into evidence because I have no intention of committing...professional suicide. The problem with that alternative is that the plaintiff will be deprived of her right to present the truth about generic Lorital to the jury."

Green broke eye contact and shifted uncomfortably in his chair. A sober cast came into his eye. He looked at Hempstead. "Do you have anything further, Mr. Hempstead?"

"Your Honor, this is the first time I've seen this document. My client, Mr. Holt, wants me to argue that this entire document should be placed into evidence, but I won't. I'm as appalled by this as you are. Ms. Hornsby is absolutely correct about asking you to do what she suggests...Absolutely."

Holt interjected, "Your Honor, if you 'tend to admit part of this document, it should be admitted in its entirety." His face was red and he looked angrily back at Hempstead.

Green frowned. "Quite frankly, Mr. Holt,"—he looked sternly at the man— "your position offends me, as I am sure it does Ms. Hornsby...and apparently everyone else standing up here. The redacted document, Exhibit 4A, is admitted and the witness can be questioned only about the redacted portions of the letter." He paused. "I'm going to take this a step further. I am imposing a gag order on this particular document. If anyone mentions the contents of this letter, other than the sentence Ms. Hornsby offers into evidence, a contempt citation against that person will be entered. Furthermore, the entirety of this document will remain under seal and never be included as part of the record of this trial. At the end of this witness's testimony, all parties are ordered to immediately surrender any and all unredacted copies of the exhibit to Ms. Hornsby. Have I made myself clear, Mr. Holt?"

"Yes, Your Honor."

No one, for a moment, said anything. Green said, "We'll take a break and let Ms. Hornsby gather her thoughts." He looked at Katie. "You can use my office and take as much time as you like. Let me know when you're ready to go." He looked directly at Holt. "The rest of you just get out of here until we come back."

Katie nodded. "Judge, I'm fine. We can continue. Thank you for your kindness."

Green studied her for a moment. "I understand. Let's go back to work."

The lawyers returned to their respective tables. Katie looked around at the packed courtroom and breathed a deep sigh of relief that the entire document had not been permitted. Out of the corner of her eye, she thought she saw a familiar face seated halfway beck in the spectator section. She quickly averted her eyes and sat down. What was he doing here?

Green leaned forward. "You may continue, Ms. Hornsby."

Bless Leslie, Katie thought. This turned out exactly as she had predicted. She stood and walked closer to Singh and handed him the redacted copy of the exhibit.

"Mr. Singh, or Mr. Lion, do you remember writing a letter to Timothy Holt earlier this year in his capacity as general counsel to Orex Pharmaceuticals in Brunswick, New Jersey?"

"I don't remember writing such a letter. No." The smirk was gone.

"Let me see if I can refresh your memory. Do you remember writing the words 'I am particularly enjoying my spying on Ms. Hornsby as per my contractual obligation for Enpact' to Mr. Holt in his capacity as general counsel to Orex Pharmaceuticals?"

"No, I don't remember."

"Mr. Singh or Mr. Lion, please take a look at the signature on this letter. Is that your signature?"

"I don't think it is. I don't remember writing this letter."

"Your Honor, at this time I offer Exhibit 4A, the report, and Exhibit 5, the sworn affidavit of an expert handwriting analyst who has examined the handwriting of the witness who has verified that this is the witness's signature."

Hempstead stood. "Objection. There has been no identification of the purported handwriting analyst, nor verification of that analyst's qualifications. It is gross hearsay."

Green nodded. "I agree. The redacted document, Exhibit 4A, may be received for identification purposes only but may not be admitted until there is sufficient verification of its authenticity."

Katie took another deep breath. Well, here goes nothing. "Mr. Singh also known as Mr. Lion, do you remember handing Exhibit 4 to me at your room in the Dearborn Ritz Carlton at the time you personally admitted to me that you'd been spying on me on behalf of Enpact?"

"You're lying. I've never met you before in my life and I've never seen this document." He gestured toward the exhibit.

Katie was surprised by his evasiveness, but his answer was not unexpected. "I'd like to have you look at proposed Exhibit 6 for a minute and, after you're done, tell the court and the jury whether or not you wish to change your answer to the question you just made." She handed Singh a photograph of the two of them seated at dinner in the Navy Club, and then distributed copies to Hempstead and the court. "Do you recognize anybody in Exhibit 6?"

"Yes."

"Would you tell the court and the jury who the two people sitting side by side in the photograph are?"

"One is me and the other may be you."

"May be? Think again. Remember, you're under oath."

Singh hesitated. Katie took the opportunity to quickly scan the audience again. He was still there. She hadn't imagined it.

Singh looked up. "It's you."

"Now, let's go back a few questions and revisit your answers. I remember you gave the following answer to one of my questions: 'You're lying. I've never met you before in my life and I've never seen this document.' Do you remember making that answer?"

"I don't remember."

Katie was frustrated at how difficult it was to pry this out of him. "Your Honor, could we have the court reporter go back about five or six questions ago and find the answer that the witness gave?"

The judge nodded and the court reporter began her search. She indicated to the judge that she'd found the place.

Katie said, "Would you please read the answer?"

The reporter cleared her throat and read from her notes. "You're lying. I've never met you before in my life and I've never seen this document."

"Do you believe in telling the truth? In giving your answer, please keep in mind that you are under oath."

"Yes."

The court reporter looked up. "Should I read further?"

Katie shook her head, turned to the witness, and resumed her questioning. "What did you tell your wife about meeting a young woman lawyer in a bar in Washington D.C. and inviting her to have dinner with you the next night at the Navy Club? Did you send her a copy of this photograph, Exhibit 6?"

"No."

Katie checked her notes. Gary had given her some simple advice in helping her get ready for this difficult cross-examination. "Quit while you're ahead," he'd told her.

She looked once more at Singh. "That completes my questions."

Hempstead stood quickly. "We'd like to meet in chambers, Your Honor."

The judge excused the jury and the group of lawyers filed into his chambers and took seats on opposite sides of the conference table. The judge sat at the end of the table. "What's on your mind, Mr. Hempstead?"

Hempstead was subdued. "Mr. Holt will address that." He nodded toward Holt.

"Judge, I don't know what's going on here. All this stuff about a relationship that Ms. Hornsby allegedly had with one of our important witnesses. The totally unfounded revelations in court the past few minutes have the potential of being misconstrued or misunderstood if the information is made public. The potential damage to Orex, a non-party to this litigation, is such that I move to sequester all of the documents produced in the examination of the last witness. The court has already ruled that the one document should be placed under seal. Your rulin' should apply to all documents."

The judge looked at Gary. "Any thoughts, Mr. Newton?"

Gary looked at Green. "Your Honor, I'd like just a few minutes to confer with Ms. Hornsby."

Gary and Katie walked into the corridor outside of Green's courtroom. Katie said, "I've got an idea. Tell me what you think about this…"

# # #

They walked back into Green's chambers. Gary spoke. "Your Honor, we'd like you to reserve your ruling on the documents in question until we present another witness. I will represent to you that following this witness's testimony, your understanding of this pending motion will make a decision much easier."

Green nodded. "Okay. Let's go back in court and hear this witness. I will reserve ruling on the pending motion until the completion of the testimony as Mr. Newton has requested."

As the jury filed back into the courtroom, Gary leaned over and whispered in Katie's ear. "You'll do great. Just make sure you listen to his responses."

Green looked at Newton. "Call your next witness, counsel."

Katie stood. "We call Everett Plimpf, IV to the stand, Your Honor."

Everyone in the courtroom, including the jurors, turned and looked as Plimpf stood. At first he had a surprised look but soon his expression turned to one of anger and his face got redder as he moved to the front of the courtroom. He stopped in front of the bench. "Your Honor, there must be some mistake."

Holt grabbed Hempstead's arm and whispered loudly in his ear. "Ya gotta stop this. Right away."

Hempstead stood. "Judge, can we approach the bench?"

Chapter 44
October 2012

The group of lawyers huddled at the side bar and Green looked at Hempstead.

"Your Honor, this is completely unexpected. We didn't know that Mr. Plimpf was going to be called as a witness. I checked plaintiff's witness list. His name is not on the list. This is a big surprise. Mr. Plimpf is the CEO of Orex. Orex is not a party in this litigation. Mr. Plimpf has nothing to do with the generic Lorital market or Enpact."

Katie stepped forward. "Judge, Mr. Plimpf was present in India at the depositions I took in this case. Also, our witness list clearly states that we are going to call a representative of Orex. I suggest that the CEO of a company is a proper corporate representative, particularly if he has traveled halfway around the world to sit in on this litigation's depositions." Katie hesitated. "And, Your Honor, if you will recall, Mr. Freidberg testified about two doctors who admitted falsifying Mark Stenson's medical records at the request, and I quote 'from a representative of the company that makes brand-name Lorital, a company by the name of Orex'. End of quote. We have also just heard from the last witness that Mr. Holt, standing before you as one of Enpact's lawyers, is also the general counsel for Orex. Exhibit 4A clearly shows Mr. Holt's position in that capacity. I will represent to the court that I intend to reveal the identity of the Orex employee who requested that the two doctors falsify the records and that, rather than identify that person right now, I would prefer to do so in the presence of the jury so that they would have a clear understanding that Mr. Newton and I were not involved in the presentation of false evidence to this court."

Holt looked at Hempstead and nodded.

Hempstead addressed Judge Green. "Your Honor, I'd like to make a suggestion at this time that the parties meet and confer regarding potential settlement. The sensitive issues that have arisen in court today are such that public disclosure may have significant negative economic impact on both Enpact and Orex."

Green didn't hesitate. "I'll send the jury home for the rest of the day." He turned and looked at the jury. "Ladies and gentlemen, an issue has come up that will take us some time to resolve. I'm going to excuse you for the rest of the day. Please be back here tomorrow promptly at 9 a.m. and we'll continue."

After the jury left the courtroom, Green looked at the lawyers. "Use my conference room. I'll be in my chambers if you need me for any reason."

Gary stood. "Judge, if you don't mind, I think it's advisable that you be present during our negotiations and serve as the moderator."

# # #

Thirty minutes later, both sides had made predictable efforts. Gary had started off with a big number and Hempstead countered with an offer that Gary said was "peanuts."

Gary focused on Holt. He knew Holt's ass was on the line if the startling disclosure about the relationship between Enpact and Orex became a matter of public knowledge. "I'll start with my original number and every minute that this trial is delayed, it will go up another hundred thousand dollars…and generic Lorital must be removed from the United States market."

Everyone in the room looked at Holt and waited for his response. The man was sweating. His face turned beet red. "Your demand is robbery. We'll offer half a billion and not a penny more."

Newton stared at Holt. "And the drug comes off the market?"

"Enpact's drug. Not Orex's…and we get a secrecy agreement."

Gary responded. "Secrecy on the amount of the settlement only. Everything else is fair game except for the court's ruling already made on the document."

Holt thought for a moment and then nodded.

Newton smiled and turned to Green. "Those terms are agreeable, Your Honor. Please give me five minutes to confer with my clients. I'll reach them by phone right now. Ms. Hornsby and I'll be right back."

Green nodded. "Take all the time that's necessary."

Katie stopped Gary in the hallway. "Why would you agree to secrecy?"

Gary looked at Katie. "I'll explain in a second. But first, this is the most exciting day of my life. Not only did I watch the greatest young lawyer in America kick some serious ass, a drug company wants to give me a half billion dollars to divide between sixty clients. I already have authority to settle for a hell of a lot less than that. Each of them is going to get a lot of money."

Katie was beaming as she let Gary's words sink in. He continued, "A secrecy provision on the amount of settlement helps them avoid nosy friends and relatives who'll come out of the woodwork to borrow money if they know how much the client has received. Also, countless numbers of lives will be saved because a terrible drug is being taken off the market and there will be no secret about that. All because of you...and your courage."

"I had to do what I had to do. My father..."

"Don't say it. I already know what you're going to say. 'It's an old saying of your father's.'" They stood in the hallway and laughed.

Gary took her by her hand and pulled her to him. He wrapped his arms around her and gave her a big hug. "Your father would be so proud. Let's go back in and wrap this up."

Chapter 45
October 2012

In the courtroom, Katie gathered the exhibits and packed them in her large brief cases that she then placed on a cart. She looked around the courtroom to make sure she hadn't forgotten anything and then headed out to the elevators down the corridor. Lance Rebus stood waiting in front of the elevators.

As she approached, he said, "Can I talk to you for a minute?"

She colored, knowing that Rebus obviously knew about her liaison with Lion. "Sure." She couldn't look him in the eye.

He stepped closer and spoke softly. "I have two things I really need to say to you. First, I'm so sorry about what you went through, what Enpact did to you. I want you to know that Hempstead and I knew nothing about it until last week. We had nothing to do with it. I told your friend as soon as I found out. I haven't been able to sleep since. Second, your courage in doing what you did today is the bravest thing I can ever imagine someone doing."

She looked up at him and saw that he was blushing. She was truly touched by his words.

He continued, "I also wonder if we can have coffee together sometime, or a drink...now that we're not on opposite sides."

Katie pretended to be serious. "You said two things. That's more than two things. More like three or four..."

He looked puzzled.

"That's a joke." She smiled. "I'd like to do that...very much."

The two stood quietly for a moment and looked at each other while waiting for an elevator. Any sense of shame and embarrassment and guilt Katie had simply dissolved within her and was replaced by a sensation unlike anything she'd ever felt before. "Thank you for saying that. I can't tell you how much it means."

They walked back to the Buhl building together. He pulled her cart with the two bulky briefcases. Leslie was absolutely right. Rebus was way more than cute.

Chapter 46
October 2012

Judge Green was nervous, nervous as hell. He drove down the street of his home where his wife and children lived without him. The session with the marriage counselor had been both tumultuous and healing. He rode slowly past the home once, turned around at the end of the block, and approached again. He pulled into the driveway and parked behind his wife's car. He took several deep breaths and silently rehearsed what he intended to say before he emerged from the car and approached the front door. He knocked.

Abigail answered the door. When she saw him, she yelled back inside the house, "It's Daddy." She opened the door and he stepped inside. Nancy walked out of the kitchen and Green looked at her.

"I know I'm violating the restraining order, but I just want to talk with you...all of you."

Nancy paused. "The other girls aren't home right now. They're at school working on a project."

Green looked down at his feet. "I'm here to say two things...make that three things. First, I'm sorry for the way I've acted. I want to come home...and I love you, love all of you so much." Tears glistened in his eyes. He stammered. "Can we sit down? There are a few things I'd like to say, I need to say...I've been such a fool."

Abigail didn't hesitate. She threw her arms around her father. "Daddy, I love you! I love you." Nancy stood and watched for a moment. She stepped forward, reached the pair and made it a group hug. The three stood and held each other silently, tears flowing freely from their eyes.

# # #

The sun was shining, the temperature was ideal, and the day was perfect for a Sunday afternoon baseball game. The Newton law firm was there to celebrate the settlement and the entire staff was seated, along with several guests, in box seats at Comerica Park to watch the Tigers attempt to avoid being swept by the San Francisco Giants in the World Series. It was a big game. The Tigers had played so well the entire season but now faced the prospect of losing a cherished Series appearance in four straight games.

Katie was seated between Leslie and Lance Rebus. The game was scoreless until the Giants just scored on a controversial play. The Giants' batter attempted a bunt with bases loaded. The ball hit the batter's knee and ricocheted onto the playing field. The runner on third scored and the batter was safe at first. The home umpire had missed seeing that the ball hit the knee of the batter. It would have been called a foul ball if he'd seen it. While the Tigers manager argued the call with the umpires, the batter stood on first and rubbed his knee where the ball had struck. The entire crowd had seen the ball strike his knee, if not when it first happened, when the scene captured on camera was replayed on the large screen in left field, not once, but several times. Katie had stood along with the rest of the full house of fans in the stands and protested the umpire's decision. The ruling was upheld and the umpire threw the Detroit manager out of the game for protesting vigorously.

Katie, along with the rest of the crowd, was disgusted. She stood and looked at their small group. She smiled at Judge and Nancy Green and their three daughters. "I'm going to get a hot dog. Anybody want anything?"

Rebus also stood. "I'll go with you." The others shook their heads. The two walked up the aisle to the pavilion area, went to the nearest concession stand, and stood at the end of the long line. The guy in front of them was on a rant about the umpire's decision.

"It isn't fair," he told them. "The guy stands on first base and rubs his knee where the damn ball hit him. Why don't they ask him if it hit him? Why doesn't he tell them?"

Katie stood there and thought for a moment about the play, the past few weeks, about everything that had happened. She looked at the guy and then at Rebus. "My dad always told me four things. 'Life is not fair,' 'Baseball is like life,' and 'You've got to do what you've got to do.'" She paused for a moment.

Rebus laughed. "I've been waiting for this opportunity. You said four. That's only three."

"You didn't let me finish, Mister Jokester." Katie grinned. She moved close and whispered in his ear. "And I've been waiting for this opportunity, too. The fourth is my favorite. 'All's fair in love and war.'" She put her arms around him and kissed him squarely on the lips.

The run turned out to be the winning run of the last game of the World Series.

TOM BLEAKLEY

Epilogue

The next day, there was a call waiting for Katie when she arrived at the office.

"This is Everett Plimpf. Congratulations on your settlement. I'd like you to consider doing some of Orex's legal work. What do you think?"

For the first time in her life, as long as she could remember, she was at a loss for words.

TOM BLEAKLEY

About the Author

Tom Bleakley is a trial lawyer who specializes in handling cases against the pharmaceutical industry as well as pro bono cases involving constitutional issues and matters of public interest. He has an extensive background in medicine and pharmacology. He has received a Ph.D. in developmental psychology and most of his trial experiences deal with various developmental defects in children whose mothers were exposed to various prescription drugs during pregnancy. He has co-authored a two-volume textbook, A Teaching Program in Psychiatry, and written two previous novels, both dealing with the subject matter of the dangers of prescription drugs.

TOM BLEAKLEY